Hiking the

SOUTHWEST'S
CANYON COUNTRY

Hiking the

SOUTHWEST'S CANYON COUNTRY

by Sandra Hinchman

SECOND EDITION

THE
MOUNTAINEERS

Published by
The Mountaineers
1001 SW Klickitat Way, Suite 201
Seattle, WA 98134

GV
199.42
.S68
H56
1997
c.2

© 1990, 1997 by Sandra Hinchman

First edition 1990. Second edition: first printing 1997, second printing 1999, third printing 2000

Published simultaneously in Great Britain by Cordee, 3a DeMontfort Street, Leicester, England, LE1 7HD

Manufactured in the United States of America

Edited by Paula Thurman
Maps by Hannah Hinchman
All photographs by the author unless otherwise noted
Cover design by Watson Graphics
Typography by Virginia Hand
Layout by Hargrave Design
Black and white photo scans by Gray Mouse Graphics

Cover photograph: *Hiker gazes out at fins from upper opening, Double O Arch, Arches National Park. (Photo © Scott Spiker)*
Frontispiece: *Paria Canyon's Sliderock Arch forms a natural tunnel. (Lew Hinchman photo)*

Library of Congress Cataloging-in-Publication Data

Hinchman, Sandra, 1950-
    Hiking the Southwest's canyon country / by Sandra Hinchman. — 2nd ed.
        p.   cm.
    Includes bibliographical references (p.) and index.
    ISBN 0-89886-492-5
    1. Hiking—Southwest, New—Guidebooks. 2. Backpacking—Southwest, New—Guidebooks. 3. Mountaineering—Southwest, New—Guidebooks. 4. Southwest, New—Guidebooks. I. Mountaineers (Society) II. Title.
GV199.42.S68H56 1997
917.9—dc21
                          97-23725
                          CIP

 Printed on recycled paper

To my best hiking buddies, Lew and Bryce

Backpackers approach Escalante River through a steep-walled side-canyon.

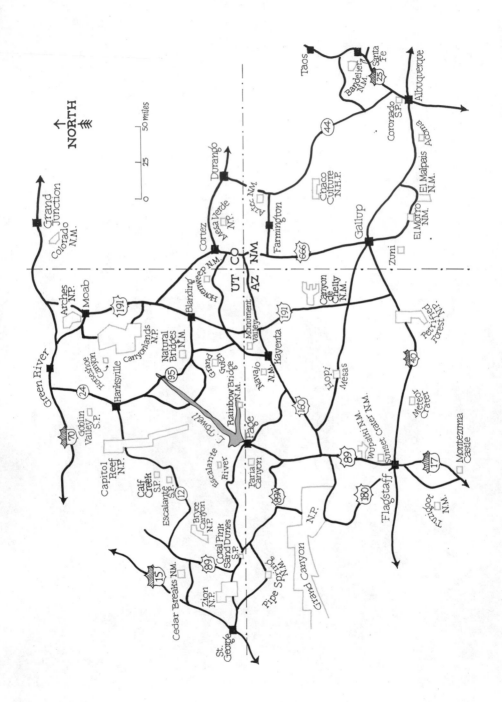

CONTENTS

Legend

——— paved road		🥾	hike
▬▬▬ dirt road		📷	overlook
═══ jeep road		⧄	camping
········· trail or route		⌂	ranger station or
Ⓢ start of hike or drive			visitor center
cliff		rock art	
mesa		⊡	ruin
butte, temple or hoodoo		pueblo	
peak or dome		ladder	
natural arch or bridge		] [	bridge
cave		[ ]	tunnel
waterfall		———	park boundary
spring		— · — · —	reservation
drive			boundary

PREFACE

When my husband, Lew, and I began traveling in the Southwest in 1974, we were long on enthusiasm but short on experience. Although Lew had hiked and camped in the Sierra Nevada range, I was new not only to backpacking but to exercise as such; being "in shape" was not even a concept for me. We had little sense of what equipment to buy, how to select a trail equal to our abilities, or how much ground we could cover each day. For our first adventure, we hiked to the bottom of the Grand Canyon on a sweltering summer afternoon, wearing stiff, uncomfortable boots and carrying everything we could cram into our packs. By the time we returned to the rim the next day, I was suffering from sunburn, blisters, heat exhaustion, and muscle cramps. Hardly an auspicious beginning! Backpacking, at that point, seemed like lunacy. But the lure of the wilderness, combined with my husband's dogged refusal to give up on me, persuaded me to try again—on a more realistic scale. Eventually, the desert insinuated its way into my soul, becoming a vital part of the way I define myself. Although I have lived in the East nearly all my life, it is the desert that feels like home.

Many years after our first, calamitous trip, I set out to write this guide to camping, hiking, and exploring the Southwest in the hope that others (especially nonjocks, like myself) might profit from both our mistakes and our successes. That such books might have a bad effect on the Colorado Plateau is an irony not lost on me. Authors risk attracting to the area people who will love it to death, transforming it from the pristine and wondrous place one knew into the kind of crowded, littered, trampled-down place one had hoped to escape. Indeed, precisely this sad scenario has played itself out in all too many locales.

I am gambling, however, that people who hike the Southwest will come to care about it and will work on its behalf: writing letters to Congress, joining environmental organizations, working on trail crews, or simply encouraging friends to treasure nature's beauty, wonder, and variety. In recent years, canyon country has been beleaguered by proposals for constructing dams, mines, power plants, nuclear waste dumps, and other assorted horrors, any one of which would cause more damage than thousands of hikers. If ecotourism can create a constituency to oppose such plans, the adverse impact of increased visitation may be worth the risk.

As a gesture toward maintaining the desert's ecological health, I pledge to donate a substantial portion of my royalties to organizations such as the Southern Utah Wilderness Alliance (1471 South 1100 East, Salt Lake City, UT 84105-2423) and Grand Canyon Trust (The Homestead, Route 4, Box 718, Flagstaff, AZ 86001). These groups have struggled tirelessly, and sometimes heroically, to preserve and enlarge

A deer browses at dawn under a Bryce Canyon cliff.

designated wilderness areas. Our world would be a much poorer place without their efforts.

Inevitably, in a guidebook such as this, errors will occur. Readers are urged to write to me in care of The Mountaineers Books, 1001 Southwest Klickitat Way, Suite 201, Seattle, WA 98134.

ACKNOWLEDGMENTS

Many people have contributed to making this book a reality. First, there are friends, too numerous to name, who provided support, ideas, or companionship on the trail. You know who you are! Second, I want to thank the savvy pros at The Mountaineers Books, especially Margaret Foster, who—over the years—has also become a friend. Collectively, they have spoiled me forever with their painstaking attention to my manuscript. Third, I am grateful to my sister-in-law, Hannah Hinchman, who lavished time and talent on the book's maps. Fourth, I appreciate the help and advice of rangers from the National Park Service (NPS) and the Bureau of Land Management (BLM) who examined portions of the manuscript with a critical eye. I am also grateful to readers who have taken the trouble to send along information and suggestions.

I have saved the most important person for last: my husband, Lew, who hiked with me every step of the way, solved my various computer problems, proofread drafts for accuracy, served as a consultant on geology, and looked after our son, Bryce, while I crunched words and pored over maps. Although Lew may sometimes wish I had taken up needlepoint instead, this book simply would not exist without his companionship, encouragement, and generosity. In this, as in all aspects of my life, he has been my sine qua non.

A collared lizard sports yellow and green markings.

Chapter 1

INTRODUCING THE DESERT

NATURAL AND HUMAN HISTORY

Most of the hikes described between these covers are within a day's drive of each other. With some notable exceptions, they are concentrated on the Colorado Plateau, near the so-called Four Corners, where Utah, Arizona, Colorado, and New Mexico meet. This is redrock country, a breathtaking landscape of canyons, fins, arches, hogbacks, and spires carved from stone. The remains of buildings constructed by prehistoric tribes that once inhabited the region are amply in evidence. Rivers that helped shape the high desert's topography—most notably, the Colorado, Green, Rio Grande, and San Juan—provide access to remote points of interest and offer, arguably, the most scenic floating and thrilling whitewater rafting in the United States. And the towering, geologically unusual mountains that frame this arid region add an extra dimension to its enchantment. Even a rudimentary grasp of the desert Southwest's natural and human history will enhance the visitor's experience.

Geology

Forces at Work. The Colorado Plateau is an exciting and accessible geologic schoolroom. Domes, spires, cliffs, goblins, arches, and alcoves stand forth starkly, usually without cover of dense vegetation and topsoil. The neophyte geologist need not search for road cuts to see the earth layered here; the geologic past is everywhere on display.

Simplifying the task of understanding Southwestern geology is the dominance of sedimentary rocks. The component materials of these rocks were deposited layer-cake style so that deeper-lying strata are almost always older than upper strata. Even an amateur geologist can distinguish the different kinds of sedimentary rock, recognizing the colorful badlands of the Morrison Formation, the weirdly eroded Entrada Sandstone goblins, the massive domes of Navajo Sandstone, and the severe, vertically fractured Wingate Sandstone cliffs. Each stratum offers clues about what kind of environment prevailed when the rock's component materials were laid down.

For instance, Coconino Sandstone in the Grand Canyon is composed of rounded sand grains of more or less equal size, arranged in layers that often lie at angles to one another (a phenomenon known as cross-bedding). This formation suggests that the present-day Grand Canyon was covered by vast dunes when the Coconino was deposited, since we can observe shifting winds arranging desert sands in exactly such patterns today.

Yet high desert geology is not as simple as rock-layer diagrams make it appear; close inspection reveals unimagined complexities. First, sedimentary rocks are never deposited in layers of uniform thickness. Ancient ecosystems of relatively limited extent—river estuaries, beaches, dunes—determined the depth and size of each stratum. Consequently, formations characteristic of some sections of the Colorado Plateau may thin out or even vanish elsewhere. For example, the Elephant Canyon Formation so prominent in the Needles District of Canyonlands National Park is entirely absent, both above and below the surface, in nearby Arches National Park.

Second, because sediments can be laid down only in basins, whenever sections were uplifted, they stopped receiving sediments and instead began eroding away. The result is an "unconformity": two layers of rock with no geologic trace of an intervening time period between them. Thus, sedimentary rocks in the Southwest offer a fragmentary and incomplete guide to the region's geologic history. Whole pages, even chapters, of that history are missing (though a "grand tour" makes it possible to reconstruct much of it).

Third, faulting and uplifting have disturbed many strata that elsewhere form unbroken beds, pushing one part of the bed above, or dropping it below, another part. The Moab Fault, near Arches National Park, provides a vivid illustration. Wingate Sandstone cliffs, capped by Navajo Sandstone, tower above the west side of the valley. On the east side, however, the Wingate layer is buried beneath the earth, while the Navajo and Entrada Sandstone form the backdrop for the Arches Visitor Center. The offset of strata along this fault reaches 1000 to 1500 feet.

Finally, ancient vulcanism and mountain-building have played dramatic roles. Areas on the periphery of the Colorado Plateau, such as Bandelier National Monument, owe their peculiar geology to vast amounts of ash and lava from ancient volcanoes. Elsewhere the region is crossed by long "folds" or "reefs," such as Utah's Waterpocket Fold and San Rafael Reef, caused when subterranean forces lifted up overlying rock strata and tilted them at crazy angles—sometimes to a nearly vertical plane. Often the uplifting occurred so slowly that preexisting streams cut into the rock as fast as it was being raised up around them, creating narrow "slot" canyons that run perpendicular to the axis of the reef.

In addition to such folds, the canyon and mesa country boasts

Gypsum veins decorate mudstone, San Rafael Reef.

several mountain ranges that rise 10,000 feet or more above sea level. Many—including the La Sals, Abajos (or Blues), and Henrys, and isolated, turtle-shaped humps like Sleeping Ute and Navajo Mountains—are "laccoliths": roughly, failed volcanoes that created large bulges in the earth but never actually erupted. The rocks in and around them are mostly igneous types, such as granite. Deep canyons, similar to the slot canyons that cut through folds and reefs, formed on the flanks of laccoliths as meltwater rushed through soft, sedimentary rock. Navajo Mountain's Bridge Canyon, the site of Rainbow Bridge, offers a choice example.

The Rock Strata. Clear and simple on a grand scale, the geology of the high desert is complex and unique for each specific area.

Some of the region's oldest rocks are displayed in the Grand Canyon. Indeed, the youngest rocks laid down there, the Kaibab Limestone Formation, date back to the late Permian age (285 to 230 million years ago). Look especially for the bands of buff-colored Coconino Sandstone near the top of the Grand Canyon and the red-tinted Redwall Limestone, somewhat lower, that form sheer cliffs for miles.

In Utah, you will find some very ancient Paleozoic strata. The Needles of Canyonlands National Park are composed of grayish-white Cedar Mesa Sandstone, as are the cliffs of Grand Gulch and Natural Bridges National Monument. Cedar Mesa Sandstone is actually a "member" of the Cutler Formation, which includes other, quite different strata. Some Cutler rock is dark red and weathers into spires, gargoyles, and "standing rocks," visible in Canyonlands' Maze District and at Fisher Towers north of Moab. In Capitol Reef National Park, look for Chimney Rock and other monoliths around the park's western boundary. These towers resemble the Cutler but are composed of the newer, Triassic-era Moenkopi Formation. A harder cap of Shinarump conglomerate retards the erosion of the mud and sandstone Moenkopi beneath.

The most spectacular formations in the region belong to the Glen Canyon Group of the Triassic and early Jurassic ages, the heyday of the great dinosaurs. Notable among these is Navajo Sandstone, the classic tan to white "slickrock" of the high desert. This stratum, over 1500 feet thick in some places, may be appreciated well when viewing the muscular domes of Capitol Reef and in Zion National Park, where it forms features such as the Great White Throne. The Navajo layer also produces nearly vertical cliffs in places like the Escalante River and the slot canyons of the San Rafael Reef.

Below Navajo Sandstone, you will usually see the reddish, easily weathered rocks of the Kayenta stratum. The Kayenta forms ledges, "Swiss cheese" rock walls, and also arches, most notably in Capitol Reef's Upper Muley Twist Canyon. Some remarkable narrows cut

Common Rock Strata of the Colorado Plateau

LAYER (Typical Maximum Thickness)	WHERE FOUND	Period
Claron Formation - 600'	Bryce Canyon, Cedar Breaks	TERTIARY — up to 65 million years ago
Mancos Shale -3500'	Capitol Reef, Book Cliffs	CRETACEOUS — 136-65 million years ago
Dakota Sandstone - 350'	Capitol Reef	CRETACEOUS — 136-65 million years ago
Morrison Formation - 400'	Arches, Capitol Reef	JURASSIC — 195-136 million years ago
Summerville Formation - 300'	Goblin Valley, Arches	JURASSIC — 195-136 million years ago
Curtis Formation - 225'	Goblin Valley	JURASSIC — 195-136 million years ago
Entrada Sandstone - 800'	Arches, Goblin Valley, Cathedral Valley	JURASSIC — 195-136 million years ago
Carmel Formation - 650'	Capitol Reef, San Rafael Reef	JURASSIC — 195-136 million years ago
Navajo Sandstone 1000'	Zion, Escalante, Arches, Rainbow Br, Capitol Reef	JURASSIC — 195-136 million years ago
Kayenta Formation - 350'	Muley Twist, Arches, Island in the Sky	TRIASSIC — 230-195 million years ago
Wingate Sandstone - 375'	Dead Horse Point, Capitol Reef, Colorado Nat. Mon.	TRIASSIC — 230-195 million years ago
Chinle Formation - 650'	Island in the Sky, Capitol Reef	TRIASSIC — 230-195 million years ago
Moenkopi Formation - 1000'	Natural Bridges, Capitol Reef, Fisher Towers	TRIASSIC — 230-195 million years ago
Kaibab Limestone - 300'	Grand Canyon, Capitol Reef	PERMIAN — 285-230 million years ago
White Rim Sandstone - 250'	Island in the Sky	PERMIAN — 285-230 million years ago
Cedar Mesa Sandstone - 1200'	Grand Gulch, Natural Bridges, Needles, Maze	PERMIAN — 285-230 million years ago
Cutler Formation - 1400'	Monument Valley, Fisher Towers	PERMIAN — 285-230 million years ago
Honaker Trail Formation - 3000'	San Juan R. Gorge, Shafer Trail, Colo./Green confluence	PENNSYLVANIAN — 325-285 million years ago
Paradox Salt - 5000'	Fisher Valley, Salt Valley (Arches)	PENNSYLVANIAN — 325-285 million years ago

through the Kayenta Formation, too, such as those in Crack Canyon near Goblin Valley State Park in central Utah.

Wingate Sandstone, a fairly hard rock that often yields long vertical fractures, is the final member of the Glen Canyon Group. Sometimes it erodes into towering, golden cliffs such as those of the Castle in Capitol Reef or along parts of the Colorado River north of Moab. Elsewhere, it weathers into isolated buttes and spires, of which the Six-Shooter Peaks of the Canyonlands Needles District offer a prime example. Usually the base of the Wingate is formed by the sloping, rubble-strewn Chinle Formation, a bearer of uranium.

Two other formations deserve mention because of the manner in which they erode. Above the Navajo in places lies Entrada Sandstone. In Arches National Park, it is a gold or reddish, fairly hard rock out of which most of the arches and fins were hewn. But at Goblin Valley, it is much softer, more crumbly, and mudlike. So here, it has eroded into grotesque and comical knobs, hoodoos, and pillars.

Farther west, at Bryce Canyon National Park, Navajo Sandstone is the oldest rock that has been found, and that only by drilling. The rest of the formations go up to the Cenozoic period (after 65 million years ago), capped by the brilliant pastel and white Claron Formation, a combination of limestone, shale, and sandstone. The Claron has weathered into the ethereal, dreamlike world of Bryce's Pink Cliffs.

Thus, if you traveled from the Grand Canyon through Capitol Reef and Zion and then on to Bryce, you would see the "grand staircase," a series of rock strata displaying geologic history from Precambrian times to the demise of the dinosaurs and the emergence of early mammals.

Topographic Glossary

Alcoves *(overhangs, amphitheaters)* are shallow caves in cliffs or fins that result from flaking or falling rock.

Anticlines are domes or ridges formed when rock layers are pushed upward and bowed by subterranean forces. They often erode in the center, leaving valleys bounded on either side by upward-tilting strata.

Arches are natural openings formed when water percolates into porous rock, such as sandstone, and gradually breaks it down either by dissolving its chemical "cement" or by freezing and thawing. **Potty arches** form when the resultant rock openings occur at the top of alcoves.

Badlands are dry, barren, clay hills, often multihued, that have been fluted by mechanical and chemical weathering.

Balanced rocks develop as the pedestal on which a caprock sits erodes rapidly, becoming ever thinner.

Buttes form when water, frost, or wind action cause mesas to weather drastically and unevenly, until only tall remnants remain. These remnants are capped with hard, resistant rock that helps protect softer layers underneath. Unlike mesas, buttes are higher than they are wide.

Canyons *(gorges, gulches)* are carved into plateaus by streams, sometimes aided by simultaneous uplifting caused by underground forces. **Arroyos** occur when streams gouge out channels that are deeper than the level prevailing on the canyon floor; this can result from flash-flooding, especially when the landscape is denuded of vegetation by overgrazing.

Desert varnish is a dark oxide stain caused as minerals in the rock are dissolved by water.

Fins and **domes** occur when parallel vertical joints in solid rock are widened by erosional agents, eventually yielding freestanding formations. **Needles** are standing rocks that result when such joints also run perpendicular to each other.

Grabens are sunken fault blocks that show on the surface as narrow valleys or trenches bounded by steep walls. Good illustrations are provided by Cyclone and Red Lake Canyons in the Needles District of Canyonlands National Park, which formed when underlying beds of salt leached away.

Hanging canyons are caused when a tributary does not cut into its bed at the same rate as the main stream but becomes suspended above it.

Streaks of desert varnish create a tapestry effect, Capitol Reef National Park.

Hoodoos *(goblins)* are standing rocks, sometimes found along the base of cliffs, that have eroded into improbable shapes.

Laccoliths are isolated mountains that form when subterranean molten materials force their way up without breaking through the earth's crust. The magma travels horizontally between thick beds of sedimentary rock, warping those layers.

Mesas (meaning "tables" in Spanish) are high, flat plateaus with sloping or cliff-bounded sides.

Monoclines appear as sudden tilts or jogs in the plane of sedimentary rock strata. The term may designate the structure of one side of an anticline; Utah's San Rafael Reef provides a classic example.

Narrows occur when canyon walls pinch very close together, for a tunnel-like effect.

Natural bridges are created by the surge of water against a rock wall—for example, when a stream cuts off a meander by breaking through a fin and enlarging the opening, making a new course for itself.

Oxbows or **goosenecks** occur when a canyon stream has meandered enough to form a loop, turning back on itself. **Entrenched streams** form when a meandering watercourse cuts into its bed as the land around it is uplifted.

Pour-offs *(dryfalls)* are found when canyon floors take sudden steep plunges, creating obstacles for hikers.

Reef is a colloquial term applied by early settlers to any barrier to travel. In the Southwest, the term refers to drastically uptilted ridges, such as Utah's Comb Ridge, San Rafael Reef, and Waterpocket Fold.

Rincons are abandoned meanders that occur as a stream cuts through a narrow neck between loops to create a new channel. Where this happens, natural bridges sometimes develop.

Slickrock is a colloquial term referring to expanses of bare, undulating sandstone (most typically, Navajo Sandstone). It is generally not slick at all, except after rainstorms.

Spires *(pillars, towers)* usually originate when relatively soft rock strata are thinned out by weathering or when erosion breaks off vertical slabs of harder rock from isolated buttes, reducing them to slender, freestanding pinnacles.

Synclines are downward slumpings of the earth's surface, the opposite of anticlines.

Climate

What makes the Four Corners region a desert is not simply the small amount of precipitation it receives (under 10 inches annually) but that most of this precipitation occurs in storms during late July and August, instead of falling evenly throughout the year. The parched, sparsely vegetated ground cannot absorb the moisture from these monsoons, so much of it simply runs off, contributing to rapid erosion. Snowfall is generally light, though winter temperatures can fall below 20°F. Summers

Whimsical hoodoos populate Goblin Valley State Park.

can be intensely hot—90°F and up—at least before the brief but sometimes torrential afternoon thundershowers cool things off. These storms can cause flash floods and quicksand in previously dry "washes," or gullies. They also moderate temperatures, replenish the supply of drinking water in streams and potholes, and kill off much of the insect population. Summer visitors to the desert can expect hot, buggy, dry conditions during the first half of the season and wetter, cooler, relatively bugless conditions during the second half. April, May, September, and October are the ideal months for most high desert travel.

Flora and Fauna

The distribution of plant and animal species in the Southwest can be explained by the "life zone" concept formulated a century ago by botanist Clinton Hart Merriam. Merriam observed that the climate and latitude of an area help determine what flora and fauna will flourish there. "Communities" of plants and animals develop as the species residing in an area grow interdependent over millennia of evolutionary changes.

However, climate and latitude don't tell the whole story. Altitude must also be factored into the equation. Air temperature decreases and precipitation increases with altitude, producing a new environment that supports different life forms. Every 1000 feet of elevation gain is equivalent to about 300 miles of latitudinal movement toward the pole.

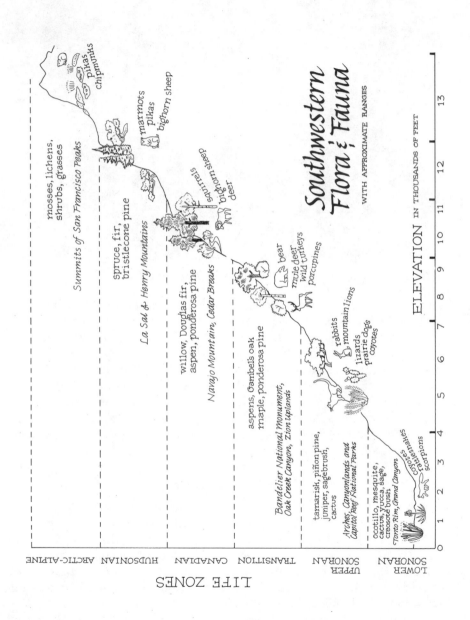

Southwestern Flora & Fauna

WITH APPROXIMATE RANGES

ELEVATION IN THOUSANDS OF FEET

LIFE ZONES

ARCTIC-ALPINE   HUDSONIAN   CANADIAN   TRANSITION   UPPER SONORAN   LOWER SONORAN

mosses, lichens, shrubs, grasses

Summits of San Francisco Peaks

spruce, fir, bristlecone pine

La Sal & Henry Mountains

willow, Douglas fir, aspen, ponderosa pine

Navajo Mountain, Cedar Breaks

aspens, Gambel's oak, maple, ponderosa pine

Bandelier National Monument, Oak Creek Canyon, Zion Uplands

tamarisk, piñon pine, juniper, sagebrush, cactus

Arches, Canyonlands and Capitol Reef National Parks

ocotillo, mesquite, cactus, yucca, sage, creosote bush

Toroto Rim, Grand Canyon

pikas, chipmunks

marmots, pikas, bighorn sheep

squirrels, bighorn sheep, deer

bear, mule deer, wild turkeys, porcupines

rabbits, mountain lions, lizards, prairie dogs, coyotes

coyotes, rattlesnakes, scorpions

Merriam postulated the existence of seven life zones, from the Tropical to the Arctic-Alpine. Several zones prevail in the high desert. These zones, and their residents, overlap considerably, and the vegetation and wildlife found where water is relatively ample (lakeshores, riverbanks, intermittent streams, springs, and even potholes) may be anomalous.

The Lower Sonoran Zone. Reaching to about the 4000-foot line, this zone includes the bottom of the Grand Canyon, the banks of the Rio Grande, and the southwestern corner of Utah. Cactus, mesquite, yucca, agave, creosote bush, blackbrush, rabbitbrush, and snakeweed are the dominant flora. The zone's wildlife include rattlesnakes, deer, coyotes, scorpions, lizards, kangaroo rats, bats, skunks, cactus wrens, and hummingbirds.

The Upper Sonoran Zone. From 3500 to 7000 feet in altitude, this zone occupies by far the largest portion of the Four Corners region. Most typical of the Upper Sonoran is the so-called pygmy forest of pinyon pines and Utah junipers—"pygmy" because these trees are dwarfed by the region's scant rainfall. Locally, junipers are often termed "cedars." Other common trees here include oak, box elder, and cottonwood, which grow where the water table is high. But the zone's bushes and shrubs are even more diverse: sagebrush, blackbrush, bottlebrush, Mormon (or Brigham's) tea, rabbitbrush, tamarisk (an "exotic" riparian bush), willow, canyon grape, mock orange, cliffrose, buffaloberry, snakeweed, and greasewood. Less welcome to most visitors are poison oak and ivy. Floral displays in late spring and early summer can be extravagant, especially in years with high precipitation. Among the flowering plants prevalent in the Upper Sonoran zone are prince's plume, mule ears, bee plant, jimson weed (sacred *Datura*), sego lily, penstemon (or beardtongue), prickle poppy, geranium, globe mallow, phlox, four o'clock, evening primrose, scarlet gilia, Indian paintbrush, sunflower, and monkeyflower. Wildlife here includes coyotes, bats, rattlesnakes, scorpions, lizards, prairie dogs, kangaroo rats, mice, rabbits, squirrels, skunks, gray foxes, pronghorn antelopes, and mule deer. Among bird species, look for canyon wrens, hawks, swallows, kinglets, owls, vultures, scrub and pinyon jays, ravens, vireos, magpies, nighthawks, horned larks, finches, western tanagers, hummingbirds, towhees, and golden and (occasionally) bald eagles.

The Transition Zone. A buffer between deserts and mountains (from 6500 to 9500 feet), this zone contains two distinct associations of plants and animals. At lower altitudes, you will discover Gambel's oak, maple, Ponderosa pine, Rocky Mountain juniper, serviceberry, chokecherry, mountain mahogany, and manzanita. Higher up, Douglas and white fir, aspen, common juniper, and mountain ash predominate. Occasional stands of bristlecone pines—the earth's oldest living trees—can also

Top left: *Barrel cactus in bloom.* Top right: *Tan lizard camouflaged on rock.* Bottom left: *A curious coyote in Salt Valley, Arches National Park.* Bottom right: *Alligator juniper sports unusual scaly bark.*

be found. You may see wild turkeys, deer, porcupines, bears, squirrels, chipmunks, foxes, marmots, skunks, bobcats, and even mountain lions. Common bird species include swallows, swifts, nuthatches, robins, flickers, jays, ravens, and chickadees.

Archaeology

Centuries before Europeans arrived in the New World, three native American cultures flourished in the high desert: the Anasazi (meaning "alien ancestors" in Navajo); the Sinagua (meaning "without water" in Spanish); and the Fremont (named after the explorer of a river valley that they inhabited). All three groups descended from the central Asian peoples who migrated across the land bridge that once connected Siberia with Alaska and then gradually moved southward and eastward to populate two continents. Relics of their ways of life are scattered throughout the Southwest, offering valuable clues to their cultures. The Anasazi, believed to be ancestors of the modern-day Hopi and Pueblo tribes, dominated the Four Corners region, with the Fremont culture concentrated north and west of the Green River and the Sinagua residing farther to the south, in Arizona.

Members of two of these Neolithic societies, the Anasazi and Sinagua, eventually lived in masonry homes and villages, some built ingeniously into deep alcoves high in south-facing cliffs for protection from the elements or from rival tribes. In addition to hunting small game and gathering nuts and berries, these peoples grew squash, beans, and corn in irrigated fields. To some degree, they may have been influenced culturally and technologically by societies from central and southern Mexico, with whom they traded for turquoise, shells, feathers, and other commodities. Like other aborigines, they had a thorough knowledge of indigenous plants, from which they would extract dyes, medicines, and seasonings and make objects such as sandals and ropes.

The Anasazi. Because their artifacts are so abundant, the Anasazi, as they are familiarly known, are particularly interesting to visitors to the Four Corners. There is a great deal of controversy over what we should call them: their Hopi descendants use the term "Hisatsinom" (meaning "ancient ones") while their Pueblo descendants prefer "Ancestral Pueblos." Other controversies swirl over how egalitarian and how ecologically responsible their societies were, and whether they might have practiced cannibalism.

Anthropologists sometimes divide the history of this culture into two broad periods—Basket Maker and Pueblo. During the late Basket Maker era, lasting until about A.D. 750, the Anasazi lived in underground pit houses in settled communities, developed bows and arrows for hunting, and began making pottery for storage and cooking to supplement the fine woven baskets they had traditionally employed. In the subsequent Pueblo phase, the Anasazi moved to surface houses and ultimately to masonry cliff-dwellings, often grouped together in small villages or even great cities accommodating hundreds of people. Increasingly, they depended on irrigated agriculture for sustenance. Also during the Pueblo phase, the pit house of yesteryear evolved into the "kiva," the Hopi word for a subterranean ceremonial chamber used for religious, social, economic, and educational functions. The usual entrance into kivas was from the top, by ladder. Each kiva also had a hole called a "sipapu," or symbolic entrance to the spirit world.

Cliff dwellings, erected in the twelfth and thirteenth centuries, often were accessible only by toe- and handholds laboriously pecked out of solid rock. These stairways were specially coded: a person had to know whether to begin climbing with the right or left foot or else risk dangerous midcliff corrective maneuvering. Rural Mormons, anglicizing the Spanish word for Hopi, called these primitive ladders "Moki" steps; they assumed that because the doors of Anasazi houses have extremely low clearance, a Munchkin-sized race they called Mokis had built them. In fact, the Anasazi, like the Fremont and Sinagua peoples, were comparable in stature to the Europeans of their day. The typical life span was comparable, as well, at 30 to 35 years, with very high infant mortality (a 50 percent death rate for children under age 5).

Below the cliff dwellings were the "middens," a sort of dump where items such as broken pottery and old sandals were discarded. The dead were sometimes buried in these middens, not out of disrespect, but because digging was easiest there. Mysteriously, however, few corpses have been found in or near cliff dwellings. Some Hopis maintain that the Anasazi, having perfected themselves through harmonious dealings with nature and one another, ascended to the fifth level of creation, leaving behind our fourth level with its suffering and strife.

Many of the Southwest's most breathtaking Anasazi sites were found and publicized by Richard and John Wetherill and their brothers in the late nineteenth and early twentieth centuries. The Wetherills were ranchers from Mancos, Colorado, who became amateur archaeologists after stumbling upon abandoned dwellings on nearby Mesa Verde. Excited by these finds, they spent years exploring the Southwest, searching for pottery and other artifacts, which they sold to East Coast and European museums to finance their expeditions. Although by today's standards this practice would be considered looting, in the nineteenth century it was neither illegal nor even regarded as unethical. During his travels, Richard Wetherill formulated the distinction between the Basket Maker and Pueblo stages of Anasazi history that remains widely in use.

The Fremonts. Primarily hunters and gatherers, the Fremont people inhabited central Utah and western Colorado between A.D. 700 and 1300. Over time, they developed irrigated agriculture, probably as a cultural borrowing from the Anasazi. But their social organization remained relatively simple. They lived in small bands, building no towns to speak of and developing no elaborate division of labor. Although they were adept at masonry and left behind many small dwellings and granaries, they lived mostly in pit houses, which have not withstood the ravages of time. Other differences between the Fremont and Anasazi cultures show up in artifacts like pottery, baskets, and footwear. Also in contrast to the Anasazi, the Fremonts used *atlotyls* in hunting and made ceremonial clay figurines.

The Fremont River valley, in and around what is now Capitol Reef National Park, was the heart of Fremont culture. Fremont Indian State Park, near Sevier, Utah, is another excellent place to learn about the tribe and study its artifacts. Like other aboriginal peoples, the Fremonts decorated rock sufaces with shamanistic art, but it is difficult to say with confidence exactly which panels are theirs. Art of the so-called Barrier Creek style, once attributed by archaeologists to the Fremont peoples, is now believed to have been created centuries earlier by the Desert Archaic culture, from which the Fremonts may have evolved. These remarkable drawings feature supernatural-looking, vase-shaped figures, sometimes horned, with geometric decorations on their bodies. The most striking examples of this style are panels in Canyonlands National Park's Horseshoe Canyon.

The Sinaguas. Having emigrated from southeastern Arizona in the seventh century, the Sinaguas made their homes around modern-day Flagstaff in the shadow of the San Francisco Peaks. For hundreds of years, they dry-farmed the land, living in one-room pit houses. Their tribal organization was loose, with isolated family gatherings as the main social units, but eventually families grouped together in villages. By the time they began erecting aboveground dwellings in the twelfth century, in places like Walnut Canyon, Tuzigoot, Montezuma Castle, and Wupatki National Monuments, they had acquired masonry techniques from the Anasazi and irrigation from the Hohokams (ancestors of the modern Tohono O'odham or Papago tribe), whose members originally inhabited the Gila River basin near present-day

Mano *and* metate, *ancient grinding tools*

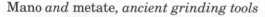

Erosion-damaged Fremont pictograph, South Temple Wash, Utah

Phoenix. Few generalizations can be made about the building styles of the Sinaguas, which varied greatly in response to local conditions. But one noteworthy structure in the Wupatki complex is a masonry ball-court, a cultural borrowing from Mesoamerica.

The Demise of the Early American Cultures. After up to 2000 years of residence in canyon country, the three groups of indigenous peoples abandoned their homes between A.D. 1100 and 1400. Some anthropologists argue that an unhappy coincidence of drought, global cooling, and resource depletion (of soil, game, and wood) made farming and hunting increasingly difficult, causing internal strife and placing an intolerable burden on the social structure. Other hypotheses stress the impact of raiders on tribal welfare and security or the rise of new, kachina-based religions that exerted a cultural and geographic pull. Perhaps the Fremonts evolved into nomadic raiders, climatic changes having affected their way of life even more adversely than those of the other groups. The Anasazi and Sinagua peoples evidently relocated to the Little Colorado and Rio Grande drainages, where their descendants live today.

Whatever motivated their exodus, the aboriginal Americans left behind not only their homes and utilitarian objects, such as pots, ropes, and sandals, but also rock art: mineral-dye paintings (pictographs) and etchings (petroglyphs). Typically, specimens are found on smooth, flat cliff faces or boulders near ruins, monoliths, springs, or canyon mouths. Designs incorporate human, animal, and spirit figures, as well as handprints, hunting implements, and geometric shapes. Attempts by modern-day descendants of the Southwest's Neolithic inhabitants to decipher the various symbols have proven fascinating, but inconclusive.

Unfortunately, an estimated 80 to 90 percent of the archaeological sites of the Southwest have been defaced or plundered. Some, however, remain in good condition. Of these, the sites at Mesa Verde National Park are the best known and generally the best preserved. But ruins of exceptional quality are also found in places like Navajo National Monument, Grand Gulch, Ute Mountain Ute Tribal Park, and Chaco Canyon. Travelers interested in learning more about the prehistoric cultures of the Southwest should visit the Edge of the Cedars Museum in Blanding, Utah, the Anasazi Heritage Center in Dolores, Colorado, or the Museum of Northern Arizona in Flagstaff.

Native Cultures Today

The present-day Native Americans of the Four Corners region include Utes, Navajos, Hopis, and Pueblos. Tribal members live suspended between two distinct worlds: the traditional, animistic world of ceremony, in which all the earth is seen as alive, and the larger society, with its high technology and metaphysical religions. Please bear in mind that when traveling on their reservations, you are a guest in another culture's homeland.

The Utes. Some anthropologists believe that the Utes descended from the Fremont peoples. Others think they descended from Shoshones, who entered the region in the twelfth and thirteenth centuries. Before being vanquished by the U.S. Army, the Utes lived as semi-nomadic hunters and warriors. Once pushed onto reservations, they were compelled to live in a more sedentary manner, dependent upon agriculture and upon rations from the Bureau of Indian Affairs. Currently, tribal members inhabit reservations in northern Utah and southwestern Colorado, adjacent to Mesa Verde National Park. Livestock raising and agriculture, their economic mainstays, have been handicapped by the absence of reliable, good-quality water supplies.

The Navajos. Calling themselves "Dineh," or "the people," the Navajos are ethnically unrelated to most pre-Columbian inhabitants of the Colorado Plateau. Like the Apaches, they descended from nomadic hunters on the plains. Their common name comes from the Spanish corruption of another tribe's word for them, "Apache de Nebahu," or "enemies with cultivated fields." Over 175,000 strong, the Navajo nation exceeds all other U.S. tribes both in population and the extent of its territory, a reservation encompassing half of northern Arizona and spilling across the borders of Utah and New Mexico. Previously, the Navajos were believed to have migrated into the region during the seventeenth century, but recent findings suggest their presence in New

Mexico as early as the 1200s. Some anthropologists have even postulated a link between the coming of the Navajos and the exodus of the area's aboriginal peoples.

In many ways, the Navajos fared better than other tribes in their dealings with the federal government. Although they endured terrible woes, including the destruction of their homes, livestock, and orchards, and the deaths of many kinsmen on a forced march to eastern New Mexico in 1864, they ultimately were able to keep their land. And that land, which at first appeared worthless to Anglos, turned out to contain natural gas, oil, uranium, and coal, which is now mined extensively on Arizona's Black Mesa. The discovery of coal was a mixed blessing, however, since with it came the construction of lucrative (for some people) but polluting power plants, which supply energy to distant cities.

Some citizens of the Navajo nation are employed as energy workers. Others earn their living by selling high-quality wool rugs and turquoise and silver jewelry, while more traditional Navajos raise sheep and goats. Unemployment rates here, as on other reservations, are high, and relatively few homes boast electricity and indoor plumbing. Although trailers and other prefabricated homes are common on the reservation, Navajo lands are also dotted with more

Noxious jimson weed produces delicate white flowers.

traditional structures such as sweat lodges, ramadas, and hogans (one-room hexagonal or octagonal dwellings, made of earth, logs, and modern materials, that customarily face toward the rising sun). An excellent source of information about Navajo culture is Santa Fe's Wheelwright Museum of the American Indian.

The Hopis. A small tribe of under 10,000 members, the Hopis have been relatively successful in preserving their cultural traditions ever since the days of Spanish conquistadors and missionaries. Their reservation is surrounded by Navajo land, which has caused great friction between these tribes over the years. In recent decades, it occasioned a bitter lawsuit over disputed joint-use territory that resulted in the displacement of many Navajo families. Unlike the Navajos, the Hopis are primarily farmers. They live on arms of Black Mesa in villages like Oraibi, the oldest continuously occupied town in the United States. Although the tribe has its outspoken faction of "modernizers," many Hopis continue to observe their old customs, evidently derived in part from Anasazi practices. Like the Navajos, the Hopis regard certain mountains in the area to be sacred, such as the San Francisco Peaks, where their nature gods, deified spirits of ancestors (or "kachinas"), supposedly reside. Another sacred spot is the "Sipapu," a travertine dome on the Little Colorado River. The Sipapu has an opening from which traditionalists believe human beings emerged into our world.

The Pueblos. This population is scattered among nineteen independent villages, mainly in the Rio Grande Valley. Conquest by the Spanish in the seventeenth century led to pillaging, enslavement, and attempts at forced conversion to Christianity. Bloody revolts and bloody reprisals ensued. Somehow the Pueblo peoples managed to retain much of their cultural integrity in the face of both long-term Spanish dominion and subsequent waves of Mexican and Anglo immigration. Today some of their villages seem relatively prosperous, with economies based on agriculture and on crafts like pottery and jewelry-making. Kivas are still in use here, as on the Hopi Reservation, though many are now aboveground structures. Sacred dances are held in the villages several times a year, in keeping with ancient rituals. Visitors are generally welcome to tour the pueblos for a small fee; photographing and sketching privileges (not available during ceremonies) cost extra.

The Havasupais and Hualapais. Members of these tribes inhabit portions of the western Grand Canyon. Both very small in number, they farm terraces inside the canyon and graze stock in high meadows along the rim, earning extra income by selling hiking and camping permits. The Havasupai town of Supai, a Shangri-la near the bottom of the canyon, is famed for its teal-blue travertine waterfalls. Reachable by an 8-mile foot trail, it is the last town in the United States to have its mail delivered by mule.

HIKING AND DRIVING

Every desert traveler should be informed about certain potential hazards and how to avoid them or at least remedy their effects. All problems included in the following list are exacerbated by remote locations and difficult terrain. A good first-aid kit and manual are essential.

Hiking Safety

Water. During the summer months, plan on at least 1 gallon of water per person each day for drinking, washing, and cooking. This amount may seem excessive, but it is not, and you shouldn't be tempted to skimp on it. In most places, you can't count on finding groundwater, so you will usually have to carry all you need. At over 8 pounds per gallon, this can be a heavy proposition.

Sometimes water will be available from springs and perennial streams. Conditions change seasonally, even weekly. Since map and guidebook information regarding possible water sources may be outdated, you must always confirm such information at local ranger stations. Avoid drinking dry any water sources you do find, since animals depend on them for survival.

Poor water quality presents an increasingly serious problem for hikers throughout the American wilderness, and the desert is no exception. Many water sources—even those that look pristine—have been contaminated by cattle, horses, and wild animals, not to mention careless campers. The main contaminant is *Giardia lamblia,* a bacterium released into water and soil as feces decompose. When ingested, this bacterium can cause severe diarrhea and dehydration. Symptoms may not appear for several weeks, but they tend to persist until treated with antibiotics.

To avoid contracting giardiasis and other water-borne diseases, follow these recommendations religiously:

- Boil all drinking water.
- Or purify water chemically with a small amount of clorox bleach (one or two drops per quart) or commercially available tablets. Shake the container well and wait at least 20 minutes before drinking.
- Alternatively, use a portable, charcoal-based filtration system. Strain the water through cheesecloth or let it settle in a canteen first, since sediment can clog the filter and dramatically shorten its useful life. (Don't drink from any canteen employed for this purpose.)
- Never drink from any source that supports no life, since it may contain arsenic or some other toxic compound.

Flash Floods. Mid-July through early September is a time of frequent afternoon thunderstorms in the Southwest. These brief but heavy

Sandstone monuments delight a hiker in Canyonlands National Park.

downpours (called "male rains" by Navajos) sometimes cause flooding even in faraway streams. You can hear a flash flood coming—it sounds like a locomotive—but you may be inconvenienced, injured, or even killed by one unless you take certain precautions:

- Never camp in or near the bed of a dry wash or in any narrow section of canyon lacking an easy and obvious escape route.
- Listen to weather reports and pay attention to natural phenomena that signal impending storms, such as sudden shifts in air temperature or wind direction.
- Avoid travel in remote areas when storms seem imminent.
- Never try to cross a wash on foot or by car during a flash flood.
- Should you be trapped in a canyon during a flash flood, find very high ground and wait for the water to subside. Never try to beat a flood out of a canyon. Sometimes it takes 12 to 24 hours for waters to recede, though minor floods will not delay you for so long. Quicksand often develops in the aftermath of flash-flooding; this can make it difficult to complete a hike.

Quicksand. Sometimes encountered in or along streambeds, quicksand rarely presents a genuine hazard. People usually sink no farther than knee- or waist-deep, and the sinking tends to be so gradual that you can pull yourself out, though you may need a rope or helping hand from one of your companions. If you are hiking alone and this happens, extend your arms, fall on your back, and pull your legs free. Stay calm and extricate yourself without making unnecessary movements. During the thunderstorm season, quicksand will form in conjunction with pools of water in normally dry canyons. If it poses enough of a problem, alter your plans.

Heat. Foot travel on hot desert days can result in dehydration, muscle cramps, heat exhaustion, or even sunstroke, a life-threatening condition. To avert such ailments, drink small amounts of water frequently—a cup or two every half hour—whether thirsty or not. Give yourself time to acclimatize before tackling strenuous trails, and rest sodium-depleted muscles at the first sign of cramping. If heat is extreme, alter your plans.

Doctors agree that the best treatment for heat-related ailments is to find some shade, remain quiet, consume cool water (to which you can add a small amount of salt or electrolyte drink powder), and wet down your clothing. In the case of sunstroke (hyperthermia), emergency medical attention is imperative. Usually the onset of heat-related illness is gradual. Initial symptoms include dizziness, weakness, nausea, headache, and disorientation. Sunstroke can result if these early warning signs are ignored. It is characterized by rapid pulse-rate, high temperature, loss of consciousness, delirium, dry skin, or profuse sweating.

Hazardous Terrain. To hikers in the Southwest, sheer drops pose a significant danger, since many of the desert's most appealing trails either descend into or wind along the rims of steep-walled canyons. Certain varieties of sandstone are notoriously crumbly, and sand on slickrock can create slippery conditions. Since medical help may be far away, prudence dictates caution on steep trails, especially for those hiking with children. Knowledge of first aid is a must. Avoid unnecessary rock climbing unless you are an experienced, well-equipped climber. Don't cut switchbacks, and never throw or roll rocks.

Getting Lost. Particularly when they traverse talus fields or slickrock, desert trails can be difficult to follow. To avoid getting lost, never proceed far until you have located the next trail marker. As insurance, tell someone in advance about your hiking plans. If you do get lost, stay where you are, signal your position in some obvious way (such as laying out colorful gear and clothes in an open area), and wait for help to arrive.

Poisonous Creatures. Although the Southwestern deserts are home to rattlesnakes, scorpions, and black widow spiders, you will rarely see these creatures. They are largely nocturnal, preferring to take shelter under rocks or in woodpiles or brush during the heat of the day. Rattlesnakes usually give fair warning of their presence. Their bites are seldom fatal, and about one in every three snakes injects no venom when it bites, having spent its reserves on its prey. The bites of black widow spiders are likewise rarely fatal, for although their venom is even more toxic than that of rattlesnakes, they inject a much smaller amount. Among scorpions, only a short and slender yellow species, averaging 2 inches in length, is potentially deadly (especially to young children or unhealthy adults); of the areas covered in the book, this species normally resides only in the Grand Canyon.

Common sense, however, does suggest certain precautions. Be careful when climbing rocks or turning them over, and try not to place your hands anywhere that you can't examine visually first. Shake out your shoes before putting them on, and inspect the underside of your tent before rolling it up. Poisonous desert creatures are more common in wet areas, such as the micro-environment around perennial streams.

If someone is injured by a poisonous creature, consult a first-aid manual for the recommended immediate treatment and obtain medical assistance as soon as possible. In general, authorities recommend that the victim be kept warm and quiet, to retard the spread of the poison through the bloodstream or nervous system. The site of a scorpion sting or spider bite can be immersed in cold water—or, preferably, treated with an icepack—to make the victim more comfortable. (Cryotherapy is not recommended for snake bites.) Painkillers can be administered, but the victim should ingest no sedatives or alcoholic beverages.

Dangerous Plants. One of the most common desert hiking injuries is getting pricked by cactus spines, which are mildly poisonous and easily become imbedded under the skin. Avoid contact with cacti by watching where you step. If you do pick up some spines, remove them,

Agave plants growing in a rock crevice

Tukuhnikivats Arch frames the La Sal Mountains, Utah.

then douse the affected area with hydrogen peroxide or some other disinfectant. The sharp tips of yucca and agave leaves can also irritate skin, though to a lesser degree. Beware, too, of poison ivy and oak.

Insect Pests. Late spring and early summer, prior to the onset of the thunderstorm weather pattern, is prime bug season on the Colorado Plateau. Aside from mosquitoes, most common in watery canyons, there are four especially annoying species. Red ants can inflict a painful sting, best treated with cold-water immersion. Biting gnats, which favor pinyon and juniper habitats, go after the tender eye and ear areas, causing itchy welts and even swollen glands to form. Like mosquitoes, gnats are most bothersome around dusk. Deerflies, concentrated in moist, reedy places where livestock have grazed, are attracted to motion and usually aim for the backs of the knees. Finally, blowflies—though they do not bite—make life unpleasant merely by their presence on the scene; they are drawn to open wounds, in which they seek to lay eggs.

Deep woods-type repellents containing DEET are effective against many of these pests. Use only unscented beauty and hygiene products while camping and hiking. Wear light-colored clothing, hats with "no-see-um" netting, long-sleeved shirts, and long pants. Choose breezy, exposed campsites and build smoky fires, if regulations allow. As a last resort when insects become intolerable, try another trail or even another park, since bugs are not uniformly distributed but vary with altitude, water supply, and other local conditions.

A Note about Safety

Travel in many parts of the desert entails unavoidable risks that every traveler assumes and must be aware of and respect. The fact that an area is described in this book is not a representation that it will be safe for you. Trips vary greatly in difficulty and in the amount and kind of preparation needed to enjoy them safely. Some routes may have changed, or conditions on them may have deteriorated since this book was written. Also, of course, conditions can change even from day to day, owing to weather and other factors. A trip that is safe in good weather or for a highly conditioned, properly equipped traveler may be completely unsafe for someone else or unsafe under adverse weather conditions.

You can minimize your risks by being knowledgeable, prepared, and alert. There is not space in this book for a treatise on general wilderness safety and safety in the desert, but there are a number of good books and public courses on the subject, and you should take advantage of them to increase your knowledge. Just as important, you should always be aware of your own limitations and existing conditions when and where you are traveling. If conditions are dangerous, or if you are not prepared to deal with them safely, change your plans! It is better to have wasted a few days than to be the subject of a wilderness rescue. These warnings are not intended to keep you out of the desert and backcountry. Many people enjoy safe trips through the desert and backcountry every year. However, one element of the beauty, freedom, and excitement of these areas is the presence of risks that do not confront us at home. When you travel in these areas, you assume those risks. They can be met safely, but only if you exercise your own independent judgment and common sense.

Driving Safety

Desert driving is usually delightful and unchallenging: vistas are grand, skies are clear, and traffic is light. Yet remote locations, extreme temperatures, and rough roads may pose unaccustomed hazards.

Because towns in the Four Corners region are few and far between, and because service stations tend to close early, it is important to keep plenty of gas in your tank and to check your car's fluid levels frequently. The low octane ratings of much of the gasoline sold in the area, coupled with above-average elevations, may adversely affect your car's performance; to prevent sluggishness, you might want to buy premium unleaded gas. Consider storing extra motor oil, coolant, battery water, hoses, belts, tools, and a shovel in the trunk, in addition to a spare tire. Turn off your air conditioner to deter engine overheating. Always have extra food and plenty of drinking water available in case your car breaks down miles from nowhere, and remember that small town service stations may have to mail-order any parts needed to repair your vehicle. Be advised that towing fees can be extremely steep.

When hiking, lock up, bring along an extra set of keys, and leave nothing valuable in your car. Although car "clouting" remains relatively uncommon in the Four Corners area, it is a growing problem, particularly at certain trailheads.

Driving on Unpaved Roads. On gravel surfaces, slow down when approaching other vehicles to avoid sustaining a broken windshield. Sharp rocks may also cause flat tires or blowouts. Dirt roads can be rough when dry and impassable when wet, either because they cross wash bottoms or because they are composed of clay-type soil. On washboards, the closely spaced, parallel ridges that often characterize dirt roads, slow down on curves to maintain control. Slow speeds are also advisable when the road is bumpy or twisty or when it descends into gullies or crosses exposed rock. The absence of guardrails on many roads poses another danger, as does the presence of unfenced livestock. Try to avoid night driving on unpaved roads; otherwise, you risk a close encounter with a deer, a cow, or a frame-bending gully. Never drive off established roads, for this practice will harm the desert (and possibly your car).

Drivers should familiarize themselves in advance with road maps, particularly if they plan to travel off the main highways. Unfortunately, maps rarely show all of an area's unpaved roads. People using such roads should seek precise directions and current road-quality information locally before starting out. The condition of an unpaved road can vary dramatically within short periods of time, mainly as a function of weather. If you will be driving on poor or remote roads, it is wise to inform someone of the route you intend to take in case you get lost or experience car trouble.

Ethics and Hygiene

The desert is a fragile ecosystem, easily harmed by thoughtless human practices. Decomposition is slow, erosion is rapid, and unsightly scars made by vehicles, fires, and even lugged soles may take decades to heal. It is therefore even more vital here than elsewhere to camp in a low-impact manner, as epitomized in the familiar motto, "Take nothing but pictures, leave nothing but footprints." In particular, visitors should abide by the following guidelines:

- Stay on trails or designated routes. Do not cut across switchbacks to shorten your hike, for this practice hastens erosion.
- Do not drive off established roads.
- Bury human waste in "catholes" 6 inches deep and at least 300 feet from water sources. Pack out your toilet paper. In the future it is likely that campers in dispersed sites will be required to have their own portable toilets.
- Do not bring pets into the wilderness. They might harm, or be harmed by, wild animals, and they often frighten or annoy other hikers.

- Resist the temptation to make souvenirs of cacti, exotic plants, rocks, pottery fragments, arrowheads, or petrified wood from protected areas. These practices violate federal and state laws.
- Avoid trampling the black, crusty, microbiotic (also called "cryptogamic" or "cryptobiotic") soil that retards erosion throughout the Southwest. Composed of lichens, mosses, algae, and fungi, this living substance stabilizes the sand, permitting larger plants to take root.
- Camp and wash dishes at least 300 feet away from all ground water. Never pollute pools or streams with dishwashing soap, even the biodegradable kind.
- Use a backpacking stove instead of building a campfire, since fire rings scar the desert. Fires are prohibited in many places. If you do make a fire where they are permitted, gather only dead wood that is lying on the ground; use a fire pan or an already-established fire ring; build your fire far away from vegetation; pack out all trash; and douse the fire with water, stirring to make sure no live coals remain.

Antiquities

Appreciation for the Southwest's archaeological heritage has led federal and state governments to make laws protecting ancient ruins, drawings, and artifacts from vandalism, damage, and theft. Simply put, it is illegal to remove, deface, or destroy any Neolithic object found

Admiring the Great Gallery's Ghost King, Horseshoe Canyon, Utah

on public land. Violation of these laws carries stiff penalties, including fines and jail terms.

Most people who harm ruin sites probably do so in an innocent manner. They don't realize that taking even the tiniest potsherd can complicate the task of scholars trying to reconstruct how pre-Columbian tribes lived. They don't stop to think that adding their initials to a petroglyph will detract from the enjoyment of others. Or they don't understand how fragile ancient artifacts are, so they touch wall plaster and rock art, camp inside ruins, walk on middens, or stand, climb, or lean on ruin walls.

Please respect all antiquities that you find. Disturb nothing, take nothing, and make sure that others follow suit.

Equipment

Outfitting yourself for backcountry desert travel need not involve extraordinary effort or expense. If you are an experienced mountain hiker, most of the gear you already own will suffice. Major items needed include a backpack, daypack, tent with "no-see-um" netting, lightweight sleeping bag, ground pad, camp stove, cooking equipment, water bottles (at least a 2-gallon capacity per person), and water purifier.

Always carry with you the Ten Essentials recommended by The Mountaineers: extra clothing, extra food, sunglasses, knife, matches, fire starter, first-aid kit, flashlight, map, and compass. In the desert, also bring sunscreen and extra water.

Summer travelers should pack clothing appropriate for warm to hot days and cool nights. Long-sleeved tops and long, loose-fitting slacks offer protection from sun, bugs, and dangerous plants. Wide-brimmed hats are advisable. For footwear, bring comfortable, high-top nylon and leather shoes; rigid, heavy-duty boots are needed only for the most rugged trails. Because some hikes involve wading, pack old boots or sneakers and plenty of extra socks.

Maps

Some of the hikes outlined in this book can be completed easily either with no map at all or with a very basic diagram of the sort provided in park brochures. Others, however, require the use of topographic maps issued by the United States Geological Survey (USGS). The maps can be purchased locally or obtained in advance from the U.S. Geological Survey, Distribution Section, Denver Federal Center, Building 41, Denver, CO 80225. Their phone number is (303) 236-7477.

Waterproof, tear-proof versions of the topo maps for many Southwestern parks are published by Trails Illustrated. Also widely available is the AAA map, "A Guide to Indian Country," which shows all the major paved and unpaved roads of the area and gives accurate distances to 0.1 mile.

Trip Planning

An enjoyable camping trip requires a good deal of advance planning. Write away for topo maps or national park literature and secure reservations months ahead for popular campsites and backcountry trails. Be advised that, increasingly, parks are charging user fees for backcountry travel.

Always inquire locally about weather, water, and insect conditions before beginning a major hike. Carefully calculate how long your chosen route will take so that you can plan and provision accordingly. If yours is not a loop or a round-trip hike, arrange for a car shuttle or hire someone to drive you to your trailhead. Rangers in national parks and employees in outdoors stores or other wilderness-related businesses sometimes can help you make contact with people eager to earn extra money in this manner.

Also consider the availability of showers, laundromats, and grocery stores in a given area. Showers pose a particular problem in the rural Southwest. Some state and national parks have shower facilities, and many RV parks will allow nonguests to shower on the premises for a few dollars. Otherwise, unless you decide to stop at a motel, you may have to settle for a dip in a lake, river, or swimming pool.

Above all, consider the capability and experience of the members of your party. Plan to step up your exercise program weeks in advance of the trip. Novices should stick to short, well-established trails through terrain that is not too rugged or challenging. Even veteran backpackers need time to adjust to the heat and elevation of the desert. A "conditioning" hike or two will help you avoid problems.

Camping. Most national and state parks have modern camping facilities, though in some cases you will have to put up with outhouses and the absence of running water. Some campgrounds close during the winter months; others remain open, offering fewer services. During the peak season, and especially on holiday weekends, try to arrive at campgrounds as early in the day as possible to avoid disappointment. If sites are full, bear in mind that much of the high desert—especially in Utah—is public land, administered by the Bureau of Land Management (BLM), and you are allowed to camp virtually anywhere on it, in the absence of "no trespassing" signs. Basically, you just turn onto a dirt road, follow it for a mile or so, and find a comfortable, level spot, preferably one that has been used before. Be careful not to run over vegetation when you pull off the road. Don't be intimidated by fences and gates on public lands, since these are generally meant to keep livestock in, not to keep you out; but remember to leave gates as you find them. The Indian reservations allow camping, if at all, only in designated areas. Please respect their property rights.

Another alternative when a full campground disappoints you is to obtain a backcountry permit for tent camping elsewhere in the park.

In most cases, regulations allow you to camp almost anyplace you want, provided you are at least a half mile off the trail. The exception to this is in archaeological parks such as Chaco and Mesa Verde, where backcountry camping is forbidden.

Using This Book

This book is designed to take some of the burden of trip planning out of your hands. It groups many of the high desert's most enjoyable trails and awe-inspiring scenic attractions into six itineraries, each about two or three weeks in length. Because the loops overlap in spots, those with extra time will find it easy to integrate them into longer trips. For illustrative purposes I have assumed that you will begin and end at a particular town, but you can join an itinerary at any point. If your home is far from the Four Corners region, you can fly to a major urban center such as Denver, Albuquerque, Phoenix, Las Vegas, or Salt Lake City, rent a car, and drive from there to intersect your chosen loop.

For each itinerary, I have minimized driving and maximized time to explore the desert on foot. As you will discover, driving is a pleasure and not a chore in the Southwest. Certain road trips are "classics," worth doing for their own sakes, such as the Burr Trail, AZ-98 across the Navajo Reservation to Lake Powell, and UT-128 north of Moab, along the Colorado River.

I built as much diversity as possible into each loop, to provide a fair sampling of local scenery and culture and to strike a balance between day-hiking and backpacking. A few itineraries may have special appeal to certain audiences. Readers especially intrigued by archaeology should select the Anasazi Loop, while serious backpackers might be happiest with the Canyons Loop.

For each hike, I specify its distance (rounded to the nearest quarter mile, except where greater precision seems vital), the time an average hiker needs to complete it (with estimates on the conservative side), and the topo map(s) that correspond to it. Moreover, each hike is assigned a difficulty rating on a scale of very easy to very strenuous.

Very easy trails have good walking surfaces and may even be paved. They are usually short, more or less level, utterly unproblematic to follow, and suitable for almost everyone. Such trails are generally found in national parks and are highlighted in their brochures.

Easy trails demand minimal physical exertion. Although they may involve some elevation loss or gain, it is of the slow, steady variety. They are usually well marked with signposts or cairns (rockpiles) and well-maintained, and although they tend to be longer than their "very easy" counterparts, they still remain good family hikes.

Moderate trails ask somewhat more of the hiker in regard to skill and endurance. Some of them, by virtue of their length, are practical

A hiker investigates Navajo Sandstone narrows.

Splashing through a tributary of the Escalante River, Utah

only for backpackers. They presuppose a certain degree of route-finding ability, in addition to a tolerance for ups and downs. Climbs may be short and steep or may be longer, with a more gentle gradient. The route may require slogging through sand or hopping boulders.

Strenuous hikes put significant demands on travelers. Often located in remote areas, they generally involve advance planning. Most are backcountry trails not suitable for day-hiking. Complications may include dramatic elevation gains on steep, exposed slopes; deep wading; rock scrambling; long waterless treks; unmarked or poorly marked routes; and precipitous drops.

Very strenuous routes are recommended only for experienced backpackers in top condition. The same hardship factors evident in strenuous hikes also apply here, but to a higher degree of difficulty, or in greater concentration.

Chapter 2

DESERT RIVERS LOOP

Utah

This 17-day itinerary promises something for everyone: natural bridges, waterfalls, narrow slot canyons, and prehistoric artifacts. Balancing day trips with backpacking, and involving minimal driving, it explores portions of the Green, Fremont, Escalante, and Paria drainages. The area's oasislike streams carve through some of the driest country around.

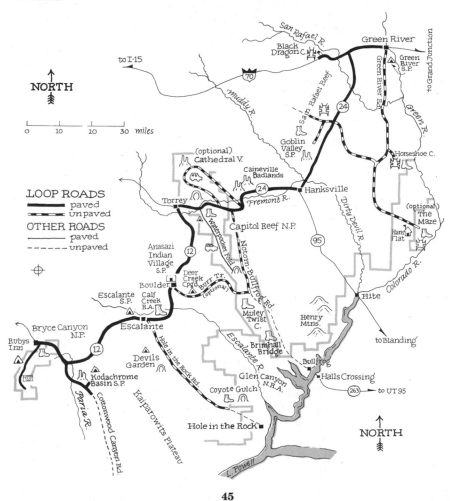

Dusk falls over the "mushroom" rocks of Goblin Valley State Park.

Day 1: GREEN RIVER TO GOBLIN VALLEY

- **A 45-mile drive along the spectacular San Rafael Reef**
- **Short, conditioning hikes amid bizarre hoodoos**
- **Camping and showers at Goblin Valley State Park**
- **Gas, groceries, and showers available in Green River**

Your trip begins in Green River (population 900), situated in east central Utah where I-70 crosses the Colorado's main tributary (see map, p. 45). A sleepy town, Green River nevertheless provides the essentials. Fill your gas tank and stock up here, for the next settlement scheduled on the loop—Hanksville, on Day 3—is even tinier than Green River!

Drive west 12 miles on I-70 and take the exit for UT-24. Turn south on this lonely road, which parallels the **San Rafael Reef** virtually all the way to Hanksville. Resembling the backbone of a stegosaurus, the reef is the eastern edge of the San Rafael Swell, a huge anticline born millions of years ago when subterranean forces thrust up and deformed overlying rock strata. It creates a striking contrast to the featureless, arid land on your left, which gives little hint of the Edenic canyons lying just beyond. Through these canyons—the Labyrinth and Stillwater sections of the Green River—one can float 120 miles from the highway bridge at Green River State Park to the Green's confluence with the Colorado, without negotiating a single rapid. Required permits are available through Canyonlands National Park.

Reach **Goblin Valley State Park** by turning right (west) onto a narrow paved road toward Temple Mountain, 25 miles south of I-70. In about 5 miles turn left at a junction marked by a sign. Now the San Rafael Reef is on your right, and inspiring views of the Gilson Buttes are on your left. Goblin Valley is 7 miles down this graded dirt and gravel road, near Wild Horse Butte (See map, p. 49).

The goblins of this magical 3650-acre park are carved out of cocoa brown Entrada Sandstone and capped by the greenish white Curtis Formation. When the area was discovered in the late 1920s, it was named "Mushroom Valley" for its wildly eroded, toadstool-shaped mud hills. The treeless campground, complete with showers, flush toilets, and other modern conveniences, will serve as your base of operations for trips into the San Rafael Reef and Swell. After setting up camp, continue down the park road to its end at Observation Point, a sheltered overlook with picnic tables and pit toilets. Access into the main part of the valley is by foot on a short path that descends from here. About 50 yards down, the trail peters out and you're left to follow your inclinations in this otherworldly setting.

Goblin Valley also has two official trails, both accessible from the Observation Point parking area. Plan to hike these today, to acclimate yourself to the temperature and altitude. The **Carmel Canyon Loop** (1.5 miles) is the shorter and easier of the two. From the northeast corner of the parking lot, it descends into Carmel Canyon, winds left through badlands toward a prominent butte called Mollys Castle, and then enters a short narrows section before climbing back to the road a few hundred yards north of the trailhead. More interesting is the undulating **Curtis Bench Trail** (2 miles), which begins near the parking area and ends at the campground. A spur trail from the benchlands affords marvelous views of the Henry Mountains to the south. This remote and wild chain was the last major range in the continental United States to be "discovered" by white people.

For further information, write to Goblin Valley State Park, Box 637, Green River, UT 84525-0093; for reservations, call (800) 322-3770.

Day 2: THE SAN RAFAEL REEF

- **A memorable day hike through narrow canyons**
- **Camping and showers at Goblin Valley State Park**

For today's hike, choose among three high-walled canyons chiseled into the San Rafael Reef: Little Wild Horse (paired here with Bell to form a loop), Crack, and Chute. All have deep narrows bounded by soaring cliffs and afford easy passage. You can complete both the Crack and Chute Canyon trips in one day if you are feeling ambitious. Be sure to fill water bottles before starting out. There are many other wonderful canyons to explore in the area, notably Ding and Dang, Eardley, Farnsworth, Coal, Three Fingers, Iron Wash, and the Chute of Muddy Creek.

Day Hike 1: Little Wild Horse and Bell Canyons

Distance: 7.5 miles round trip
Time: 1 day
Map: topo for Wild Horse
Difficulty: easy to moderate

With its extensive, tight narrows, Little Wild Horse Canyon is a visual and tactile delight (see map, p. 49). Its southern end joins Bell Canyon, making for an exciting but leisurely loop hike. It is also a cool one, for the sun penetrates these deep slots only at midday. Do not enter the canyons if rain threatens; few exit routes are available.

The access road to Little Wild Horse Canyon is 5.75 miles west of the Goblin Valley Entrance Station. Leave the state park and turn left at Wild Horse Butte onto a generally good dirt road. You may have trouble at mile 2.75, where the road crosses Wild Horse Creek; gun it here to avoid getting stuck in the sand. At mile 5.75, a sign on the main road reads, "High clearance vehicles only." Turn right just past the sign and follow the jeep track as far as you feel comfortable driving; the road extends for about a mile. Park when you start feeling nervous. Past a grove of cottonwoods you climb or skirt two dry waterfalls in quick succession. After that, you come to a fork. Bell Canyon is to the left. You turn right here, into **Little Wild Horse.**

Before long you reach the twisty Navajo Sandstone narrows that continue, on and off, about two-thirds of the way up the canyon. At times you must turn sideways and remove your daypack to proceed. You may also have to jump or wade across small pools. Where the canyon opens out at its end, there are several minor chockstones and pour-offs.

After about 3.5 miles, a jeep road crosses the canyon. Turn left here and follow the road for about 1.25 miles over a pass to the head of **Bell Canyon.** Upper Bell is narrower, prettier, and shadier than upper Little Wild Horse, and a rough dirt road extends into it almost as far as its narrows section. Despite some obstructions near the upper end, you can maintain a rapid pace. In no time, you'll be back to the Little Wild Horse junction and your car.

Day Hike 2: Crack Canyon

Distance: up to 7 miles round trip
Time: up to 3.5 hours
Map: topo for Temple Mountain
Difficulty: moderate

Although you can enter this canyon from either the bottom (via Wild Horse Creek, near the butte) or the top (from a road that parallels the reef), the latter access avoids a sandy slog over 2 miles of featureless

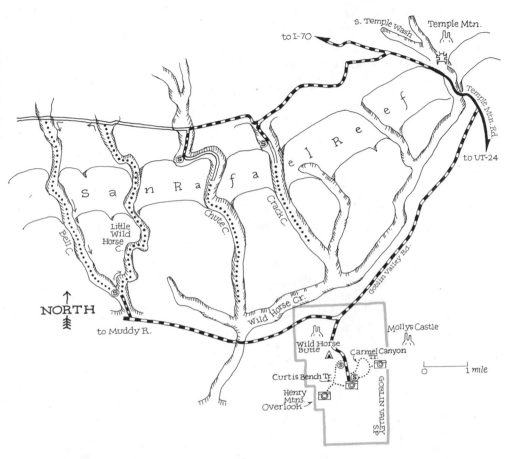

desert (see map, above). Leave Goblin Valley and drive northeast on the Goblin Valley road for 7 miles to its junction with the road to Temple Mountain. Turn left (north). In about 0.75 mile look for the South Temple Wash Fremont pictograph panel on the cliffs to the right. A half mile farther, the pavement stops, and 1.25 miles past that point, turn left (west) onto a good dirt road, normally suitable for all vehicles as far as Chute Canyon. Magnificent views of **Temple Mountain**—a prime source of uranium for the Manhattan Project of the 1940s—and the top of the San Rafael Reef can be enjoyed here, marred only by abandoned shacks, cars, and debris left by miners.

The entrance to **Crack Canyon** is 4.25 miles down this road. A jeep track extends south into the canyon for about 0.75 mile. As it slices through the reef, the canyon exposes the Navajo and Kayenta Formations. Each stratum contains a colorful set of narrows. Though very short, the Navajo narrows, with rock pockmarked like Swiss cheese, feature a subway-type overhang. The Kayenta narrows, much longer and deeper, begin about 2 miles down the canyon. A few dryfalls and other obstacles make these narrows somewhat tricky to negotiate, so those without moderate athletic ability may wish to stop here. When you have seen enough, backtrack up the canyon to your car.

Day Hike 3: Chute Canyon

> **Distance: 5 miles round trip**
> **Time: 2.5 hours**
> **Map: topo for Wild Horse**
> **Difficulty: very easy**

This canyon is Crack's nearest neighbor to the west; some people combine the two into a long loop hike. Since that involves a dusty trek down Wild Horse Creek and nearly 2 miles of road-stomping north of the reef, investigating each canyon separately seems more sensible. With no obstructions or tight narrows, Chute is an easy walk (see map, p. 49).

High-walled canyons cut through San Rafael Reef.

Approach **Chute Canyon** from the dirt road at the top of the San Rafael Reef (see Day Hike 2, Crack Canyon). The entrance into Chute is 6.75 miles down this road, or 1.75 miles past Crack. The road itself actually goes a long way into Chute before climbing out to the west. A good place to turn back is at the end of the narrows section, before the canyon joins Wild Horse Creek.

Day 3: GOBLIN VALLEY TO CAPITOL REEF

- **A drive through the desolate Caineville Badlands**
- **Short hikes in the Waterpocket Fold country**
- **Camping at Capitol Reef National Park**
- **Gas, groceries, and showers available in Hanksville**

Leave the Goblin Valley area today and head 19.5 miles south on UT-24 to Hanksville, where the Fremont River and Muddy Creek unite to form the Dirty Devil, so named by Major Powell's party because of the quantity of silt it transports. Gas up and reprovision in Hanksville, buying 2 days' worth of food. From here it is 37 miles to Capitol Reef National Park. Continue on UT-24, which follows the Fremont River drainage to an eye-blinker of a town, Caineville, in 20 miles. The Henry Mountains rise to the south. The road passes through the gray and tan **Caineville Badlands,** which are most appealing when the sun is low in the sky; watch for prominent **Factory Butte** to the north. The landscape becomes more lush and inviting as you near **Capitol Reef National Park.**

Called "the land of the sleeping rainbow" by Navajos, this photogenic and geologically unusual park is off the beaten track. Water erosion here has created intricate canyons, arches, spires, and domes. One of the largest domes, composed of Navajo Sandstone, resembles the Capitol Building in Washington, D.C., and gives the park its name.

The dominant landform is the 100-mile-long **Waterpocket Fold,** a rocky ridge warped and uplifted 60 million years ago by subterranean pressures. Many canyons bite into the fold, exposing its tilted strata. As you travel from east to west through these gorges, you move forward in geologic time, beginning with the Chinle Formation and passing through the majestic Glen Canyon Group: Wingate Sandstone, the Kayenta Formation, and Navajo Sandstone. Throughout the region, numerous small potholes, or "pockets," in the rock collect rainwater. The Fremont River, named to honor the nineteenth-century explorer John C. Fremont (of Civil War fame), drains the area.

Between A.D. 800 and 1200, Fremont Indians lived along the river, and their rock carvings are still amply in evidence; a large grouping of petroglyphs can be seen at a marked pullout about 1.25 miles east of the visitor center. In later centuries, the area was frequented by Ute and Paiute Indians, law-evading polygamists, and members of Butch Cassidy's "Wild Bunch." The Fremont River valley was settled by

Mormons who planted and irrigated orchards that the Park Service still maintains; in season, visitors may pick and purchase fruit.

Capitol Reef presents wonderful opportunities for day or overnight hikes. After selecting a campsite, orient yourself by taking the 25-mile, round-trip Scenic Drive from the visitor center to Capitol Gorge. The Gorge served as the original route for travelers through the Waterpocket Fold. Where the road ends at a parking lot and sheltered picnic area, you will find trailheads to the Tanks and the Golden Throne. Other day hiking possibilities are described below.

For more information, write to the Superintendent, Capitol Reef National Park, Torrey, UT 84775.

Day Hike 1: The Tanks

> **Distance: 2 miles round trip**
> **Time: 1.5 hours**
> **Map: topo for Capitol Reef National Park**
> **Difficulty: very easy, with optional, moderate climb**

Beginning at the Capitol Gorge picnic shelter, this popular hike leads to the **Tanks,** a series of water-filled potholes (see map, p. 54). The route is level, except for an optional 150-foot climb at the end. Around the 0.5 mile mark is a Pioneer Register, where westward migrants recorded their names on the smooth, sandstone cliffs. About 0.25 miles farther on is the first of the Tanks, to the left; others are out of sight, directly above. In years past, these waterpockets provided welcome refreshment for pioneers and their stock animals.

To see the higher pools, continue 100 yards downstream to reach a sign. Turn left and climb, following cairns, for about 0.25 mile to a small natural bridge. Backtrack to your car.

Day Hike 2: Golden Throne

> **Distance: 4 miles round trip**
> **Time: 2 hours**
> **Map: topo for Capitol Reef National Park**
> **Difficulty: moderate**

This trail, which ascends 1100 feet to a viewpoint below the base of a gold-colored dome, begins a few yards up the road from the Capitol Gorge picnic shelter (see map, p. 54). The climb, although initially steep, takes advantage of natural sloping ledges of slickrock and compressed dirt. It hugs the rim of Capitol Gorge, digging in toward the north several times to head side-canyons.

The trail is logical and clearly marked, but it provides little shade. At the top, hikers enjoy magnificent views of the Navajo Sandstone domes that dominate this part of the park. Although you cannot get very close to the **Golden Throne** itself, it does photograph well, especially in late afternoon, when it seems to glow from an inner fire. Return the way you came.

Day Hike 3: Hickman Bridge

> **Distance: 2 miles round trip**
> **Time: 2 hours**
> **Map: topo for Capitol Reef National Park**
> **Difficulty: moderate**

The well-marked trailhead to **Hickman Bridge** (see map, p. 54), named after a local man instrumental in securing federal protection for the area, is 2 miles east of the visitor center on UT-24. For a short distance, the trail follows the river before climbing rapidly about 400 feet to the canyon rim. Where the trail splits, 0.25 mile from the trailhead, take the left fork, which drops into a shallow wash before arriving at the 130-foot-long Kayenta Formation bridge, 0.75 mile past the junction. Delights along the way include an ancient granary, a pit house, and two small natural bridges, plus striking views of **Capitol Dome,** Pectols Pyramid, and other petrified dunes. On the far side of Hickman Bridge, a short loop ascends for a better view before dropping back to the main trail.

Day Hike 4: Fremont River Overlook

> **Distance: 2 miles round trip**
> **Time: 1.5 hours**
> **Map: topo for Capitol Reef National Park**
> **Difficulty: initially very easy, then strenuous**

The Fremont River Trail (see map, p. 54) begins at the back end of the Capitol Reef campground. The first 0.5 mile is a level, leisurely walk along the riverbank, past orchards and horse pastures. Look for yellow-bellied marmots in the bushes. Passing through a gate, the trail begins a merciless 800-foot ascent up rocky switchbacks to the ridgetop. Here you enjoy views of sandstone domes and of the canyon of the upper Fremont River cutting into Boulder Mountain. Currently, that canyon can be hiked (a strenuous trip involving many stream crossings), though county officials have proposed building a dam upstream.

Day Hike 5: Grand Wash

> **Distance: 2.25 miles one way**
> **Time: 1.5 hours**
> **Map: topo for Capitol Reef National Park**
> **Difficulty: very easy**

Grand Wash has carved through the Waterpocket Fold a sheer-walled canyon with a short but unusually beautiful narrows section. The

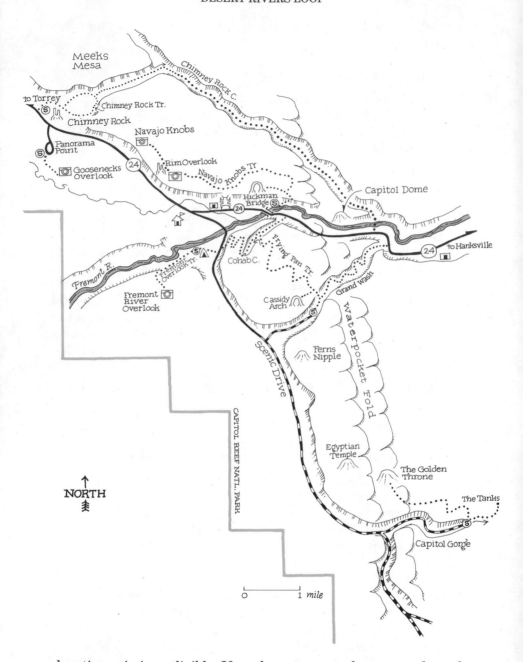

elevation gain is negligible. If you have two cars, leave one where the hike terminates, at a marked pullout on UT-24, 4.5 miles east of the visitor center. Otherwise, plan to retrace your steps.

Start your hike at the end of a spur 3.5 miles south of the visitor center along the Scenic Drive (see map, above). A trail parallels the streambed on the right for about the first 0.25 mile, but most of the way you walk in the wash. Because this 500-foot-deep canyon has few exit routes, do not enter it when rain threatens. Within about a mile, the narrows begin; at some points the canyon is only 20 feet wide. After another mile, the canyon opens up again somewhat, and you soon reach the highway.

The short side-canyons branching east from Grand Wash are worth exploring. Especially enjoyable are Bear Canyon, which intersects the main canyon just before the narrows, and an unnamed slot at the heart of the narrows, where the wash bends sharply to the left.

Day Hike 6: Chimney Rock Trail

> **Distance: 3.5 miles round trip**
> **Time: 2 hours**
> **Map: topo for Capitol Reef National Park**
> **Difficulty: moderate**

This hike begins at the Chimney Rock parking area, 3.25 miles west of the visitor center (see map, p. 54). In about 0.25 mile, the trail divides. Turn right here and ascend several hundred feet to a mesa top. You are treated to glorious views of Chimney Rock, a Moenkopi pillar with a cap of Shinarump Sandstone (a member of the Chinle Formation). After a flat stretch, the trail heads east to another mesa. A Wingate formation called Mummy Cliff dominates the scene. Crossing over to the back of the second mesa, you descend significantly to meet the trail that goes toward Chimney Rock Canyon. At the junction, turn left (south) to loop back to the parking lot. The trail climbs a low saddle before dropping down toward the highway.

Day 4: MORE IN CAPITOL REEF

> • **Narrow canyon or ridgetop hike**
> • **Camping at Capitol Reef National Park or Cedar Mesa Campground**
> • **Gas, groceries, showers, and laundry available in Torrey**

Choose today among four long trails, all with incredible allure. Two traverse high, exposed benchlands, while the others explore dark, sinuous canyons. Sometime today, decide whether to elect a backpacking trip (see Days 5 and 6) in Upper or Lower Muley Twist Canyon. Secure a permit at the visitor center, and purchase 3 days' supplies in verdant Torrey, 10 miles west of the park on UT-24.

Camp at Capitol Reef Campground or Cedar Mesa Campground, 20 miles down the Notom-Bullfrog Road (see Days 5 and 6 for directions). Take along several gallons of water per person, as Cedar Mesa Campground and most of the hikes in the lower part of the park are dry.

Day Hike 1: Frying Pan Trail

> **Distance: 6.25 miles one way, including side trip to Cassidy Arch**
> **Time: 4 hours**
> **Map: topo for Capitol Reef National Park**
> **Difficulty: moderate**

Most of the Frying Pan Trail traverses the slickrock terraces of the Kayenta Formation overlooking the park. Because parts of this trail can become ovenlike at midday without a stiff breeze, begin the trip in early morning. To reach the trailhead (see map, p. 54), drive south from the visitor center on the Scenic Drive to the Grand Wash spur. Turn left here and continue to the road's end, where the hike begins.

After 0.25 mile, your trail branches off to the left, climbing briskly about 900 feet to the canyon rim. In 1 mile, a 0.5-mile spur trail to the left leads to **Cassidy Arch,** a graceful span named after the outlaw Butch Cassidy.

Back at the main trail, go left. The trail climbs a few hundred feet more, winding through eroded uplands. After leveling out for a short distance, it descends to cross the shallow arm of a canyon, and then ascends a low pass before dropping into the **Cohab Canyon** drainage, about 3 miles beyond the junction with the Cassidy Arch spur. The vistas are phenomenal.

Upon entering Cohab Canyon, turn left, proceeding up the canyon to its head. This narrow chasm, with its Swiss cheese rock walls and

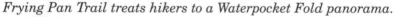

Frying Pan Trail treats hikers to a Waterpocket Fold panorama.

even narrower side-canyons, was once a refuge for Mormon polygamists, or "cohabitationists," trying to evade federal marshals. From the canyon's end, the trail drops steeply in the next mile, switchbacking down a precipitous cliff to the Scenic Drive and campground, 3.5 road miles north of your car.

Day Hike 2: Navajo Knobs Trail

> **Distance: 9 miles round trip**
> **Time: 5 hours**
> **Map: topo for Capitol Reef National Park**
> **Difficulty: moderate to strenuous**

This beautiful, well-constructed trail takes off from the Hickman Bridge parking lot, 2 miles east of the visitor center on UT-24 (see map, p. 52). Although it involves a substantial climb, the ascent is mostly on gently tilted slickrock ramps. Take along an appropriate amount of water, and start early in the day in hot weather.

Follow the Hickman Bridge Trail for 0.25 mile, climbing, until you arrive at a fork amid black lava boulders. Go right at the fork. After crossing a wash, the trail slowly and steadily ascends, offering views of Pectols Pyramid. At about mile 1, you come to another signed junction. The main trail continues to the right, but it is worthwhile to detour first onto the short spur to the left, which leads to an overlook of Hickman Bridge.

Returning to the main trail, turn left. The trail heads a few shallow side-canyons as it climbs toward **Rim Overlook**, at mile 2.25. From here you can see the Henry Mountains and Waterpocket Fold country to the east, the gorges of Sulphur Creek and the Fremont River to the south, and Thousand Lake Mountain to the west. Gnats may be fierce at the overlook during late spring and early summer.

Past the overlook the trail drops somewhat, rounds a large bay, and climbs to a ridge on which there is a radio tower. The formation called the **Castle** comes dramatically into view. You descend to the midpoint of another large bay, skirting the Castle, and then start a big climb on a slickrock ramp toward the **Navajo Knobs.** A cairned route leads to the top of one of these knobs, where you can relax before your return trip.

Day Hike 3: Chimney Rock Canyon

> **Distance: 9 miles one way**
> **Time: 6 hours**
> **Map: topo for Capitol Reef National Park**
> **Difficulty: moderate**

Narrow Chimney Rock (aka Spring) Canyon runs parallel to the axis of the Waterpocket Fold for many miles before cutting through it. The trail into this exquisite canyon starts at the Chimney Rock pullout north of UT-24 (see map, p. 54), about 3.25 miles west of the visitor center. **Chimney Rock** itself can also be visited by those with time and energy to spare. Otherwise, the hike is slightly downhill and relatively shady most of the way.

From the trailhead, climb onto the tableland behind Chimney Rock to the junction with the **Chimney Rock Trail.** Continue straight ahead toward the soaring Wingate cliffs of Meeks Mesa. You soon pass the other end of the Chimney Rock Trail loop on your right. Following a drainage, you descend gradually to intersect **Chimney Rock Canyon,** 2.5 miles from the parking lot. There is a drift fence here. Go right and follow the canyon for 6.5 more miles down to its confluence with the Fremont River.

Chimney Rock Canyon, chiseled out of Wingate Sandstone and the Kayenta Formation, is narrow, twisty, and spectacular, its depth averaging about 500 feet. Navajo Sandstone domes loom above. At one point, you'll have to climb a bit onto the eroded left bank to avoid some pour-offs, but otherwise you remain in the streambed. About halfway down the canyon, look for a natural arch on the left. Just past an enormous alcove, Chimney Rock Canyon meets the **Fremont River**, 3.5 miles east of the visitor center on UT-24. Cautiously ford the river. From here it is 6.75 miles by road back to your car.

Day Hike 4: Sulphur Creek Narrows

> **Distance: 5 miles one way**
> **Time: 3 hours**
> **Map: topo for Capitol Reef National Park**
> **Difficulty: moderate; strenuous in high water levels**

The trailhead for this one-way, downstream hike is across the highway from the Chimney Rock parking lot, 3.25 miles west of the visitor center (where the hike concludes). Check on weather before starting out, since the narrow canyon is no place to be caught in a storm. Avoid this trip, too, if the water in the creek is cold or its level is high.

The route remains in the washbed virtually all the way. It begins by dipping into a side-canyon of Sulphur Creek. A minor obstruction in the side-canyon should pose little difficulty. After about 0.75 mile, you join Sulphur Creek. Here the canyon is shallow, with a hard-packed dirt floor, and you can expect to make good time. As the creek cuts into older, uplifted rock layers, the canyon narrows considerably, and you enter the "goosenecks," where the streambed doubles back on itself repeatedly.

About 0.5 mile beyond the goosenecks, your progress is impeded by a series of obstacles, mainly falls, of which the first two present the greatest challenge. Both can be skirted, carefully, on the right bank. If water is flowing in the wash, it may be deeper in this vicinity. When the canyon widens out again, about 0.75 mile past the first of the falls, travel becomes quicker and easier.

From the last obstruction, a waterfall that you can avoid by keeping left, it is about another mile to the end of the hike. Just past this obstacle, a side-canyon comes in on the right, but you stay in the main channel. A few more meanders bring you within sight of the highway bridge. Go left here on a cairned trail to the visitor center.

Capitol Reef's domes, seen through Hickman Bridge

Days 5 and 6: MULEY TWIST

- **A drive down the Notom-Bullfrog Road along the Waterpocket Fold**
- **An overnight canyon wilderness excursion**
- **Arches, alcoves, and breathtaking scenery**

Upper and Lower Muley Twist match any canyons in the Southwest for aesthetic appeal. Reserve an extra day for Lower Muley Twist if

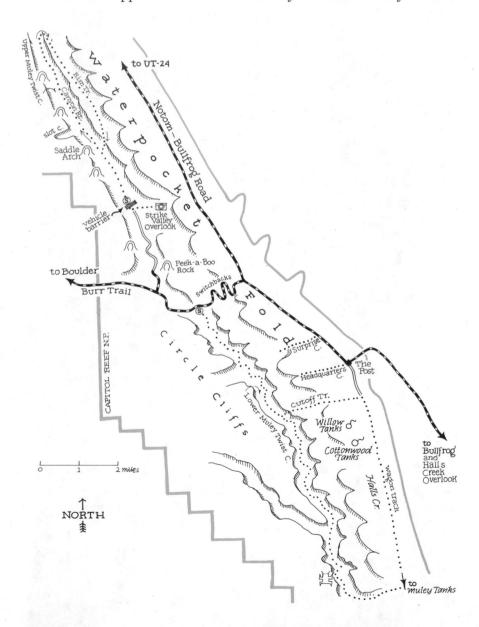

you plan to investigate side-canyons and/or walk back to the parking lot. Get an early start, and carry at least a gallon of water apiece per day. It's also possible to take day hikes in these canyons instead of backpacking them. An excellent day hike nearby, to Brimhall Double Bridge, is another alternative.

The trips described take off from the (mostly unpaved) Notom-Bullfrog Road connecting UT-24 with Lake Powell. It is a 1.5-hour drive from the visitor center to the Muley Twist trailheads, and about 30 minutes farther to the trailhead for Brimhall Bridge. From the visitor center, drive east on UT-24. Just past the park boundary, turn right (south) onto the Notom-Bullfrog Road. Cedar Mesa Campground, a primitive campground with five sites, is 20 miles distant.

For Muley Twist, turn right onto the famous **Burr Trail** about 15 miles past Cedar Mesa Campground. The Burr Trail climbs to the top of the Waterpocket Fold on a thrilling set of switchbacks. After 2.5 miles, once the road has topped out, a sign indicates access into Lower Muley Twist Canyon, on the left. The turnoff for the Upper Muley trailhead is a mile up the road beyond this point, on the right.

The alternate hike to Brimhall Double Bridge begins at **Halls Creek Overlook**. To get there, proceed south toward Bullfrog Marina instead of ascending the Burr Trail switchbacks. Soon the road veers sharply east, away from the Fold. About 45.25 miles from UT-24, you reach a T intersection. Turn right here, toward Bullfrog Marina. In about 1.5 miles, there will be a Y intersection, where you bear right for Halls Creek Overlook, 2.5 miles distant. Especially near its end, this road is rough and requires a high-clearance vehicle.

Whatever trip you choose, camp near Boulder on the evening of Day 7, perhaps at one of the national forest campgrounds north of town on UT-12. Calf Creek Recreation Area south of town also offers camping, but its sites fill quickly. For the most direct route to Boulder, continue west through Long Canyon on the Burr Trail. Deer Creek Campground is located near the road's end, about 26.5 miles past the turnoff for Upper Muley Twist. All of the 36.25-mile-long Burr Trail, except for the section in Capitol Reef National Park, is paved, but the road is narrow and not suitable for trailers.

Backpack (or Day Hike) 1: Lower Muley Twist Canyon

> **Distance: 17.5 miles (or 6.5 miles) one way**
> **Time: 2 to 3 days (or 1 full day)**
> **Map: topo for Capitol Reef National Park**
> **Difficulty: easy, with strenuous exit on Cutoff Trail**

This historically important, exceptionally scenic canyon received its name from Mormon pioneers, who declared it sinuous enough to "twist a mule." Running in the Waterpocket Fold, the canyon is chiseled out of the Navajo, Kayenta, and Wingate Formations. Although the entire canyon offers outstanding hiking, a Cutoff Trail allows you to do a 6.5-mile day trip (see map, p. 60). Unless you have two cars, plan on walking back up the Burr Trail to your car, 4.25 miles from the Post, on the Notom-Bullfrog Road, where the trail ends. Keep in mind that the canyon has no reliable water. Also, because flash-flooding poses a danger, consult rangers about the weather forecast.

Park at the trailhead near the top of the Burr Trail switchbacks and descend into the canyon. About 2 miles down Muley Twist, a large side-canyon comes in from the right; bear left here. After 4 miles, a sign on the left marks **The Post Cutoff** in the red Kayenta Formation. A slickrock campsite on the east bank is a short distance up the canyon from this sign.

If you have opted for a day trip, leave the canyon here and take the Cutoff Trail, which ascends a tributary of Muley Twist to the crest of Waterpocket Fold. From here on, the strenuous trail prefers slickrock. Because the way down is not always predictable, be sure to locate each cairn before proceeding. Your route traverses far to the right, sometimes climbing unexpectedly or passing through notches in the low Navajo Sandstone domes near the top of the reef. Eventually, the trail plunges into the reddish Kayenta Formation. At the bottom it crosses a wash to arrive at a spur road, 2 miles from the start of the Cutoff. Turn left at the spur road, passing a corral, and within another 0.5 mile you will reach the Post on the Notom-Bullfrog Road.

If you continue your hike down Muley Twist instead of taking the Cutoff Trail, you have 8 more miles to the end of the canyon and 5.5 more miles back to the Post. Past the Cutoff, the serpentine canyon slices deeply into the Kayenta and Wingate Formations, older strata than the white Navajo Sandstone above them. After encountering some tremendous overhangs in the next few miles, you arrive at a major drainage entering from the right. This tributary showcases nature's artistry, with its remarkable desert varnish, Swiss cheese cliffs, and hat-wearing gremlins, and it can be easily explored for about 1.5 miles, until a dryfall and some narrows impede upstream progress.

Back in Muley Twist, a long, straight, golden cliff defines the left side of the canyon. Where a small side-canyon comes in on the right about a mile past the major tributary, slickrock benches offer excellent camping. There are more alcoves between here and the point where the canyon finally forces its way through the fold. On the rear wall of the largest and southernmost of these amphitheaters, at a big bend, numerous cattlemen from years gone by carved their names. Unfortunately, an overabundance of cow chips makes this an unappealing place to spend the night, but there are nicer spots in the mile remaining between here and the canyon's 90-degree turn into the reef. The canyon walls pinch in, to open up again near the junction with Halls Creek.

At the junction, turn left (north) and follow a deteriorated wagon

Gold-hued walls bound serpentine Muley Twist Canyon.

track toward the Post, 5.5 miles distant. If you are short of water, you can detour 0.5 mile to the south and refill canteens at Muley Tanks, pools of water located near a grove of cottonwoods. The only other water sources in the vicinity are Cottonwood Tanks and Willow Tanks, over a mile south of the Post.

About 0.5 mile below the Post is the east end of the Cutoff Trail. You can return to your car via this trail, revisiting the northern section of Lower Muley (6 miles). Or you can simply proceed to the Post, returning to your car from there along the Burr Trail (4.25 miles).

A final note: two spectacular day hikes into narrow box canyons originate in this vicinity. The trail to **Headquarters Canyon** begins at the Post, while the trail to **Surprise Canyon** is about a mile to the north. Each of these hikes is 2.25 miles, round trip, and is rated easy to moderate.

Backpack (or Day Hike) 2: Upper Muley Twist Canyon

> **Distance: 9.5 miles (or 4 miles) round trip from**
> **vehicle barrier; 14.5 miles (or 9 miles) round trip**
> **from beginning of jeep road**
> **Time: 1.5 to 2 days (or 1 day)**
> **Map: topo for Capitol Reef National Park**
> **Difficulty: initially easy, with strenuous climb to**
> **the Fold**

This visual feast of a hike regales you with magnificent views both within the canyon itself and along the crest of the Waterpocket Fold. Your mileage depends on the kind of vehicle you drive, for the 3-mile access route is designated a jeep road after the first 0.5 mile. With high clearance you may be able to go the full distance; the worst stretch of road comes at the very beginning. Those who must walk the road will find the extra 5 miles (round trip) quick, easy, and highly scenic. Look for Peek-a-Boo Rock (a window in the Navajo Sandstone) on the right and two unnamed red Kayenta Formation arches on the left.

The turnoff for the jeep road is 1 mile beyond the Lower Muley trailhead at the top of the Burr Trail switchbacks (see map, p. 60). At the end of the jeep road is a large parking area; the easy **Strike Valley Overlook Trail** (0.75 miles round trip) is on the right, with the main canyon straight ahead, past a vehicle barrier. The first 2 miles of Upper Muley Twist beyond the barrier are nearly flat and would make a suitable day trip for nearly all age and ability groups.

Immediately before Saddle Arch at mile 2, the second of two significant Kayenta Formation arches on the left, a sign on the right indicates the **Rim Trail,** a cairned route to the top of the Waterpocket Fold. Consider establishing a camp either on one of the benches near Saddle Arch (never in the canyon, because of flash flood danger) or, preferably, on top of the Fold via the cairned route. Campsites become scarce as the canyon continues to narrow, and much of the route is very difficult, even treacherous, with a backpack. If you set up camp in this vicinity, you can hike the rest of the canyon with only a day pack containing water and other essentials.

Between Saddle Arch and the upper end of Muley Twist, several more arches come into view. About 0.5 mile past Saddle, a slot side-canyon opens on the left; a chockstone complicates your exploration of the grotto on the other side. Within another 0.5 mile, you skirt a very short set of narrows by ascending slightly up the right bank. After about 100 yards, drop back to the streambed and follow it for the next mile.

At a sharp bend to the right, a small jug-handle arch appears directly in front of you. The true narrows start 0.25 mile past this point, or 4 miles from the vehicle barrier. Leave the canyon floor and climb steeply up the right bank, following a challenging but clearly marked route. The route stays high above the chasm for about 0.75 mile. Watch your footing, especially where there are sheer drops.

Once the narrows end, the trail returns briefly to the stream level. Adventurous hikers can scramble to the head of the canyon, 6.5 miles beyond the vehicle barrier. Others will prefer to proceed to the Rim Trail, which begins immediately after a small chute, 0.25 mile past the narrows, at mile 4.75. Although the cairned trail to the rim seems nearly vertical at times, requiring some hand-over-hand climbing, it is not as dangerous as the narrows section.

At the top is a prominent Navajo dome with a tall sign reading "Canyon Route." From here you must travel freestyle south along the rim. The route is generally uncairned, so take your bearings by close observation of the side-canyons, arches, and other landmarks you saw from below. On the knife-edged ridges between domes, passage is often hazardous and difficult. But you may be energized by the stunning tableau to the east, incorporating Strike Valley, the Henry Mountains, the Little Rockies, Tarantula Mesa, and Halls Creek.

Near Saddle Arch, the cairned Rim Trail route descends to the canyon through an obvious break in the otherwise impenetrable Navajo Sandstone cliffs. The descent is not difficult, but spotting the unobtrusive sign marking its beginning may be. The aptly named Saddle Arch is your best guide. At the bottom, go left to return to your car.

Day Hike 3: Brimhall Double Bridge

> **Distance: 4.5 miles round trip**
> **Time: 5 hours**
> **Map: topo for Capitol Reef National Park**
> **Difficulty: strenuous**

Brimhall Double Bridge is a spectacular span in the remote southern part of the park. Because it involves a long drive and a difficult trek, it is less often visited than many of Capitol Reef's other attractions. It can, however, be spotted from Halls Creek Overlook (which is often gnat-infested), where the trail begins.

Look for the trailhead sign at the north end of the parking lot. The trail cuts boldly down the top part of the cliffs and then traverses north for several hundred yards before plunging to the canyon bottom within the first mile. Loose rock on the descent mandates attentive hiking.

Lower Waterpocket Fold harbors a double-spanned natural bridge.

Halls Creek contains welcome cottonwoods and, in the summer, un-welcome deerflies. Turn left here and proceed down the wash. A sign at the bottom points the way to Brimhall Bridge.

The bridge is in **Brimhall Canyon,** the first side canyon on the right. Enter the side-canyon and proceed about 0.25 mile. Here you encounter the first of three obstacles, a slope that requires a short friction climb. At the top of the slope, there may be pools to wade or swim across. Within a few hundred yards comes the second obstacle, a chockstone and boulder field. The final obstacle is a dryfall that cannot be climbed by ordinary mortals; avoid it by ascending a steep scree hill on the right. The bridge is visible from the ridgetop.

Drop back into the canyon and walk in the brushy wash bottom. Exercising care, you probably can make it to a point under the bridge, on the left side of the wash. Return the way you came.

Day 7: CALF CREEK, Grand Staircase-Escalante N.M.

- **A brief visit to an Anasazi village**
- **A hike to a desert waterfall**
- **Camping and showers at Escalante State Park**
- **Gas and groceries available in Escalante**

If you camped near Boulder, you won't have far to drive today. Your first stop, **Anasazi Indian Village State Historical Park,** is in Boulder on UT-12. This excavated, multiroom structure was abandoned by its Neolithic residents around A.D. 1300. Nearby are a museum and a full-scale replica of an intact pueblo.

South of Boulder, UT-12 switchbacks down a narrow ridge between two canyons in the Escalante system. At the bottom, where the road bends sharply, **Calf Creek Recreation Area** is on the right; look for the entrance between mileposts 75 and 76, 11.5 miles past Boulder. Park at the picnic area and fill your canteens in preparation for today's hike to Lower Calf Creek Falls. Nearby, Upper Calf Creek Falls provides a less crowded but more challenging alternative.

At the conclusion of your hike, you will drive southwest on UT-12 to the small town of Escalante (population 800), located 28 miles beyond Boulder. The drive is engaging, especially after you cross the river and ascend to a viewpoint east of town. Resupply in town, and then go west about a mile on UT-12 to the turnoff for **Escalante State Park,** on the right, where you will camp. Here you can take the short Petrified Forest Trail and the adjoining Sleeping Rainbow Loop (which together total 1.75 miles round trip). Originating at the campground, these trails ascend to a mesa top and wind through beautiful petrified wood deposits. Other attractions include fossilized dinosaur bones and prehistoric Fremont artifacts. Please resist the temptation to pocket "souvenirs."

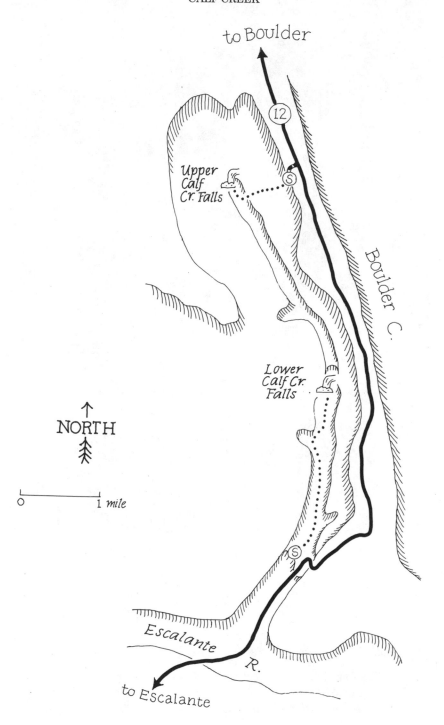

to Boulder

12

Upper
Calf
Cr. Falls

S

Boulder C.

Lower
Calf Cr.
Falls

NORTH

0   1 mile

S

Escalante

R.

to Escalante

Calf Creek's lower falls create a pellucid pool.

For additional information, contact the Bureau of Land Management, Escalante Interagency Office, P.O. Box 225, Escalante, UT 84726; and Escalante State Park, P.O. Box 350, Escalante, UT 84726.

Day Hike 1: Lower Calf Creek Falls

> **Distance: 5.5 miles round trip**
> **Time: 3 hours**
> **Map: topo for Calf Creek**
> **Difficulty: easy**

The main attraction of this pleasant, interpretive trail is a 125-foot waterfall, but it also offers various archaeological treasures (see map,

p. 67). Proximity to a verdant streamside campground makes this an immensely popular destination for families.

From the picnic area, walk a short distance up the road through the campground; look for the trailhead on the left. The trail, mostly over sand, runs along the left bank of the perennial creek. In addition to pictograph panels, there are two ruins in the Navajo Sandstone cliffs: one in the main canyon and another in a side-canyon on the left. Below the waterfall, in a sort of grotto, is a large, idyllic pool. Sheer cliffs around the falls prevent the trail from going farther; double back to return to your car.

Day Hike 2: Upper Calf Creek Falls

> **Distance: 3 miles round trip**
> **Time: 2 hours**
> **Map: topo for Calf Creek**
> **Difficulty: moderate to strenuous**

The trail to this oasis begins 5.5 miles north of the entrance to Calf Creek Recreation Area on UT-12 (see map, p. 67). Take the second dirt road on the left past milepost 81. Follow this short, rough dirt track for 100 yards to the parking area.

From the register box, the trail descends a steep slope, following occasional cairns, to the inner rim of Calf Creek. The first half of the trail is over slickrock, while the rest is mostly over sand, for a total elevation loss of about 600 feet.

Once you reach the inner rim, the trail plummets to the base of the waterfall, which forms a pool. The pool is situated in a cool, shady grotto that is framed, in season, by monkey flowers, traduscantia, and wild roses. Back at the inner rim, you can lateral around to see the top of the falls (be careful here) and more pools, farther upstream. Double back to the parking area.

Day 8: BRYCE CANYON NATIONAL PARK

- **Scenic drive along the canyon rim**
- **Day hikes amid the hoodoos**
- **Camping at Bryce Canyon National Park**
- **Gas, groceries, laundry, and showers available at Rubys Inn; some services at Bryce Canyon**

This should be a relaxing day, involving only a 1-hour drive to the Bryce Canyon entrance station and a trip down the scenic road, punctuated by stops at overlooks and by short hikes. From Escalante, follow UT-12 west for about 45 miles, and then turn south on UT-63 near **Rubys Inn**. Entering the park, select a campsite at North or Sunset Campground. Then continue south toward Yovimpa and Rainbow Points.

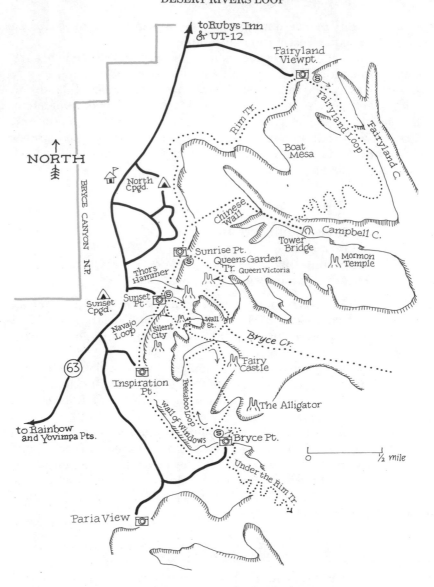

Bryce Canyon is one of those special places that stir the imagination and encourage metaphor—at least in some people. The Paiute Indians, whose myths depicted the spires as individuals petrified and painted by the god Coyote, called it "red rocks standing like men in a bowl-shaped canyon"; but to Ebenezer Bryce, the immigrant rancher after whom the canyon was named, it was simply "a hell of a place to lose a cow." Technically, it is not a single canyon at all, but a series of amphitheaters biting into the Paunsaugunt Plateau. Like neighboring Cedar Breaks, Bryce's high altitude—up to 9100 feet—makes it a much cooler and more comfortable place to visit in the summer months than most of the region's other parks.

Over 60 miles of trails wind through the park's pastel needles and hoodoos, which were carved out of the Claron Formation by mechanical and chemical weathering. All of the trails from the rim to the floor of the canyon are at least moderately difficult, requiring tough climbs of several hundred feet, but other trails are suitable for people of any ability level. You will have the opportunity to sample several trails during your 2 days in the park.

For further information, contact the Superintendent, Bryce Canyon National Park, Bryce Canyon, UT 84717.

Day Hike 1: Navajo Loop

Distance: 1.5 miles round trip
Time: 1 hour
Map: topo for Bryce Canyon National Park
Difficulty: moderate

The Navajo Loop and the Queens Garden Trail (see Day Hike 2, below) can be hiked independently or together. They are Bryce Canyon's most popular routes, for they allow visitors access to the hoodoos in the heart of the park.

The **Navajo Loop** begins at Sunset Point (see map, p. 70). Just below the rim, the trail forks. Take the left fork and descend 520 feet on switchbacks to the canyon floor, enjoying close-up views of the Two Bridges, the Pope, and Thors Hammer, a slender orange pinnacle capped by a mallet-shaped stone. Within 0.75 mile, the connector to

Evening light accentuates ethereal formations of Pink Cliffs.

the Queens Garden Trail comes in on the left. Bear right to continue on the Navajo Loop. Rounding a bend, you soon reach Wall Street: a narrow, steep-walled gully. The trail threads through this passageway to begin its steep climb to the rim. Near the top, a short spur on the left leads to an overlook of the Silent City.

Day Hike 2: Queens Garden Trail

Distance: 1.5 miles round trip
Time: 1 hour
Map: topo for Bryce Canyon National Park
Difficulty: moderate

Beginning at Sunrise Point (see map, p. 70), the **Queens Garden Trail** is the "easiest" of the trails that descend to the floor of the Bryce amphitheater. It winds down 320 feet, past Gullivers Castle and Queens Castle, before ending at a viewpoint of the Queen Victoria profile formation. From here you can retrace your steps back to the rim or take the connecting trail to the Navajo Loop. If you do ascend to Sunset Point on the Navajo Loop, a very easy 0.5-mile stroll to the north along the Rim Trail will return you to Sunrise Point.

Day Hike 3: Rim Trail

Distance: variable, up to 11 miles round trip
Time: up to 4 hours
Map: topo for Bryce Canyon National Park
Difficulty: easy

The Rim Trail follows the lip of Bryce Canyon from Fairyland View to Bryce Point (7800 and 8300 feet, respectively). Since it connects with Sunrise, Sunset, and Inspiration Points, all accessible by car, there are many different places to begin and end the hike (see map, p. 70). Arguably the most beautiful section extends from Sunrise to Inspiration, where the walking is especially easy.

Day Hike 4: Bristlecone Loop

Distance: 1 mile
Time: 30 minutes
Map: topo for Bryce Canyon National Park
Difficulty: very easy

This lovely trail connecting Rainbow and Yovimpa Points starts at the southern end of the park road, near the Rainbow Point parking lot. It involves little elevation change as it passes through forested uplands, swinging out to a high, exposed overlook with 180-degree views. You feel as though you were on the prow of a ship. The trail loops back to the parking area, with a short spur at the end leading to Yovimpa Point.

Day Hike 5: Mossy Cave

> **Distance: 0.75 mile round trip**
> **Time: 30 minutes**
> **Map: topo for Bryce Canyon National Park**
> **Difficulty: easy**

This trail is accessed not from the park road but from UT-12, east of Rubys Inn, between mileposts 17 and 18. From the parking area south of the highway, the route follows a stream, which it crosses on two bridges. After the second bridge, the trail forks. The left fork heads to **Mossy Cave,** an alcove sheltering a perennial spring. The right fork leads to a small waterfall and a good view of windows in the canyon cliffs. Retrace your steps back to the car.

Day 9: MORE EXPLORATION OF BRYCE CANYON

- **Glorious day-hiking amid spires and needles**
- **Camping at Bryce Canyon**
- **Gas, groceries, showers, and laundry available at Rubys Inn; some services at Bryce Canyon**

Each of the following outings gives you a chance to see the strange and wonderful formations of Bryce Canyon close up.

Day Hike 1: Fairyland Trail

> **Distance: 8 miles round trip**
> **Time: 4 to 5 hours**
> **Map: topo for Bryce Canyon National Park**
> **Difficulty: moderate**

One of the longest day hikes in the park, the delightful Fairyland Loop can be walked in either direction. It can also be shortened by 2.5 miles with a car shuttle from Sunrise Point to Fairyland View.

From the trailhead at Fairyland Viewpoint near the park entrance, the route descends 850 feet along a scenic ridgeline to cross the upper reaches of colorful Fairyland Canyon (see map, p. 70). After rounding Boat Mesa in a series of moderate ups and downs, and passing exotic formations such as the Palace of the Fairy Queen and the Ruins of Athens, you enter Campbell Canyon. The trail then intersects a short spur on the left leading to **Tower Bridge,** one of two significant natural arches in the park. Past the spur, the trail starts its ascent, affording views of the Chinese Wall. At the top it forks; the path on the left leads immediately to Sunrise Point, while the Rim Trail on the right climbs to North Campground, hugging the lip of the bowl back to Fairyland View.

Day Hike 2: Peekaboo Loop

> **Distance: 5.5 to 7 miles round trip, depending on trailhead**
> **Time: 3 to 4 hours**
> **Map: topo for Bryce Canyon National Park**
> **Difficulty: moderate**

With its continual ups and downs, the Peekaboo Loop deters the more casual visitor. Another deterrent is the sights and smells left by horse concession operations that use this trail. Unpleasantries are quickly forgiven, however, when you catch sight of the Alligator, the Fairy Castle, the Silent City, the Wall of Windows, and other interesting formations along the route.

The Peekaboo Loop is connected to the rim by trails leading down from Sunset, Bryce, and Sunrise Points; the round-trip mileages are 5.5, 6.5, and 7, respectively (including in each case 3.5 miles on the loop itself). The ascent to Bryce Point is about 300 feet greater than it is to the other trailheads—a factor to consider when selecting a point of departure (see map, p. 70). From Bryce Point, the trail takes off to the northeast and then doubles back and descends rapidly on

Trails descending into Bryce Canyon allow an intimate look at Pink Cliffs.

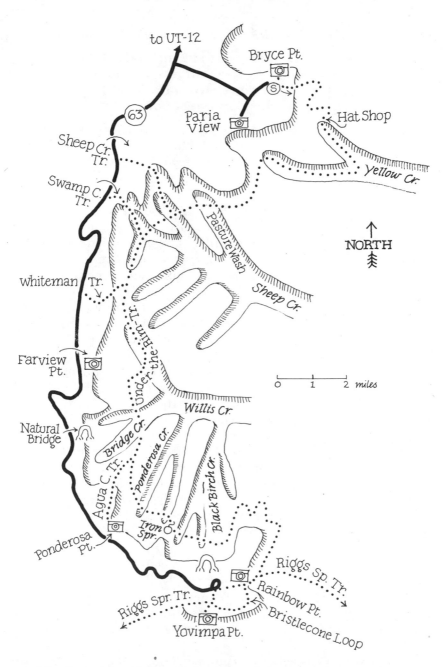

switchbacks to meet the Peekaboo Loop. Proceed clockwise around the loop, arriving at a picnic area with pit toilets. The trail continues past the Wall of Windows and Inspiration Point on the left and then reaches the junction with the trails from Sunrise and Sunset Points. Catch your breath before following the signs to complete the loop and the steep return climb to Bryce Point.

Day Hike (or Backpack) 3: Under the Rim Trail

Distance: variable, up to 22 miles one way
Time: variable, from a half day to 3 days
Map: topo for Bryce Canyon National Park
Difficulty: moderate to strenuous

The Under the Rim Trail, along with the adjoining 8.5-mile Riggs Spring Loop, offers Bryce Canyon's only backpacking experience (see map, p. 75). Many people, however, prefer to day-hike the trail in segments, particularly because water may be in scarce supply. Camping is restricted to designated sites and requires a permit from the visitor center.

The trail extends from Bryce Point at 8300 feet to Rainbow Point at 9100 feet, with several connectors, each about a mile long, to the park road. Although much of the trail is through forested country, and the Pink Cliffs are not always in view, there are numerous compensations, such as solitude and serenity. Since this is not a loop, you must set up a car shuttle or some equivalent.

On the northern end, the trail commences at Bryce Point. Within 1.5 spectacular miles, you descend almost 1000 feet to the **Hat Shop,** a collection of pink and tangerine needles with white, erosion-resistant caps. In this vicinity, there are also bristlecone pines, a species whose members can live thousands of years. Beyond the Hat Shop, continue descending for 1.5 miles until you reach the right fork of Yellow Creek. This is the lowest elevation on the route and the location of its northernmost backcountry campsite.

Continuing south, follow the Yellow Creek upstream through scrubby terrain to a spot beneath Paria View. The rhythm of the hike over the next few miles is undulating, involving many ups and downs. You descend into Sheep Creek (at mile 9) and the right fork of Swamp Canyon (at mile 10). These drainages both contain campsites and offer connecting trails to the park road. The **Sheep Creek Connecting Trail** climbs steeply through heavy timber, while the **Swamp Canyon Connecting Trail** is an easier route to the rim.

The Under the Rim Trail gradually ascends Swamp Canyon until it intersects the Whiteman Connecting Trail, at roughly the trip's halfway mark (mile 11.5). The Whiteman Connecting Trail, which follows an old roadbed, is the easiest of the connectors; it meets the park road about 0.25 mile north of a picnic area, after climbing for 1 mile.

After the junction with the Whiteman Connecting Trail, the Under the Rim Trail levels out and winds through an aspen grove. It descends into heavy timber, following Willis Creek below Farview Point and threading between the rim and an isolated battlement. An unnamed pass takes you into the Bridge Creek drainage. You may notice a window or two up in the cliff wall. Crossing the arms of Bridge Creek, you arrive at another official campsite. Nearby, in a fire-scarred clearing, look toward the rim to pick out **Natural Bridge.** This 85-foot span is actually an arch, since its opening was not formed by running water.

Somewhat farther on, at about mile 16, the **Agua Canyon Connecting Trail** branches off to the right. This trail, which leads to Ponderosa Viewpoint on the park road, is longer and steeper than the other connectors, but its well-engineered switchbacks on a rocky, sparsely vegetated slope offer grand vistas.

In the next few miles, you cross many arms of Ponderosa and Black Birch Creeks, separated by saddles. A sandy pass with a hoodoo at about mile 17.25, between two branches of Ponderosa Creek, provides an ideal rest stop. Soon after comes a level walk through forested country, memorable for an aspen glade. At about mile 18.5, you notice the orange, mineral-stained water (not potable) flowing from Iron Spring. From here the trail laterals around a point before crossing the Black Birch drainage. Look up at the ramparts to spy a big arch.

You now begin the long, final push to the rim. The altitude may make the climb tiring. But, visually, this is the crescendo of the trip: you can see an extensive section of the Pink Cliffs, plus Navajo Mountain beckoning in the distance. Eventually you attain a red, knife-edged ridge. Beyond the ridge, you continue to ascend steadily, switchbacking through white and Douglas fir to Rainbow Point.

Day 10: KODACHROME BASIN

- **Encountering "sand pipes"**
- **Camping and showers at Kodachrome Basin State Park**
- **Gas and groceries available in Escalante**

Tomorrow you will start a 3-night backpack trip in the Escalante River drainage. You may wish to prepare by purchasing supplies and obtaining a backcountry camping permit at the Escalante Interagency Office just west of town on UT-12.

The turnoff to **Kodachrome Basin State Park** is 12 miles east of Bryce Canyon on UT-12. Go south for 7.75 miles on the Cottonwood Canyon Road, which follows Cottonwood Wash. The state park is a left turn off the road. Set up camp and then explore this geologically singular area. From the valley floor rise almost 70 tall, tan spires called "sand pipes"—columns of rock produced by subterranean pressures and then exposed as the surrounding Entrada Sandstone eroded away. Hiking opportunities here include the Shakespear Arch Trail (0.75 mile round trip); the interesting and varied Panorama Trail (3 miles round trip), which inspects sand pipes at close range; the Angels Palace Trail (0.5 mile round trip); and the treacherous Eagles View Trail (1.25 miles round trip, with a steep, 450-foot climb to a pass).

For further information, contact Kodachrome Basin State Park, P.O. Box 238, Cannonville, UT 84718.

Slender spires in Kodachrome Basin assume fanciful shapes.

<u>Days 11–14</u>: ESCALANTE RIVER

- **Discovering four major natural spans**
- **Splashing through a watery canyon**
- **Narrows, alcoves, and gardens galore**

Today, you will begin a superb backpacking trip in the recently created Grand Staircase–Escalante National Monument. Several alternatives in the vicinity are given below. After reprovisioning and filling canteens in Escalante, drive east on UT-12 about 4.5 miles past town to the **Hole in the Rock Road.** This road received its unusual name from an event in Mormon history: a party of settlers, stymied by the sheer walls of Glen Canyon, blasted a notch through the cliffs, lowered their wagons and livestock, and forded the Colorado River. The unpaved road runs parallel to the Kaiparowits Plateau. Drive to the parking area for Hurricane Wash, 33 miles from the UT-12 turnoff. The parking lot is adjacent to a big cottonwood on the right, just before the road dips into a gully.

The Escalante River, named for a Spanish missionary who pioneered the exploration of the Southwest, is a tributary of the Colorado. Placid and shallow (except when in flood), it was the last major river in the continental United States to be "discovered" by white people; Major John Wesley Powell's second expedition down the Green and Colorado Rivers, in 1872, is credited with this achievement. Much of the river's lower end is now part of Lake Powell, created when Glen Canyon Dam was built in 1963.

The serpentine, cottonwood-lined canyons of the Escalante, with their fantastic arches, amphitheaters, and hanging gardens, contain flowing water (which you will need to treat). Because you'll be wading for some of the way, wear old boots or sneakers and bring along extra socks. Patches of quicksand often develop during the rainy season; if it is present near the beginning of your hike, it is likely to pose a significant problem as you proceed down the canyon. Carry about 1 gallon of water apiece as insurance until you start seeing pools and springs.

Where you decide to camp at the conclusion of your trip will depend on how early you get out and how keen you are for food and showers. One suggestion is to reprovision in Escalante and spend the night in a national forest campground off UT-12 on Boulder Mountain, between Boulder and Torrey.

For more information, write to the Bureau of Land Management, Escalante Resource Area, P. O. Box 225, Escalante, UT 84726, and the National Park Service, Glen Canyon National Recreation Area, Escalante Ranger District, Escalante, UT 84726.

Backpack: Escalante River via Coyote Gulch

Distance: 26.5 miles round trip
Time: 4 days
Maps: topos for Big Hollow Wash, King Mesa, and
    Stevens Canyon South
Difficulty: moderate

This hike starts at the Hurricane Wash parking lot, 33 miles down the **Hole in the Rock Road** (see map, p. 80). On foot, pick up a jeep road heading east, which enters **Hurricane Wash.** After a level, dry, and sandy stretch, the Navajo Sandstone cliffs gradually rise. At about 5.5 miles from the trailhead, the wash empties into Coyote Gulch. Camping is good in this vicinity. Turn right here, continuing downstream past

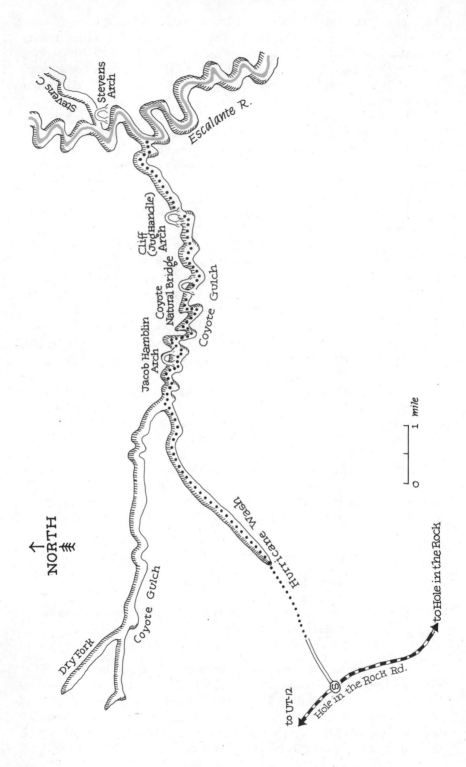

NORTH

Stevens C.

Stevens Arch

Escalante R.

Cliff (JugHandle) Arch

Coyote Natural Bridge

Coyote Gulch

Jacob Hamblin Arch

Dry Fork

Coyote Gulch

Hurricane Wash

0   1 mile

to UT-12

Hole in the Rock Rd.

to Hole in the Rock

ABOVE: A rainbow arcs over the Colorado River, Utah.

RIGHT: Mule ears, common spring flowers in Goblin Valley State Park

OVERLEAF: Fisher Towers glow red hot at sunset.

FACING PAGE: Cottonwood leaves turn golden-yellow in autumn.

The San Juan River slices through colorful strata near Mexican Hat.

Narrows of lower Buckskin Gulch are gothically spooky.

Hikers explore Farnsworth Canyon narrows, San Rafael Reef.

RIGHT: A cottonwood adds serenity to Escalante tributary.

BELOW: Cottonwoods lean toward soft pastel cliffs.

FACING PAGE: Reflection at noon, Paria River

A storm blackens the sky above Toroweap campground, Grand Canyon.

Oak Creek Canyon, a verdant oasis

two dramatic erosional formations: **Jacob Hamblin Arch** (at mile 7) and **Coyote Natural Bridge** (at mile 8.5).

About a mile past Coyote Bridge, the trail climbs onto the left bank of the canyon above a rockfall and then arrives at a series of pour-offs. Skirt the one near Cliff (aka Jug Handle) Arch on the right at mile 10.5. The canyon deepens and narrows near its mouth, and you have to climb the cliff to the right. Cairns mark the place where you go up.

Approaching the **Escalante River,** at mile 13.25, you come within sight of exceptional **Stevens Arch** far above the stream. Unless the lake level is too high, you should be able to turn left at the river and splash upstream about 0.5 mile or so to a sandy bank on the left, where you can camp if there is no flash flood danger. When ready, double back to your car.

Optional Side Trip: Devils Garden

Devils Garden is a BLM area located 12.5 miles south of UT-12 on the Hole in the Rock Road. Follow a signed spur road on the right for 0.25 mile to the parking and picnic area. Kids of all ages will love the goblins, arches, and strange erosional forms to be found here. There are no trails, but you can wander around at will.

Mano and Metate Arches, named after stone implements used by aboriginal peoples to pulverize grain, are a few hundred yards to the south of the picnic ground, and a shallow, sheer-walled red canyon is less than 0.5 mile down the wash.

Optional Day Hike: Dry Fork of Coyote Gulch

> **Distance: 4.25 miles round trip**
> **Time: 3 hours**
> **Map: topo for Big Hollow Wash**
> **Difficulty: moderate**

To reach the trailhead, drive 26.5 miles south of UT-12 on the Hole in the Rock Road. Turn left at the sign that says, "Dry Fork, 1.7." Proceed, bearing left at the Y, to the parking lot at the road's end (see map, p. 83).

Strike out for the canyon rim and hunt for a break in the cliff. There is a cairned route into a side-canyon of **Dry Fork.** Upon reaching Dry Fork itself, detour to the left (upstream) to visit a short, picturesque narrows section. Returning to the point where your side-canyon intersects Dry Fork, walk downstream.

The first side-canyon on the left past this intersection is **Peek-a-Boo Gulch.** Since it is a hanging canyon, you will need to scramble up a 10- to 15-foot dryfall, aided by foot- and handholds that have been chipped into the rock. In Peek-a-Boo Gulch, you will find a double bridge, spiral-staircase turns, and Swiss cheese holes on the canyon floor. Ascending slightly, you top out after 0.25 mile and must retrace your steps.

To visit **Spooky Gulch,** continue downstream in Dry Fork for about 0.5 mile. Follow a trail going off to the left, which leads up a low, sandy saddle. Cross to the other side to enter the drainage. (Don't worry if you miss this shortcut; you can pass through a short set of narrows in Dry Fork, after which Spooky Gulch enters from the left.) Spooky Gulch may be the narrowest slot canyon negotiable by human beings. Plan to take off your daypack and ease yourself sideways through the tight spots. After about 0.25 mile, you arrive at a 6-foot pour-off, which requires free-climbing skills to ascend. Return the way you came.

Hikers scale a pour-off to enter Peek-a-Boo Gulch.

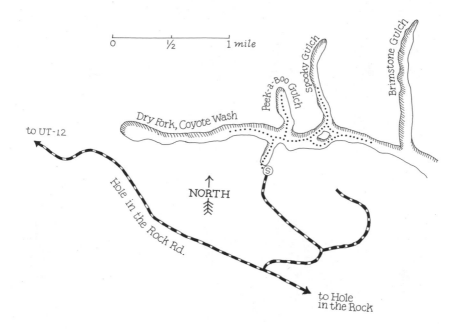

If you like, you can stroll farther down Dry Fork. There are other narrows, with tumbleweed graveyards and chockstones that may impede your progress. When you are finished exploring, double back to your vehicle.

Day 15: CATHEDRAL VALLEY

- **A loop drive through phenomenal badlands with more day hikes in Capitol Reef**
- **Camping at Capitol Reef National Park**
- **Gas, groceries, showers, and laundry available in Torrey**

This morning, drive over Boulder Mountain on UT-12 toward the town of Torrey (35 miles from Boulder), enjoying views of the Henry Mountains and Waterpocket Fold country along the way. After resupplying in Torrey, select a campsite in Capitol Reef.

If your car is a "low rider," you should not attempt the Cathedral Valley loop described below. Instead, hike one of the Capitol Reef trails you missed before (see Days 3 and 4). If your car has reasonably good clearance, however, the road to Cathedral Valley should present no problem, as long as you take it slow. The half-day drive leads to the wild and remote northern sector of the park, frequented more by cowboys than by tourists. Check at the visitor center to make sure that the roads are in decent condition, and avoid them in the event of rain, since their clay beds make them impassable when wet.

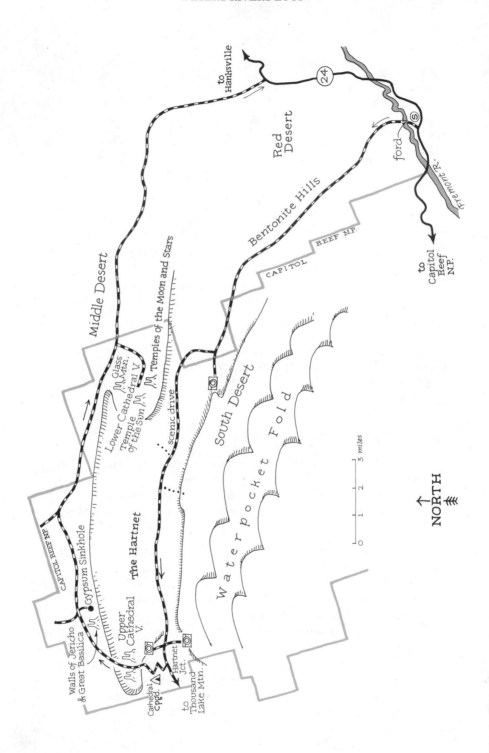

to Hanksville

24

to Capitol Reef N.P.

ford

Fremont R.

Red Desert

Bentonite Hills

CAPITOL REEF N.P.

CAPITOL

Middle Desert

Temples of the Moon and Stars

Glass Mtn.

Lower Cathedral V.

Temple of the Sun

scenic drive

South Desert

Waterpocket Fold

The Hartnet

Gypsum Sinkhole

CAPITOL REEF NP

Walls of Jericho & Great Basilica

Upper Cathedral V.

Cathedral Cpgd.

Hartnet Jct.

to Thousand Lake Mtn.

NORTH

0 1 2 3 miles

Scenic Drive: Cathedral Valley

Distance: 59 miles
Time: half day

To begin the scenic loop, drive east on UT-24 for 11.5 miles past the visitor center. Turn left at a sign for the Fremont River ford (see map, p. 84), testing the rocky-bottomed stream for depth before crossing. For the first several miles, you pass through the rainbow-hued Bentonite Hills. This area, with its barren, claylike mounds, is geologically younger than other sections of the park, a part of the uranium-bearing Morrison Formation. The Henrys dominate the southern horizon. At miles 14 and 27 (from the UT-24 turnoff), spur roads lead to overlooks of the **South Desert** basin, bounded on the west by the Waterpocket Fold. An overlook of Upper Cathedral Valley is located 0.5 mile up another spur just short of mile 27.5.

Immediately past this spur, turn right at Hartnet Junction and descend on switchbacks into **Upper Cathedral Valley.** The road veers close to the flank of Thousand Lake Mountain, going over rough, rocky terrain. The Park Service maintains a small, primitive campground (Cathedral Campground) in this vicinity. At the bottom of the switchbacks are fluted rock pyramids composed of Entrada Sandstone. Here begins the most scenically compelling part of the drive, which continues as you descend slowly toward **Lower Cathedral Valley.** You pass the Walls of Jericho and the Great Basilica on your right at mile 31, continuing straight ahead at a junction 2 miles down the road. Be sure to notice the Layercake Wall, with its tortelike horizontal bands of sandstone, on the right about a mile after crossing the irregular boundary line of the park. Past here, a spur road on the right goes to the Temples of the Sun, Moon, and Stars and to sparkling Glass Mountain, a gypsum formation. Look for a small arch about 4 miles beyond the spur.

Rejoining UT-24, turn right to the Capitol Reef Campground, 20 miles away. As a bonus on the way back, notice the granary in a shallow cave on the left side of the highway between mileposts 90 and 91, near the ford.

Day 16: HORSESHOE CANYON

- **The Great Gallery pictographs**
- **Camping on the rim of Horseshoe Canyon**
- **Gas, groceries, and showers available in Hanksville**

Drive east on UT-24 to Hanksville, and resupply for an overnight backpack trip in Horseshoe Canyon, a detached unit of the Maze District of Canyonlands National Park. At Hanksville, continue north on UT-24 (a left turn) for about 19 miles to a sign for the Maze, just south of the turnoff to Goblin Valley. Turn right here, and proceed on this dirt road for 24 miles. When you arrive at a fork, go left onto the Green River Road and continue for 5 more miles, following signs. Then turn right onto another dirt road. Proceed for about 2 miles (the last mile or so may be rough) to the lip of the canyon. To prevent vandalism and environmental damage, the Park Service no longer permits camping in Horseshoe Canyon. However, it is permissible to camp on the BLM land near the west rim, provided that you do so in a low-impact manner. It is best to avoid the area during the busy spring season and on Labor Day weekend.

For more information, contact the Superintendent, Canyonlands National Park, 2282 S. West Resource Boulevard, Moab, UT 84532.

___

Day Hike: Horseshoe Canyon

Distance: 6.5 miles round trip
Time: 1 day
**Map: topo for Sugarloaf Butte or Maze/NE Glen
    Canyon**
Difficulty: easy, with a moderate ascent

Horseshoe Canyon (see map, p. 87), a tributary of the Green River, contains some exquisite pictograph panels, including the famous 200-foot-long Great Gallery, which is the Louvre of the Southwest. Since springs are not reliable, bring along plenty of water.

An abandoned jeep road leads from the parking area to the canyon floor. Near the top you pass a vehicle barrier and then an old trough and water tank. Cairns mark the 800-foot, 1.5-mile descent. The first half of the hike is over slickrock, though the roadbed turns to sand near the bottom. At the bottom, turn right and proceed up the canyon. Within 0.5 mile, look for two pictograph panels, one on each wall.

Just after another vehicle barrier is Water Canyon, on the left. From here it is a leisurely, hour-long stroll to the **Great Gallery,** 1.75 miles upstream on the right, where the canyon widens slightly. Most archaeologists attribute the life-sized pictographs in this panel to Archaic Age nomads, who roamed the area 2000 or more years ago. The figures, with their small heads and elongated, jug-shaped or trapezoidal bodies, probably had religious significance. The most remarkable painting depicts a white, ghostlike being. On your return, stop at a large alcove on the left, about halfway back to the vehicle barrier, to see a fourth panel. This one, unfortunately, has been vandalized.

It is sometimes possible to find water in Barrier Creek near the Great Gallery. In addition, there may be a flowing spring about 0.5 mile up Water Canyon, located among some cattails to the right of the streambed. You can investigate this charming tributary for over a mile until it ends in a box canyon.

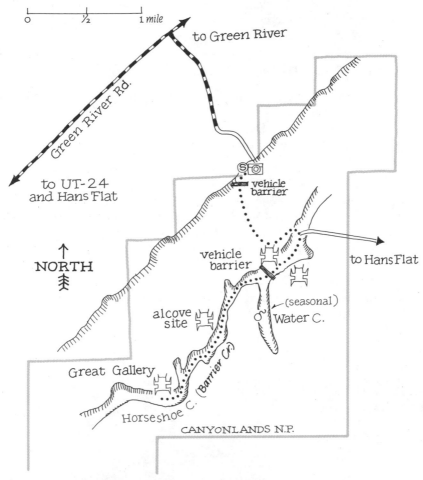

Day 17: BLACK DRAGON CANYON

- **Studying sublime pictographs**
- **Camping and showers at Green River State Park**
- **Gas, groceries, and laundry available in Green River**

The last day of your trip begins at the Horseshoe Canyon parking lot. From here, drive back to Green River Road, turning right toward the town of Green River, 42 miles to the north.

In town, resupply, and pitch a tent, if you wish, at Green River State Park. Then head west on I-70 for 15 miles in order to examine the rock art of Black Dragon Canyon. About 0.75 mile beyond the I-70 bridge across the San Rafael River, near milepost 145, is a good dirt and gravel road to the north. Pass through a cattle gate and drive over a mile until you come to a wash. This is **Black Dragon Canyon.**

Park off the road here, or drive a short distance until you reach a large overhang. Although the pictograph panels are quite close to the mouth, you may want to walk farther up the canyon. Return to the campground in preparation for tomorrow's trip home.

Day Hike: Black Dragon Canyon

Distance: up to 5 miles round trip
Time: up to 3 hours
Map: topo for San Rafael Desert
Difficulty: very easy

This lovely canyon of Navajo, Kayenta, and Wingate Sandstone slices through the San Rafael Reef to join the San Rafael River to the east. About 400 yards up the canyon on the right, around a big bend, is a Fremont pictograph panel high on the cliff. The most unusual of the drawings resembles a dragon (red, not black). Other drawings here, composed entirely of short lines, have a dynamic, "expressionist" quality.

Black Dragon Canyon can be hiked through the reef and beyond. Past the pictographs the canyon widens. A jeep road makes the walking fast and relatively easy. Double back to your car when you have seen enough.

This Fremont "dragon" pictograph suggests a prehistoric pteradactyl.

Chapter 3

REDROCK LOOP

Colorado, Utah

Originating in Grand Junction, this circuit minimizes driving time by confining itself to the eastern side of the Green and Colorado Rivers, a fractured landscape replete with exquisite arches, snow-capped mountains, and sweeping panoramas. It is ideal for people interested in devoting vacation time to relatively short and easy day hikes and backpacking trips. White-water rafting options add to the excitement of this loop.

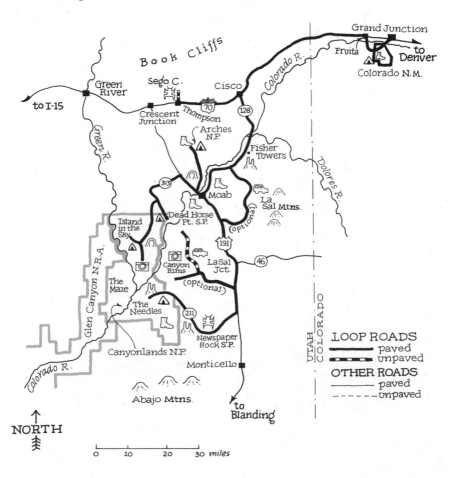

Day 1: COLORADO NATIONAL MONUMENT

- **Wonderful views of Grand Valley**
- **Day hikes amid soaring pinnacles**
- **Camping at Colorado National Monument**
- **Gas, groceries, showers, and laundry available in Grand Junction and Fruita**

Grand Junction, a pleasant city of 35,000 near the Utah border, is different from the other towns in this region, both in its size and in the diversity of its services. Poised on the western flank of the Rockies,

Monument Canyon Trail swings past the Coke Ovens.

within easy reach of the high desert, it's a natural gateway community. Buy food, ice, and other supplies here. Your first destination is very close: **Colorado National Monument** (see map, below). Take CO-340 across the river to the east entrance station and begin the spectacular, 23-mile Rim Rock Drive, which traverses the park and returns to CO-340 near Fruita. The visitor center and campground are at the western end of the drive.

The national monument occupies a mesa on the Uncompahgre Plateau, which erosion has cut into a series of deep canyons and isolated sandstone towers. Up to 2000 feet higher than the surrounding desert, it offers exciting views into the valley below and north to the Book Cliffs. Because the Colorado River was once known as the "Grand," the valley in which the towns of Grand Junction and Fruita sit is now called by that name. Irrigated patchwork fields add an amber and green contrast to the mesa's redrock wilderness.

Several trails of varying lengths either hug the rim of the mesa or

descend into the canyons from breathtaking overlooks. Especially memorable are two easy trails near the east end of Rim Rock Drive: the **Serpents Trail** (2.5 miles one way), which follows the incredibly crooked bed of the old road into the national monument, and the adjacent **Devils Kitchen Trail** (1.5 miles round trip), which crosses No Thoroughfare Canyon before ascending to a sandstone rock garden. Shorter paths from the scenic road lead to the Coke Ovens, Grandview Point, and the Pipe Organ. You may wish to stop at some or all of these on your way to the visitor center and campground, where nature trails originate. Establish your campsite, and then drive back to the Coke Ovens area and take the Monument Canyon Trail.

For further information, contact the Superintendent, Colorado National Monument, Fruita, CO 81521.

Day Hike: Monument Canyon Trail

> **Distance: 5.5 miles one way**
> **Time: 3 to 4 hours**
> **Map: topo for Colorado National Monument**
> **Difficulty: moderate**

This fascinating trail (see map, p. 91), like many others in the area, was built early in the century by John Otto, a wilderness enthusiast who sought national park status for these cliffs and buttes. You will need a car shuttle to complete the hike.

Originating at the Coke Ovens Overlook, the shadeless path quickly switchbacks to the floor of **Monument Canyon,** 600 feet below. (The total descent is 1400 feet.) At the bottom, the trail turns left and parallels the rim, descending gradually much of the way. Along the route, which cuts through the Wingate and Chinle Formations to Precambrian rock, views of many of the monument's most prominent buttes appear, including the Kissing Couple and Independence Monument.

Near Independence Monument, the trail veers to the right, passing a boulder garden formed as the sandstone cliffs weathered. At the bottom of the canyon, bear left, walking alongside the fence until the trail intersects CO-340 close to the monument's west entrance.

Day 2: SEGO CANYONS AND FISHER TOWERS

- **Exceptional prehistoric pictographs**
- **A scenic drive along the Colorado River**
- **A hike through tall red spires**
- **Camping in the Moab area**
- **Gas, groceries, showers, and laundry available in Moab**

Hikers enjoy the redrock wilderness below Fisher Towers.

Leave Colorado National Monument and head west for 69 miles on I-70 from Fruita. Your first destination is the aboriginal pictographs of Sego Canyon, near the whistle-stop of Thompson, Utah. The country becomes drier and bleaker with each passing mile; you would hardly guess that the Colorado River is gouging out Horsethief, Ruby, and Westwater Canyons, with their outstanding rafting opportunities, immediately to the south. Equally hard to imagine is that the desolate-looking, 250-mile-long **Book Cliffs** region to the north is cut by fairly well-watered canyons, through which Neolithic hunters and gatherers once roamed.

The rock drawings of these indigenous peoples are located north of Thompson, at the junction of **Sego** and **Thompson Canyons.** Take exit 185 off I-70 and enter Thompson on UT-94, crossing the railroad tracks. Continue for 3.5 miles past the tracks until the canyon opens up. Park in the small lot on the left just after the road crosses a wash. Three major panels are on the left side of the road, and two additional ones (on private land) are about 100 yards up the canyon on the right. These remarkable pictographs are probably from the Fremont culture. Some contain vase-shaped figures like those in Horseshoe Canyon's Grand Gallery.

From Thompson, backtrack eastward on I-70, taking exit 212 toward sleepy Cisco (no services). Within a few miles you pick up UT-128, a classic among desert roads. After traversing a barren plateau, the road suddenly dips to cross the **Colorado River,** which it then parallels all the way to Moab, 47 miles from the interstate. Next to the new bridge is its more charming predecessor, Dewey Bridge. Soon the cloud-covered **La Sal Mountains,** a high laccolithic chain, come into view. River rafting from here to Moab is wonderful— long placid stretches alternating with exciting rapids and riffles. Whether by car or boat, the trip through the canyon is a textbook lesson in Four Corners geology. Most of the way, Wingate cliffs predominate, dipping beneath the earth's surface north of Moab to be succeeded by Navajo Sandstone bluffs.

In the shadow of the La Sals, around milepost 21, loom the **Fisher Towers**—brick-colored monoliths hewn from the Moenkopi and Cutler Formations. Look for a dirt road on your left, which leads in 2 miles to a parking lot, picnic area (with pit toilets), and trailhead, all maintained by the BLM. This is where you begin your day hike.

At the hike's conclusion, continue driving southwest on UT-128, passing Big Bend Recreation Area between mileposts 7 and 8. When you reach US-191, turn left (southeast) toward Moab (population 5000), your base of operations for the next few days. You have several camping options, including RV parks in town (where showers are available) and public campgrounds such as the ones at Big Bend Recreation Area on the river and Little Lions Back near the Slickrock Bike Trail. You can also check on site availability at the Arches National Park entrance station, 5 miles north of town on US-191. Consider stopping at the Moab Information Center in the town center.

Day Hike: Fisher Towers

> **Distance: 4.5 miles round trip**
> **Time: 2.5 hours**
> **Map: topo for Castle Valley**
> **Difficulty: moderate**

The trailhead is adjacent to the picnic area. After crossing a shallow canyon on the right, the trail gradually ascends, winding along the right side of a cliff broken into a series of striated pinnacles. Views are splendid along the entire route. To the west is Professor Valley; to the south is labyrinthine Onion Creek, with its maroon cliffs and interesting section of narrows. The base of the **Titan,** tallest of the towers at 900 feet high, is a mile up the trail. The end of the trail rewards you with an outstanding panorama of the La Sal Mountains and the buttes of Castle Valley.

Day 3: ARCHES NATIONAL PARK

- **Four fabulous day hikes**
- **Camping in Arches National Park**

Arches National Park is a slickrock wonderland situated on a plateau above the canyon of the Colorado River. The park is celebrated for fins and towers, balanced rocks, petrified sand dunes, and over 2000 natural arches and windows, formed by the action of ice, water, and wind on Entrada Sandstone. An 18-mile road bisects the park, providing access to these treasures.

At the visitor center, reserve a spot in a ranger-led hike into the Fiery Furnace. Also, obtain a permit for overnight camping near Dark Angel on Day 4. Although water is available at the campground from mid-March to mid-October, the visitor center is a convenient place to fill canteens.

Leave the visitor center and take the park road up a well-engineered set of switchbacks, which climb a golden cliff-face. The ascent treats you to exceptional views of Spanish Valley, the Colorado River and its "Portal" (where the canyon closes in again after the river has crossed the valley), and the impressive La Sal Mountains. Along the road, take advantage of the many scenic viewpoints and short trails the park has to offer.

A dusting of snow complements Balanced Rock, Arches National Park.

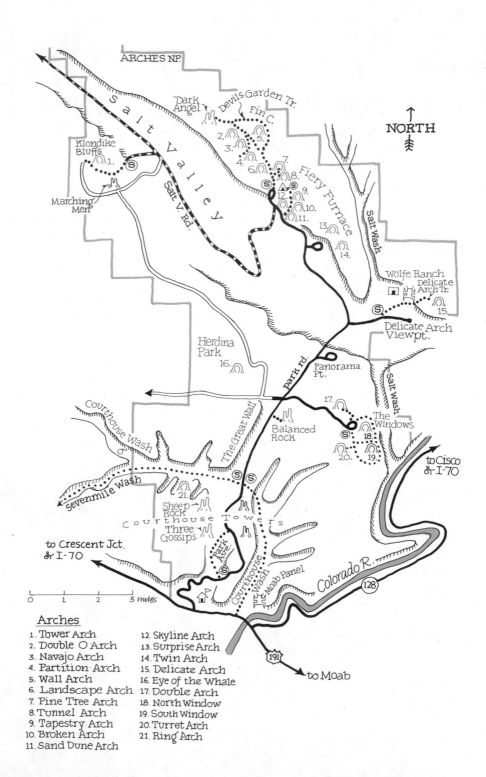

ARCHES N.P.

Dark Angel

Devils Garden Tr.

Fin C.

NORTH

Klondike Bluffs

Marching Men

Salt Valley

Salt V. Rd.

Fiery Furnace

Salt Wash

Wolfe Ranch
Delicate
Arch Tr.

Delicate Arch
Viewpt.

Herdina
Park

park rd.

Panorama
Pt.

Salt wash

Courthouse Wash

The Great Wall

The Windows

Balanced
Rock

Sevenmile Wash

Sheep
Rock

Courthouse Towers

Three
Gossips

Park Ave.

Courthouse Wash

Moab Panel

to Cisco
& I-70

Colorado R.

128

to Crescent Jct.
& I-70

0   1   2   3 miles

191

to Moab

Arches

1. Tower Arch
2. Double O Arch
3. Navajo Arch
4. Partition Arch
5. Wall Arch
6. Landscape Arch
7. Pine Tree Arch
8. Tunnel Arch
9. Tapestry Arch
10. Broken Arch
11. Sand Dune Arch
12. Skyline Arch
13. Surprise Arch
14. Twin Arch
15. Delicate Arch
16. Eye of the Whale
17. Double Arch
18. North Window
19. South Window
20. Turret Arch
21. Ring Arch

For further information, write to the Superintendent, Arches National Park, P.O. Box 907, Moab, UT 84532. For camping reservations in Arches or Canyonlands National Parks, call (435) 259-4351.

Day Hike 1: Park Avenue

> **Distance: 1 mile one way**
> **Time: 0.5 hour**
> **Map: topo for Arches National Park**
> **Difficulty: easy**

A must for visitors to Arches is a leisurely stroll down Park Avenue, 2 miles from the entrance station, in the **Courthouse Towers** section. The easy, well-marked trail (see map, p. 96) gently descends 325 feet toward Courthouse Wash and its massive buttes. You walk between cliffs topped by flat, waferlike Entrada Sandstone projections reminiscent of Egyptian bas-relief. At the end, either retrace your steps or follow the road back to the parking lot.

Day Hike 2: The Windows

> **Distance: 1 mile, if all trails are hiked**
> **Time: 1 hour**
> **Map: topo for Arches National Park**
> **Difficulty: very easy**

The popular Windows section is reached by turning right off the park drive onto a 2.5-mile paved spur road near **Balanced Rock** (see map, p. 96), 9 miles past the visitor center. Short, well-groomed paths lead to several major arches, including **Double Arch, Turret Arch,** and **North** and **South Windows.** Climb the rocks on the left behind North Window for a "framed" view of Turret Arch. From South Window a primitive trail drops behind the arches to return to the parking area.

Day Hike 3: The Fiery Furnace

> **Distance: 2 miles round trip**
> **Time: 2 hours**
> **Map: topo for Arches National Park**
> **Difficulty: moderate**

The mazelike **Fiery Furnace** (see map, p. 96), a natural amusement park of sorts, is not for the claustrophobic hiker. It's strongly advisable to take the ranger-guided tour your first time through because even an experienced person could get lost easily in this confusing, nearly trackless area, or miss some of its special attractions, such as **Surprise** and **Twin Arches.** The parking lot is off a short spur to the right of the park road, at about mile 14.5. Reservations, which are required, must be made in person at the visitor center. Permits are also needed for unguided travel here.

Day Hike 4: Sand Dune, Broken, and Tapestry Arches

> **Distance: 2.25 miles round trip**
> **Time: 2 hours**
> **Map: topo for Arches National Park**
> **Difficulty: easy**

Winding through the upper Fiery Furnace is a cairned trail to Broken Arch (see map, p. 96), with a spur to its unique neighbor, Sand Dune Arch. This is a fine after-dinner hike, for it starts at the rear of the campground, ending at a designated pullout on the park road about 16 miles from the visitor center. Your first landmark, **Tapestry Arch,** is a few hundred yards in on the left. Its backdrop and namesake is a wall coated with long, black streaks of "desert varnish" (composed of iron and manganese oxide). Then the trail passes through **Broken Arch,** whose "break" is revealed upon close inspection to be illusory. After crossing an open area, take the left-hand spur, which passes through fins to **Sand Dune Arch.** Notice the drifts around and below it. The highway pullout is only 100 yards past the trail junction. You can walk back to the campground along the park road (1.75 miles).

Day 4: ARCH HUNTING IN ARCHES

- **The Parthenon of arches and several others**
- **Backcountry camping in the Devils Garden area**
- **Gas, groceries, showers, and laundry available in Moab**

Today is an arch-finding extravaganza. In the morning, hike to Delicate Arch (bring water). After purchasing food for 2 nights in Moab, put on your pack and walk through the arch-studded Devils Garden to your chosen backcountry campsite.

Day Hike: Delicate Arch

> **Distance: 3 miles round trip**
> **Time: 2.5 hours**
> **Map: topo for Arches National Park**
> **Difficulty: moderate**

This perfect freestanding arch frames the La Sals in the distance. To reach the trailhead, drive 11.5 miles past the visitor center on the park road (see map, p. 96) to a signed junction. Turn right and go about 1.5 miles to the parking lot on the left at **Wolfe Ranch,** a pioneer cabin.

Landscape Arch, as wide as a football field

The trail itself is spectacular. First you cross a suspension bridge over Salt Wash (it may be buggy here), and then you pass through Morrison Formation badlands and begin a brisk 500-foot ascent up a slickrock ramp. At the top, look carefully for trail markers. The trail goes up a small wash and then hugs the right wall of a canyon, where it has been blasted out of sandstone. A large potty-type arch is straight ahead, and a "window" in the rock above the trail affords a tantalizing glimpse of **Delicate Arch.** The trail rounds a bend to a steep-sided bowl. Delicate Arch sits at the bowl's far end. With caution, you can safely make your way there. Like the park's other arches and fins, it is composed of Entrada Sandstone.

Retracing your steps to your vehicle, you can stop at a Ute petroglyph panel near the right bank of Salt Wash by turning right on a path at the end of your descent, before reaching the bridge. Follow the cliff for about 100 yards; the petroglyphs are in the rocks to the right. For a different perspective on Delicate Arch, drive past the Wolfe Ranch parking area to the end of the spur road and walk 100 yards to a viewpoint.

––––––

Backpack (or Day Hike): Devils Garden

> **Distance: 5 miles round trip**
> **Time: 4 hours (or overnight)**
> **Map: topo for Arches National Park**
> **Difficulty: very easy to Landscape Arch, moderate thereafter**

This trail system (see map, p. 96) is much traveled, and with good reason. Along its paths are seven major arches. Although the circuit described below can be completed in half a day, this fascinating area warrants a longer visit. Pack in 1.5 gallons of water apiece for an overnight. The trailhead and parking area are at the end of the park road.

For most of the way, the trail threads through pinyon and juniper vegetation. Less than 0.25 mile from the parking lot is a branch trail to your right, which soon divides, with one fork leading to **Tunnel Arch** and the other to **Pine Tree Arch.** Retrace your steps to the main trail and continue on toward **Landscape Arch.** Just before reaching it, you pass a trail on the right that winds through Fin Canyon on its way to Double O Arch. Landscape Arch, the length of a football field, is among the largest in the world.

The trail gets rougher here and begins to climb, following cairns. After passing Wall Arch on the right, take the short spur trail on the left to **Navajo** and **Partition Arches,** 0.25 mile away. Past this junction, the main trail favors slickrock and often goes along the tops of fins. From Fin Canyon Overlook, try to pick out Black Arch. **Double O Arch** consists of a large, round opening on top of a smaller one in a sandstone fin. Ease your way through the arch to the other side and continue 0.5 mile to rocket-shaped **Dark Angel.** The trail here, although cairned, is hard to follow at times; it bends to the left, arriving at a vantage point with stunning views of Salt Valley and the La Sal Mountains. As always, be sure to avoid walking on cryptogamic soil.

From Dark Angel, backtrack a short distance past Double O Arch. Return to the parking lot, if you wish, via scenic **Fin Canyon,** a slightly longer (3.5 vs. 2.5 miles) and more rugged route. It begins near Double O Arch and rejoins the main trail near Landscape Arch.

Light snowfall dusts petrified dunes.

Day 5: HIKER'S CHOICE

- **Afoot in more remote parts of Arches National Park**
- **Camping at the campground**

This afternoon, after registering for a site in the campground, you can stroll up or down Courthouse Wash or visit Klondike Bluffs. Carry at least 2 to 3 quarts of water per person.

Day Hike 1: Lower Courthouse Wash

> **Distance: 6 miles one way**
> **Time: 4 hours**
> **Map: topo for Arches National Park**
> **Difficulty: easy**

This pleasant day hike begins where the park's main road crosses **Courthouse Wash,** 4.25 miles past the entrance station (see map, p. 96). Head downstream (a right turn from the bridge). Very soon the Navajo Sandstone cliffs rise and the canyon narrows. Because intermittent water may be in the wash, wear old boots or sneakers.

Courthouse Wash is quite pretty and interesting and requires little skill or physical stamina. You may, however, meet up with deer-flies in reedy places and quicksand in the last 0.5 mile of the canyon (which you can avoid by picking up a trail on the bank). The hike ends at US-191, about 2 miles southeast of the Arches entrance station. There is a parking area just north of here. Bighorn sheep are occasionally seen in this vicinity. Before returning to your car, climb to admire the **Moab Panel** of pictographs, on the cliff face to the left, paralleling the highway.

Day Hike 2: Upper Courthouse Wash

> **Distance: 6 miles one way**
> **Time: 4 hours**
> **Map: topo for Arches National Park**
> **Difficulty: easy to moderate**

Like the previous trip, this hike begins inside the park, at the bridge over Courthouse Wash. It requires a car shuttle (see map, p. 96). The route ends where **Sevenmile Wash,** a side-canyon, intersects US-191, north of the turnout to the Arches entrance station. Much of the time you will be splashing along in shallow water, so wear suitable footgear. There may be mud and brush to contend with at the start as you drop into the wash from a small side-canyon. In compensation, you receive stunning views of the Courthouse Towers section of the park. Within the first mile, look for **Ring Arch** in the cliffs on the left. At about mile 3, the canyon forks. The left fork, which is the one you want, is Sevenmile Wash; but before heading that way, you may want to visit the Courthouse Wash narrows above the confluence.

Courthouse Towers brood below Park Avenue.

The 3-mile walk up Sevenmile Wash remains easy until it ends in a box canyon. An old, very steep cattle trail on the left leads up and out toward US-191, just south of its junction with UT-313 to Dead Horse Point and the Island in the Sky.

Day Hike 3: Klondike Bluffs

> **Distance: 3 miles round trip**
> **Time: 2.5 hours**
> **Map: topo for Arches National Park**
> **Difficulty: moderate**

Reach this unspoiled destination by turning west from the main park road onto a dirt road near Skyline Arch, 17 miles from the visitor center (see map, p. 96). The road, which is impassable when wet, runs the length of Salt Valley. The turnoff to the **Klondike Bluffs** parking lot is about 8 miles up the road, on the left.

The trail begins to the left of the parking lot. It rapidly ascends a cliff, treating hikers to gorgeous views of the Fiery Furnace and Devils Garden as well as the lower end of the Island in the Sky. Then it veers to the right between widely spaced rock walls, descending slowly toward a drainage. Look for an unnamed arch on the left near the trail's low point. Crossing the wash, the trail climbs a sandy hill and then turns right and continues for about 0.25 mile. From this spot, **Tower Arch** is visible in a fin to the right. An enormous pinnacle next to the arch lends this span its name. On the arch's right abutment is an inscription carved by Alexander Ringhoffer, a founding father of Arches Park, who operated a mine in Salt Valley in the 1920s. Just 100 yards to the south, in another fin, is an unnamed double arch. On your way out, detour downstream in the wash you crossed earlier to admire a row of monoliths called the **Marching Men.**

An easy—but longer (4 miles) and less shady—alternative route back begins near the small sign for Tower Arch. This cairned route climbs in a westerly direction to join a jeep track. Where this road swings hard to the left is an interesting slickrock mass. At the half-way mark, an intersecting jeep road leads toward Balanced Rock, but you continue straight ahead. Cresting a hill, the road drops down and eventually meets the Salt Valley Road, where you turn left. After a few hundred yards, another left onto the Klondike Bluffs spur road returns you to your car.

Day 6: FOUR HIKES NEAR THE RIVER

- **A canyon-bottom or canyon-rim day trip**
- **Camping at Dead Horse Point State Park**
- **Gas, groceries, showers, and laundry available in Moab**

This morning, drive into Moab and stock up on 3 days' worth of groceries, water, and supplies. If you are interested in taking a float trip on the Colorado later in the week (see Days 9 and 10), make reservations with one of the local companies. Then select one of the day hikes described below.

Tonight, after your hike, you'll camp at Dead Horse Point State Park. To reach the park from Moab, drive northwest 9 miles on US-191 to UT-313 and turn left. The road crosses railroad tracks and climbs to the mesa top, offering views of nearby **Monitor** and **Merrimac Buttes** as well as of a good portion of Arches National Park. About 29 miles from Moab, the road forks. Tomorrow you'll take the right fork, leading to the Island in the Sky. Tonight, however, turn left and proceed to the state park, 4 miles away. The campground offers covered shelters, running water, and even electric lights. **Dead Horse Point** juts out over the erosional basin of the Colorado River and is connected to the main body of the mesa by an isthmus 30 yards wide. According to local legend, the point got its name when wild mustangs were rounded up and accidentally left to die on the mesa. The vista from the point, especially at sunset, is one of the most dramatic in the Southwest. The river makes a bowknot bend directly below, and buttes, needles, and benchlands extend as far as the eye can see. The rock strata visible here, from top to bottom, include the Entrada, Navajo, Kayenta, and Wingate Sandstone layers as well as the Chinle, Moenkopi, Cutler, and Honaker Trail Formations.

For more information on the trails featured below, contact the Bureau of Land Management, Moab Field Office, 82 East Dogwood, Moab, UT 84532; the phone number is (435) 259-6111. For camping reservations (recommended) contact Dead Horse Point State Park, P.O. Box 609, Moab, Utah 84532-0609; or call (435) 259-2614.

Day Hike 1: Negro Bill Canyon

> **Distance: 4 miles round trip**
> **Time: 3 hours**
> **Map: topo for Moab**
> **Difficulty: easy**

A tributary of the Colorado River, lovely **Negro Bill Canyon** got its name from William Granstaff, a nineteenth-century mulatto prospector, farmer, and rancher who grazed his cattle here. In the late 1970s, the canyon was the scene of a skirmish in the "Sagebrush Rebellion" by pro-development Westerners resisting federal efforts to designate land as wilderness. But the Negro Bill system is also noteworthy for Morning Glory Bridge, an enormous Navajo Sandstone span at the end of a side-canyon.

Drive 3 miles northeast on UT-128 from the Colorado River bridge at Moab; Negro Bill Canyon (see map, p. 105) is the second canyon on your right. Park in the designated lot.

The canyon floor is green, thanks to a perennial stream that supports cottonwoods and Gambel's oaks. Beginning on the left side of the canyon, a primitive hiking trail crosses and recrosses the stream. About 1.5 miles from the highway, turn up into the second side-canyon on the right. Follow the trail on the left bank of this box canyon 0.5 mile to impressive, 250-foot-long **Morning Glory Bridge,** one of the Southwest's largest. Underneath this vaulting span is a pool, created by a seep spring. But beware of poison ivy, which thrives here. You can explore farther up Negro Bill—it extends for some 10 miles toward its origin in the La Sal foothills—before backtracking to your car.

Day Hike 2: Moab Slickrock Bike Trail

> **Distance: 2.25 miles for practice loop, or 10.25 for**
> **main loop, round trip**
> **Time: 1.5 hours for practice loop; 1 day for main**
> **loop**
> **Map: topo for Moab**
> **Difficulty: moderate**

Although designed originally for motorcyclists and used now almost exclusively by mountain bikers (advanced biking skills are mandatory), this trail offers opportunities for hiking on petrified Navajo Sandstone

FOUR HIKES NEAR THE RIVER

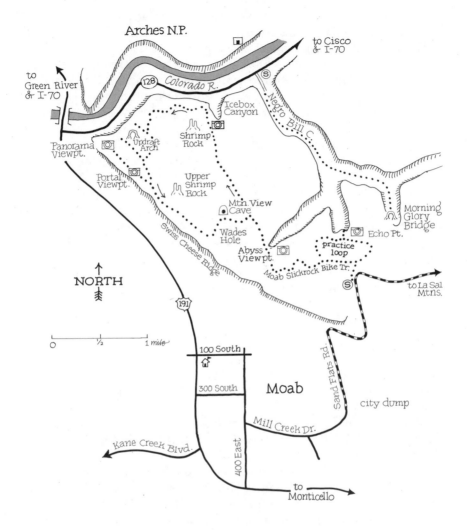

Arches N.P.

to Cisco
& I-70

128 Colorado R.

to
Green River
& I-70

Icebox
Canyon

Negro Bill C.

Shrimp
Rock

Updraft
Arch

Panorama
Viewpt.

Portal
Viewpt.

Upper
Shrimp
Rock

Mtn. View
Cave

Wades
Hole

Swiss Cheese Ridge

Abyss
Viewpt.

Morning
Glory
Bridge

Echo Pt.

practice
loop

Moab Slickrock Bike Tr.

to La Sal
Mtns.

NORTH

0   ½   1 mile

100 South

300 South

Moab

Sand Flats Rd.

city dump

Mill Creek Dr.

Kane Creek Blvd.

400 East

to
Monticello

dunes. Avoid the area on weekends, holidays, and in the spring "high season" when it receives especially heavy mountain bike traffic.

From Moab, turn east off US-191 onto 300 South (see map, above). Follow this street to a T intersection with 400 East and bear right. Two blocks down is Mill Creek Drive, which soon runs into Sand Flats Road; look for signs. Proceed up Sand Flats Road for over 2.25 miles, passing the city dump. The trailhead and parking lot are on the left 0.5 mile beyond the entrance booth. There is a campground here also. Camping is limited to official sites, and fees apply for both camping and day use.

The main biking and hiking route is indicated by white dashes painted on the slickrock. Alternate routes, usually more challenging, are marked by black diamonds. To stay out of the way of bicyclists, who generally have a tough time of it, keep to one side of the line.

The practice loop takes off to the right after 0.25 mile. Its highlight is **Echo Point,** overlooking a side-canyon of the Negro Bill system. A nice 3.75-mile trip involves hiking the practice loop, continuing on to **Abyss Viewpoint,** and then returning on the main trail to your car.

Past Abyss Viewpoint, the main trail forks. Take the right-hand trail to Shrimp Rock, an oddly shaped butte on the edge of Icebox Canyon, whose intermittent waters feed into the Colorado River. The rock gets its name from a nearby pool that contains fairy shrimp and other tiny creatures. Please do not disturb any potholes you may encounter. Three short spurs lead to other spectacular overlooks. From the first and second of these, you can admire potty-type **Updraft Arch;** the third goes to Portal and Panorama Viewpoints. The main trail then swings south to close the loop near Wades Hole.

Day Hike 3: Corona, Bowtie, and Pinto Arches

> **Distance: 3 miles round trip**
> **Time: 2.5 hours**
> **Map: topo for Moab**
> **Difficulty: moderate**

Corona Arch, formed from the weathering of a fin, is also known as "Little Rainbow Bridge" because it resembles famous Rainbow Bridge on the Utah-Arizona border. Two other arches, Bowtie and Pinto (aka Goldbar), are close by.

To reach the trailhead, drive north from Moab on US-191 (see map, p. 118). About 1.5 miles past the Colorado River bridge, turn left on UT-279 (Potash Road) and proceed about 10 miles. Following the west bank of the Colorado, this road passes through the Portal at mile 2.75, where the river abandons Spanish Valley and slices back through Navajo Sandstone domes, becoming entrenched again in a deep gorge. You will notice some rock art panels and a turnout for dinosaur tracks as you progress down the road. A sign indicates where to park for the hike.

The cairned trail ascends a steep embankment to cross railroad tracks. **Pinto Arch** is barely visible in the distance to your left. Beyond the tracks, walk toward the fence, and pass through by means of a hiker zigzag. The trail goes to the right of a shallow gorge, climbing gradually while heading left toward gold-hued cliffs. Nearing the cliffs, it contours to the right and rounds a bend. At a small scallop in the cliff, wire cables, carved-out footholds, and a ladder help you negotiate rough spots.

From the top of the ladder, Bowtie and Corona Arches are visible in the next bay over. You can freelance across the slickrock to these giants. **Bowtie** is the potty arch at the midpoint of the amphitheater, while its even more impressive companion, **Corona,** dominates the bowl's far end. Poetry in stone, this arch measures almost 150 feet across, and from it you gain splendid views into the railroad canyon. Double back to your car.

Day Hike 4: Hidden Valley/Moab Rim

> **Distance: 5 miles one way**
> **Time: 3.5 hours**
> **Map: topo for Moab**
> **Difficulty: strenuous**

Completing this hike in its entirety requires a car shuttle. But the trip has so much scenic beauty to recommend it that you could hardly go wrong by walking part way in from either end and doubling back. A topo is essential, since much of the route is unmarked.

To reach the Hidden Valley trailhead, drive 3 miles south of Moab on US-191 (see map, p. 118). Turn right onto Angel Rock Road, and go two blocks to Rimrock Road. Turn right again, and proceed to the parking lot. A sign indicates the trailhead, just below the cliffs on the perimeter of Behind the Rocks.

The **Moab Rim Trail** is sometimes used (incredibly!) by 4-wheel-drive enthusiasts. At the south end of Moab, turn west off US-191 onto Kane Creek Boulevard. Follow this road for 2.6 miles, passing through the river "portal," to a marked pullout about 150 yards past a cattle guard. Park here.

The **Hidden Valley Trail** ascends briskly on rocky switchbacks to a wide, level passageway between cliffs. It tops a saddle, crossing into another part of Hidden Valley, before continuing over another, higher pass. Views are superlative. The total elevation gain to this point is 700 feet.

The route now drops down into a slickrock wilderness to intersect the Moab Rim jeep road in about 0.25 mile. Follow the jeep road in a northwesterly direction, passing two spurs that lead to viewpoints. The road descends a sand hill and then climbs steadily as it parallels Navajo Sandstone fins and domes.

Near the crest, at mile 3.5, you reach an overlook of Moab and Spanish Valley. From here the road contours along the top of the cliffs toward the river. It then plunges 950 feet on fractured Kayenta Formation ledges. Look for scrapes and dents in the rock, made when jeeps bottomed out on this challenging route.

Day 7: TOURING THE ISLAND

- **Day hikes to craters, arches, and overlooks**
- **Watching the sunset from Grand View Point**
- **Camping at Canyonlands National Park**

On today's agenda is a leisurely exploration of the Island in the Sky, a district of **Canyonlands National Park.** Bring water along, for it is unavailable here.

Rugged and magnificent, Canyonlands is several parks rolled into one. This 337,570-acre preserve, divided into three separate zones by the confluence of the Green and Colorado Rivers, includes some of the wildest land in the Lower 48. The park has everything an adventurer could want, including turbulent whitewater in Cataract Canyon, ancient pictograph panels in the Maze, canyons studded with ruins and arches, hair-raising jeep roads, and panoramic vistas of spires, buttes, and goosenecks.

Return to the fork you took to Dead Horse Point (see Day 6) and turn left toward **Island in the Sky,** 4.5 miles distant. Like Dead Horse Point, the Island is joined to the rest of the plateau by a narrow neck. This high, rolling mesa, dotted with pinyons and junipers, drops precipitously to the **White Rim,** a terrace almost 1000 feet above the Green and Colorado Rivers. From the Neck, a mile south of the ranger station, you receive outstanding views into both Taylor Canyon (a tributary of the Green) and Shafer Canyon (a tributary of the Colorado). To the left is the beginning of the **Shafer Trail,** a jeep road that switchbacks to the White Rim and eventually hooks up with UT-279. The waterless Willow Flat Campground is off the Green River Overlook spur, near the end of the park road. Select a campsite, stop at overlooks, and hike one or more of the following short trails.

For information, write to the Superintendent, Canyonlands National Park, 2282 S. West Resource Boulevard, Moab, UT 84532, or call (435) 259-4351.

Canyon views are spectacular from Island in the Sky.

Day Hike 1: Mesa Arch Trail

Distance: 0.5 mile round trip
Time: 0.5 hour
Map: topo for Canyonlands National Park
Difficulty: very easy

This nearly level loop trail to Mesa Arch leaves the park road 5.75 miles past the ranger station (see map, p. 110). The Navajo Sandstone arch is poised on the edge of a 500-foot drop-off into Buck Canyon, which itself cuts down 700 feet to the White Rim. Framed through the arch is the formation called the **Washerwoman,** a distinctive butte with a small window.

Day Hike 2: Aztec Butte Trail

Distance: 1.25 miles round trip
Time: 1 hour
Map: topo for Canyonlands National Park
Difficulty: very easy, with a moderate climb to the
butte

The turnout for this hike is located roughly opposite the start of the Green River Overlook spur road (see map, p. 110). Of the two rock mounds visible from the trailhead, **Aztec Butte** is higher and farther away. The trail ascends 200 feet up the face of the butte, whose summit boasts a roofless, one-room ruin. The ruin explains the name of the formation—early settlers believed that cliff dwellings were built by Mesoamerican Indians.

Back at the main trail, look for another spur, very faint, almost directly opposite the first. (You should be able to spot it from Aztec Butte.) Follow this spur to the top of the low mound, and then bear right along the rim until you notice a break. Just below the break is a pair of granaries in excellent condition. Return the way you came.

Day Hike 3: Upheaval Dome Overlook

Distance: 1 mile round trip
Time: 1 hour
Map: topo for Canyonlands National Park
Difficulty: easy to first viewpoint, moderate to
second

From the end of the scenic drive on the western side of the Island (see map, p. 110), this trail climbs 200 feet in less than 0.5 mile to an overlook of **Upheaval Dome.** Once believed to be an eroded salt dome, it is now regarded by most geologists as a meteorite impact crater. Tomorrow's itinerary will offer you a chance to circumambulate the

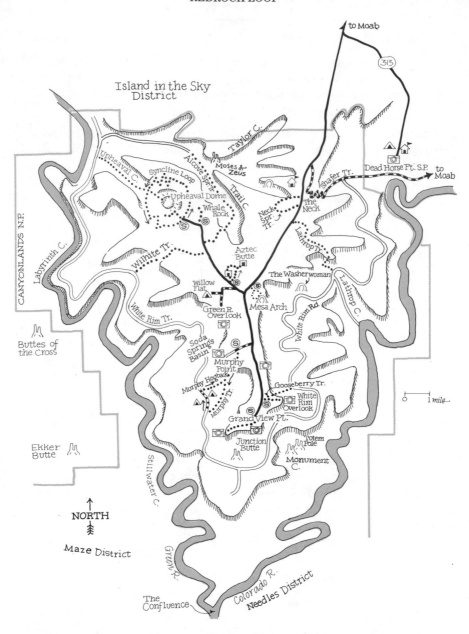

gigantic crater and enter it from the bottom. For now, content yourself with walking along the rim of the 1000-foot-deep, mile-wide depression, marveling at the colorful, tilted badlands at its center. A rather steep and rough trail extending another 0.5 mile from the initial vantage point affords an even better view. It veers to the left and plummets down a sandstone defile, with the aid of hacked-in steps, before reaching a second overlook.

Day Hike 4: Whale Rock

Distance: 0.5 mile round trip
Time: 0.5 hour
Map: topo for Canyonlands National Park
Difficulty: easy

While in the vicinity of Upheaval Dome, admire the view from adjacent **Whale Rock** (see map, p. 110). With the aid of handrails, climb 100 feet to the summit of this slickrock mass on a cairned route. From this lofty perch you peer into Trail Canyon, a tributary of Taylor. You can also see the entire perimeter of Upheaval Dome.

Day Hike 5: White Rim Overlook Trail

Distance: 1.5 miles round trip
Time: 1 hour
Map: topo for Canyonlands National Park
Difficulty: very easy

Near the south end of the mesa, a short, level hike on a finger of sandstone leads to **White Rim Overlook** (see map, p. 110), an uncommonly scenic place that affords vistas into sheer-walled **Monument Basin.** This canyon sports rows of chocolate-colored, Organ Rock Shale pinnacles wearing erosion-resistant White Rim Sandstone "hats." The most impressive of the pinnacles is called the **Totem Pole.** People sometimes hike to the White Rim from this vicinity on the Gooseberry Trail (see below), but the only nontechnical way to enter Monument Basin itself is from the Colorado River.

Day Hike 6: Grand View Trail

Distance: 2 miles round trip
Time: 1.25 hours
Map: topo for Canyonlands National Park
Difficulty: easy

At the southernmost tip of the Island is **Grand View Point** (see map, p. 110), whose name contains no exaggeration. The views, though similar to those from Dead Horse Point, are vaster in scope; the surrounding landforms are more remote and even surreal. The rivers (not visible from the overlook) flow 2000 feet below, and on a clear day you can pick out landforms up to 100 miles distant. Off to the right of Grand View Point is a cairned, mostly level trail that follows the rim to the tip of the peninsula. From the overlook, Junction Butte is immediately to the south, and the intricate canyons, fins, and standing rocks of the Maze District of Canyonlands Park are almost palpable.

Day 8: ISLAND DAY HIKE

- **Into the backcountry**
- **Camping at Willow Flat Campground**

Assuming that the Island isn't too hot or too buggy, you can choose one of the long day hikes described below. They also could be done as backpack trips, although lack of water might pose a problem. All are strenuous hikes that descend between 1300 feet and 1600 feet to the White Rim. A fourth, easier alternative remains on the mesa top. A limited number of backpacking permits are available at the visitor center for a small charge. Call (435) 259-4351 for reservations.

Several other wonderful trails drop down from the Island in the Sky. These include the **Gooseberry Trail** (6 miles round trip and very vertical, with boulder-hopping at the base of the Wingate cliffs); the **Wilhite Trail** (10 miles round trip, well-constructed through the Wingate, featuring an Anasazi granary in addition to some old mining claims); and the "easier" **Alcove Spring Trail** (10 miles round trip, leading to dramatic spires, Moses and Zeus, near the junction of Trail and Taylor Canyons).

Day Hike (or Backpack) 1: Murphy Trail

> **Distance: 9 miles round trip**
> **Time: 1 full day (or overnight)**
> **Map: topo for Canyonlands National Park**
> **Difficulty: strenuous**

This shadeless loop begins at a pullout about 1 mile down the dirt road to Murphy Point, an overlook (see map, p. 110). The trail strikes out toward the rim of the canyon and then cuts across Kayenta Formation ledges, dropping about 100 feet to a break in the Wingate Sandstone. The next mile of trail, though carefully constructed, traverses steep and rocky terrain. Low walls minimize the risk of injury and a rickety footbridge helps you cross a chasm. Plunging through the Wingate layer in a knee-busting 750-foot descent, the trail deposits you at the base of the cliff. At the fork, go left; you'll return via the other path.

The trail follows the canyon bottom for a few miles, slowly descending, until it intersects the White Rim Road, which contours around the base of the Island in the Sky. Turn right here, walking along the jeep road to the top of **Murphy Hogback.** Expect outstanding views, particularly as you peer into Soda Springs Basin to the north.

Past the Hogback's primitive campgrounds on the right, leave the White Rim Road to rejoin the Murphy Trail and complete the loop. From here to the cliff base, the trail is level and the scenery sublime. Rest a while as a prelude to the grueling climb to the top.

Day Hike (or Backpack) 2: Syncline Loop

> **Distance: 8 miles (or longer) round trip**
> **Time: 1 full day (or overnight)**
> **Map: topo for Canyonlands National Park**
> **Difficulty: strenuous**

This glorious trail (see map, p. 110) provides access into Upheaval Dome through its outlet, Upheaval Wash, and permits easy exploration all the way to the Green River's Labyrinth Canyon. Because those options add, respectively, 3 miles and 6 miles round trip to the hike, they are best reserved for backpackers.

The two ends of the Syncline Loop begin a short distance up the Upheaval Dome Overlook Trail. Turn right onto the loop. After a long, fairly level stretch, the trail drops steeply through the Breach, a wide gap between Navajo Sandstone cliffs. Reaching crescent-shaped **Syncline Valley,** you continue to descend, first gently and then very rapidly, even treacherously, at an enormous pour-off. The views here are outstanding, but watch your step on the loose, slippery scree. You may find springs at both the top and the bottom of this drop. The trail then proceeds to the junction with the signed, unmaintained route into **Upheaval Dome,** on the left.

Backpackers might consider camping in this vicinity and trekking into the dome (or down to the river) without full gear. The route into the dome follows Upheaval Wash, with cairns guiding you around some minor obstructions. After about 1.75 miles, the wash forks amid unearthly badlands. Both forks are worth exploring.

Back at the junction, the Syncline Loop dips to the floor of Upheaval Canyon. Within several hundred yards it intersects a big side-canyon on the left, which you enter in preparation for the tough 1300-foot climb to the Island. Your efforts are compensated with views into the canyon of the Green River that improve with each step. The trail levels off in the last mile.

Day Hike (or Backpack) 3: Lathrop Trail

> **Distance: 11 miles round trip**
> **Time: 1 full day (or overnight)**
> **Map: topo for Canyonlands National Park**
> **Difficulty: strenuous**

Unlike the two options described above, the shadeless, waterless Lathrop Trail starts on the eastern side of the Island, 1.75 miles south of the visitor center (see map, page 110). From the parking lot, it crosses Grays Pasture in its first, easy 1.5 miles, passing Navajo Sandstone domes as it beelines toward the rim.

Descending somewhat, the trail contours to the right for about a mile until reaching a rockslide that produced a break in the Wingate cliffs. Although the trail's steep switchbacks look intimidating, they are well-designed. At the bottom, in the Chinle Formation, the trail follows a deteriorated prospecting road, passing an old mine on the left (it is dangerous; do not enter) at mile 3. It then arrives at Moenkopi terraces which afford unforgettable views of a big bend in the Colorado River. The whole area has a Grand Canyon feel about it.

At about mile 4.5, the trail leaves the jeep track and drops into a shallow wash. From here it is about another 0.5 mile to the White Rim Road. Adventurers with camping permits may wish to continue down Lathrop Canyon all the way to the river, for an extra 8 miles round trip.

Day Hike 4: Neck Springs Trail

> **Distance: 5 miles round trip**
> **Time: 3 hours**
> **Map: topo for Canyonlands National Park**
> **Difficulty: moderate**

Drive south from the visitor center to the Neck, where the Taylor and Shafer canyon systems nearly converge (see map, page 110). Park your car in the lot, and cross the road to the trailhead. The trail descends 300 feet into an arm of Taylor Canyon. It laterals past **Neck Springs,** located in two neighboring alcoves. The first of these is one of the best echo chambers around.

Beyond the springs, the trail climbs a sand hill and levels off, paralleling the canyon. It offers a bird's-eye view of a large arch between the Kayenta and Navajo strata. Then it swings left into Cabin Spring Canyon, which sometimes contains shallow pools, and climbs up a slickrock draw to the rim, near unusual sandstone domes. An old trough on the rim calls to mind the grazing that once occurred in the area. The last 2 miles are very easy, crossing a slickrock bench to return to the road and parking lot.

Days 9 and 10: LANDLUBBER'S DELIGHT

- **White-water rafting on the Colorado**
- **Day-hiking options**
- **Or an overnight stay "Behind the Rocks"**
- **Camping on Day 9 at Newspaper Rock Recreation Site**
- **Gas, groceries, showers, and laundry available in Moab or Monticello**

Visitors in the mood for a different kind of experience can participate in one of the many river-running expeditions that depart from Moab. Common destinations include Westwater and Cataract Canyons, with their ferocious rapids, and the much tamer float trip from Fisher Towers to a take-out point north of town (called "the Daily" in local parlance). Make arrangements in advance to join such trips. Also, you may need to camp closer to Moab than at Island in the Sky prior to the excursion. If your raft trip lasts only 1 day, use the following section to brainstorm about Day 10.

From Island in the Sky, return to Moab and buy food for 2 days. Your destination is **Behind the Rocks,** a slickrock wonderland of domes, fins, and arches. There are few trails on this high, broken plateau, but jeep roads provide good access to the most picturesque spots, and cross-country hiking opportunities for skilled orienteers are superb. The only problem is a dearth of water, which mandates full canteens (1 gallon per person per day for summer backpacking). For people preferring to take day hikes, some options are presented below.

When you emerge from Behind the Rocks, you'll have plenty of time to shower, wash clothes, and buy food for the next 4 nights before heading toward your campsite at Newspaper Rock Recreation Site. From Moab, drive south on US-191, stopping to appreciate **Wilson Arch,** along the highway south of La Sal Junction. About 42.5 miles past Moab, you'll pass Church Rock on the left. Turn right (west) on UT-211 at the sign for the Needles District of Canyonlands National Park. The road descends from the plateau and follows the Indian Creek drainage to the Needles, 34 miles from the turnoff. Where you reach Indian Creek and the road bends to the right, look for enchanting **Newspaper Rock,** called Tse Hani ("rock that tells a story") by area Navajos. This flat slab of Wingate Sandstone is decorated with 2000

Many cultures contributed inscriptions to Newspaper Rock.

years of petroglyphs from many cultures: Desert Archaic, Anasazi, Fremont, Navajo, and Ute. Across the highway, along the creek, is a small, primitive campground. No drinking water is provided.

For more information about Behind the Rocks, contact the Bureau of Land Management, Moab Field Office, 82 East Dogwood Avenue, Moab, UT 84532.

Backpack (or Day Hike) 1: Pritchett Canyon

> **Distance: 10 miles round trip**
> **Time: 1 day (or overnight)**
> **Map: topo for Moab**
> **Difficulty: easy, with moderate climbs to the arches**

Pritchett Canyon's awe-inspiring beauty is enhanced by three major arches and several unnamed ones, all surrounded by breadloaf-shaped domes of Navajo Sandstone. Although it's possible to day hike part or all of the canyon, backpacking will permit more leisurely exploration.

To enter this redrock heaven, head south on US-191 from the center of Moab and turn right onto Kane Creek Boulevard, on the eastern bank of the Colorado River (see map, p. 118). Follow this road for about 4.5 miles, stopping to appreciate rock art in Moon Flower Canyon at mile 3.25. Park downstream from **Pritchett Canyon's** mouth, beyond the end of the pavement. The owner of the land at the mouth has been charging people to enter the canyon, but authorities are negotiating to end this practice.

Begin by walking a jeep road toward the canyon's head, passing several side-canyons on the left. At about mile 2, the road forks, and a spur enters one of the side-canyons; detour 0.25 mile here to visit a small natural bridge. The main trail bears right at the fork. Around mile 3, it climbs to cross a weathered fin separating two branches of Pritchett Canyon. **Window Arch,** with its huge triangular opening, is in this fin. Dropping back down, you can spot Pritchett Arch looming ahead.

Here the road forks again. To visit Halls Bridge, 0.5 mile distant, turn right past the **Ostrich,** a distinctively shaped butte, and then take another right, passing the roads that lead toward Pritchett Canyon's upper reaches. The road you want is the one that heads back down the canyon a short distance, closely following the rim. When it ends, pick up a faint path marked by a cairn, which enters the left fork of the first side-canyon. It is a bit dicey, especially where it climbs up a slickrock slot to avoid a dryfall. Continue on for a few hundred yards until muscular **Halls Bridge** (really an arch) appears in the fin to your right. You can climb up the cleft at the head of the side-canyon and cautiously work your way underneath the arch from the back.

Hikers who are very skilled at reading topo maps can proceed cross-country over high slickrock terraces to Pritchett Arch. But the more

A short scramble takes hikers under thick-walled Halls Bridge.

common route involves backtracking to the jeep road between the Ostrich and Window Arch. Follow this road up the canyon to a pass, and then descend into upper Hunters Canyon, which parallels a massive escarpment. In the valley, after going by an isolated rock obelisk and a small arch, the road crosses a wash twice, forking at the second crossing. Go right here and follow the spur to its end under the cliffs. Pritchett Arch will be visible on the ridge to the right.

Look for a cairn indicating the obscure footpath that ascends to the mesa top through a notch behind a split column of sandstone. Once on top, bear right, contouring around the base of the cliff into a hanging side-canyon. Within the next 0.25 mile you will see a cave and a potty arch. The trail peters out except for an occasional marker, but you continue straight ahead. Near the far end of this hanging side-canyon, **Pritchett Arch** peeks out from behind a slickrock mass on the left. You can climb the slope to get underneath the arch, a classical and graceful span. Follow the side-canyon just a bit farther to an overlook of Pritchett Canyon. Then retrace your steps to your car.

Day Hike 2: Hunters Canyon

> **Distance: 6 miles round trip**
> **Time: 4 hours**
> **Map: topo for Moab**
> **Difficulty: easy**

Lower Hunters offers delightful day-hiking before it ends in a box canyon. Its sandy mouth, distinguishable by a parking area and jeep track (which continues for a short distance), is about 8 miles from

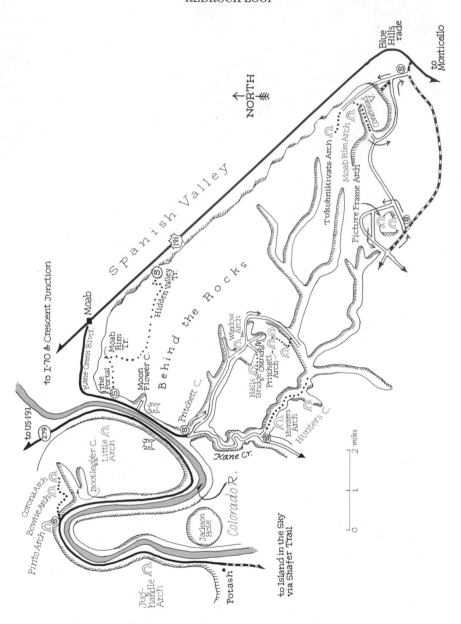

Moab on Kane Creek Boulevard (see map, above). Be sure not to confuse Hunters with a short canyon near a dripping spring at the bottom of the Kane Creek switchbacks.

The narrow, watery gorge contains several spans, including unusual **Hunters Arch** at mile 0.5 and an unnamed beauty up a significant side-canyon on the right at about mile 2. Past this side-canyon, progress is hampered by heavy brush. Hikers who persist will reach a pour-off grotto 3 miles above the canyon mouth, complete with a pool and a small natural bridge. To continue past the pour-off into upper Hunters Canyon and the Pritchett Arch area requires free-climbing skills.

Day Hike 3: Conehead Valley

Distance: 4 miles round trip
Time: 3 hours
Maps: topos for La Sal Junction and Hatch Point
Difficulty: easy, with moderate climb to
Tukuhnikivats Arch

The fascinating dome-bounded area that some locals call Conehead Valley (see map, p. 118) marks the southern end of Behind the Rocks. Excellent day-hiking possibilities abound on the rough jeep tracks that honeycomb this otherwise wild and unspoiled area. To get there, drive 13 miles south of Moab on US-191 to the top of a grade. Locate a marked BLM dirt road on the right. Although this dirt road soon deteriorates, its initial section does not require high clearance. After 0.5 mile on the dirt road, turn right at a fork and park along the shoulder.

Hike this road in the direction of Conehead Valley, clearly visible about a mile distant. Continue straight ahead past intersecting jeep tracks and dirt roads until you reach a triple fork. You will return on the left fork, but for now take a hard right along the rim. The view toward the La Sals is incomparable as you walk past the upper end of Conehead Valley and **Moab Rim Arch.** Reaching another fork, go right and continue to the road's end. A small, unusual arch will appear on the left horizon. To get there, climb the moderately steep side-canyon in front of you, skirting small pour-offs on the left. At the top, go left about 25 yards to see the formation named **Tukuhnikivats Arch** ("land where the suns shines longest") after the mountain peak it frames.

Backtrack down the side-canyon to the road, and proceed to the upper end of **Conehead Valley,** about 0.5 mile past Moab Rim Arch. Although there is no trail to guide you, it is easy to enter the valley, where you soon intersect a jeep road. As it leaves the valley's lower end, this road climbs rapidly up a steep sand hill. From the top you can spy all three of southern Utah's mountain ranges. The road leads back to the three forks mentioned earlier. Turn right here to return to your car.

Day Hike 4: Picture Frame Arch

Distance: 0.75 mile round trip
Time: 1 hour or less
Map: topo for Hatch Point
Difficulty: easy

If your car has high clearance, you can inspect lovely Picture Frame Arch (see map, p. 118) nearby, 5.75 miles from US-191. From the

Petrified dunes are visible through Picture Frame Arch.

highway, take the same dirt road as for the Conehead Valley hike, but turn left rather than right at the fork at mile 0.5. Follow the signs for Pritchett Arch until you reach the short Picture Frame spur, which loops around a redrock mass just past a dune area on the right. Park here and tackle the 0.75-mile spur road on foot. Walking counterclockwise around the base of the cliffs, you pass a large, unnamed arch within the first 100 yards before coming to **Picture Frame Arch,** around the back of the mesa. Picture Frame is accessible from a sloping terrace, provided you can negotiate a low cliff. The old ladder positioned here may be unsafe. Just behind the arch's square opening is a chamber that offers a shady place to relax. Continue on the road around the mesa to loop back to your car.

Days 11–13: NEEDLES DISTRICT

- **Wandering through cities of stone**
- **Making a pilgrimage to Druid Arch**
- **Camping at Chesler Park and Devils Kitchen**
- **Gas, groceries, and showers available seasonally at Needles Outpost**

Today you'll begin your stay in the Needles District of Canyonlands Park, an area defined by standing rocks in all colors, shapes, and sizes. On your left as you approach the park are the distinctive **Six Shooter Peaks** (Chinle Formation slopes topped by Wingate Sandstone). You pass Davis and Lavender Canyons, whose upper arms are full of arches and ruins. **Wooden Shoe Arch** stands guard over Squaw Flat Campground inside the park.

Reservations are highly recommended for overnight stays in the backcountry, especially during the busy spring and fall seasons. Backcountry campsites fill quickly, and permits—required for backpacking, camping, and motoring into Salt, Davis, and Lavender Canyons—are limited. Fees are charged.

At the visitor center, obtain a 2-night permit to camp in Chesler Park and Devils Pocket. Inquire about the water situation (you'll probably have to carry a gallon each). On Day 13, plan to camp at Squaw Flat after you've showered and resupplied at Needles Outpost, on the park boundary.

For further information, contact the Superintendent, Canyonlands National Park, 2282 S. West Resource Boulevard, Moab, UT 84532. The reservation office phone number is (435) 259-4351.

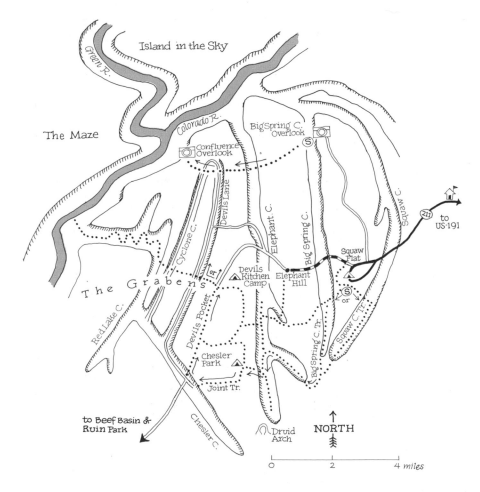

Backpack: Chesler Park

Distance: 22 miles round trip
Time: 3 days
Map: topo for Canyonlands National Park
Difficulty: moderate

Chesler Park (see map, p. 121), a meadow surrounded by sandstone towers, is one of the great beauty spots of the desert. In late spring and early summer the area is carpeted with globe mallow, larkspur, and other flowers characteristic of the Colorado Plateau.

At Squaw Flat's Campground A, take either the **Squaw Canyon** or the **Big Spring Canyon Trail,** roughly equal in length, which intersect (to make a nice 7.5-mile loop) in about 3.75 miles. Because the Big Spring route crosses a slickrock pass, it is harder, but also more scenic. Soon after the trails converge, the path seems to disappear on a slickrock bench, but it actually goes through a narrow fracture to the right between two fins. Logs jammed into this joint make the passage easier. Shortly thereafter, you hop a pass into a tributary of the Elephant Canyon system, aided by ladders.

At Elephant Canyon proper (mile 6), bear left, heading toward its source. Springs and pools may appear intermittently. You'll be grateful for these miniature oases in the summer months, for Elephant Canyon can get very hot around midday. Treat any water you find here.

Plan to spend your first night in magical **Chesler Park.** The trail from Elephant Canyon to Chesler Park (which begins 6.25 miles from Squaw Flat) climbs rapidly through remarkable country dominated by row upon row of spindly Cedar Mesa Sandstone monoliths. A loop trail defines Chesler Park's perimeter. Camping is restricted to designated areas.

In the morning, leave your packs behind (taking along valuables and essentials, plus any canteens that need refilling) and return to Elephant Canyon for a memorable side trip. Up the canyon about 2 miles is magnificent, 200-foot-tall **Druid Arch,** with its twin vertical openings. Water may be available in shallow pools nearby.

From Druid Arch, backtrack to Chesler Park, retrieve your pack, and locate the start of the **Joint Trail.** This trail, under a mile in length, follows a fissure between towering sandstone walls. The narrow passageway sometimes opens into cool, dark grottoes. Where the joint ends, the trail drops into Chesler Canyon. Turn right here on a jeep road, picking up a trail into Devils Pocket, where there is a designated campsite.

Farther on is Devils Kitchen 4-wheel-drive camp. Take either of the two jeep roads from Devils Kitchen to **Elephant Hill.** The road to the left is somewhat longer but perhaps more interesting, as it incorporates the Silver Stairs, a challenging roadbed formed of slickrock.

Stonehenge-like Druid Arch dominates Elephant Canyon.

Descend Elephant Hill on the jeep road, passing a parking lot to the right (as far as regular cars can go). From this point you have about 3 easy miles of road-stomping back to Squaw Flat.

Day 14: A TRIP TO THE CONFLUENCE

- **Watching the Green merge with the Colorado**
- **Camping at Squaw Flat**
- **Gas, groceries, and showers available at Needles Outpost**

This journey takes you to a viewpoint about 1000 feet above the junction of the Green and Colorado Rivers. Although it can be completed in one long day, you may prefer to backpack. For backpacking, permits are required, reservations are recommended, and fees are charged.

Day Hike (or Backpack): Confluence Overlook

Distance: 11 miles round trip
Time: 1 day (or 2 days)
Map: topo for Canyonlands National Park
Difficulty: moderate

The trail to Confluence Overlook starts from the road to Big Spring Canyon Overlook, 3.5 miles north of Squaw Flat Campground (see map, p. 121). The most tiring part of the hike occurs at the beginning (and end, since you'll be doubling back) when you cross Big Spring Canyon. Expect little shade and no water along the route.

The trail lacks some of the drama that characterizes its rivals in the area. But it does acquaint you with the lower reaches of Elephant Canyon, and from a high ridge more than halfway to the confluence you can feast your eyes on the needles around Chesler Park. Here you descend and cross Cyclone Canyon, one of the "grabens" that continue the rest of the way to the Colorado River.

In Cyclone Canyon you join a jeep road, which you follow to its end. **Confluence Overlook** is 0.5 mile farther on, near the top of a rise. The Green River, coming in from the northwest, is indeed noticeably greener than the muddy Colorado. Inside the "V" of their confluence lies the Island in the Sky District, while the Maze District is directly across the river.

Sandstone and sky define a slickrock hiker's world.

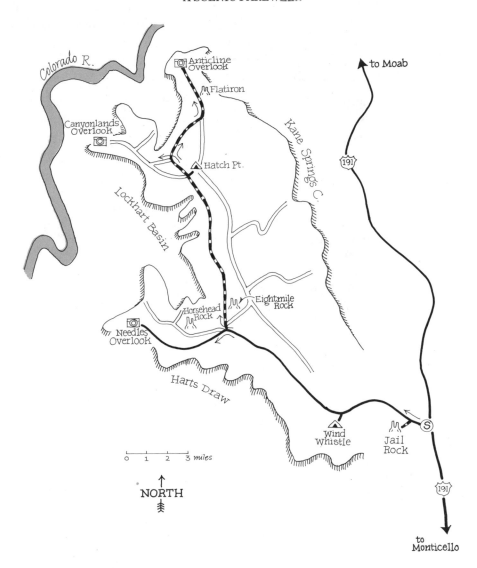

Day 15: A SCENIC FAREWELL

- **Car touring the Canyon Rims**
- **And/or the lofty La Sals**
- **Returning to Grand Junction**

On your way back to Grand Junction, you can opt for scenic drives in Canyon Rims Recreation Area and/or the La Sal Mountains. The La Sals trip replaces most of the drive between Moab and Fisher Towers on UT-128.

For more information, write to the Bureau of Land Management, Moab Field Office, 82 East Dogwood Avenue, Moab, UT 84532; and the Moab District Ranger Station, Manti–La Sal National Forest, 125 West 200 South, Moab, UT 84532.

Scenic Drive 1: Canyon Rims

Distance: up to 74 miles round trip
Time: 3 hours

Canyon Rims Recreation Area, administered by the BLM, is perched between the La Sal Mountains and the gorge of the Colorado River (see map, p. 125). From the Needles District, turn north on US-191, and drive 7 miles to a signed road on the left, where you turn off. Overlooks provide outstanding views of the canyon system created by the Colorado River. The road winds past Jail Rock and Wind Whistle Campground before arriving at a junction at mile 15. The left fork continues to **Needles Overlook,** 22 miles from the main highway, while the right fork is a gravel road that leads toward Hatch Point Campground, at mile 23, and beyond. Visiting **Canyonlands Overlook** nearby requires 4-wheel drive. Seven miles from Hatch Point, the road terminates at dizzying **Anticline Overlook,** with vistas of the Colorado River and its tributary, Kane Creek.

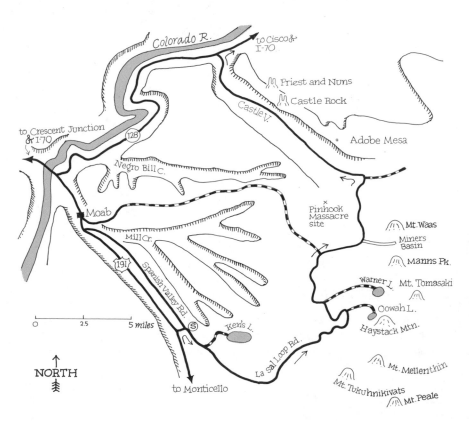

Scenic Drive 2: La Sal Mountains Tour

Distance: 36.5 miles one way
Time: 1.5 hours

This interesting and varied route ascends to alpine uplands and meadows above Moab (see map, p. 126). A 61-mile loop beginning and ending in town requires about 3 hours, but the route below is substantially shorter. People with jeeps can anticipate extra enjoyment following old mining roads.

Begin at milepost 118 south of Moab on US-191. Turn right here and then right again a mile farther on. The winding road rises steadily out of Spanish Valley, heading up Mill Creek on its way to the peaks. Often snowcapped even in summer, the geologically young La Sals are laccoliths, or igneous intrusions exposed when surrounding sedimentary layers eroded away. **Mount Peale,** at 12,700 feet, is the tallest in the range.

Near the top of the loop are spur roads to Oowah and Warner Lakes. Normally, passenger cars can negotiate these roads with little trouble. Both lakes have campsites, tables, and outhouses and are beautifully situated in basins below the peaks. Farther on, you pass a road to Miners Basin, a cirque in which prospectors established a little community during the 1890s. Nearby is the site of the 1881 Pinhook Massacre, where members of a white posse were killed by Indians accused of murder and horse theft.

Up in the aspen belt you enjoy unblocked views of both the La Sals above and the red rocks below. You soon drop down into breathtaking **Castle Valley,** which is bounded by two unusual formations, Castle Rock and the Priest and Nuns. Eventually you meet UT-128 south of Fisher Towers. Turn right to continue toward I-70.

Chapter 4

CEDAR MESA LOOP

Utah

Most of this short loop explores the Cedar Mesa country between the Abajo Mountains and the San Juan River (see map, p. 129). Prehistoric ruins, natural bridges, and high-walled canyons add to the circuit's allure. Since the towns in this part of Utah are small and rustic, offering few amenities, the tour demands that you be willing to "rough it." It is, moreover, a very active tour, with substantial walks or short backpacking trips scheduled for almost every day. Opportunities to raft the San Juan River and tour Lake Powell by boat are also available.

Day 1: BLANDING TO NATURAL BRIDGES
- **Meeting the Anasazi**
- **Driving through a spectacular monocline**
- **Camping at Natural Bridges National Monument**
- **Gas, groceries, showers, and laundry available in Blanding**

Unlike the other "host" cities in this book, Blanding (population 3200) is not located on an interstate highway. But this southeastern Utah community can be reached in a few hours from either I-70 or I-40 via US-191. The town's ultra-wide streets and ban on the sale of alcohol are legacies of its Mormon heritage. A more subtle influence is provided by local Utes, whose reservation south of here was established in the early 1920s in the wake of a skirmish that killed two of their people. Blanding is nestled under the **Abajo** (aka Blue) **Mountains,** laccolithics whose peaks soar to over 11,300 feet. Buy gas, ice, and groceries for 3 days before striking off.

On the outskirts of Blanding is **Edge of the Cedars State Park,** an Anasazi complex. It consists of a cluster of six buildings (some unexcavated) above shallow Westwater Canyon. A short trail winds around their ruins, passing an unusual "great kiva," the northernmost of its kind in Utah. Unlike smaller kivas, associated with each household, great kivas were employed by the community as a whole for religious and social functions. The masonry style here shows mainly Mesa Verdean influence but also some degree of borrowing from Chaco Canyon in New Mexico. The park museum ranks among the best of its kind, providing exhibits and information about prehistoric sites on

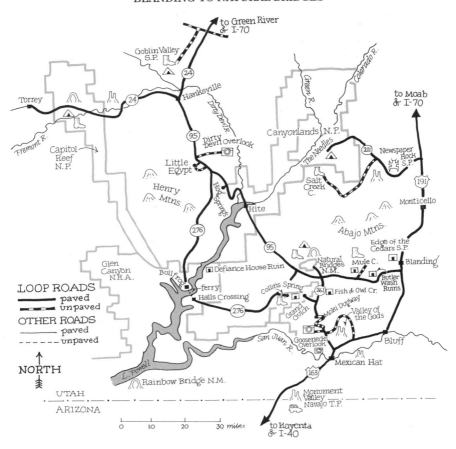

Cedar Mesa, as well as a superb collection of pottery. Free tours of the ruins are available.

For further information, contact the Superintendent, Edge of the Cedars State Park, Box 788, Blanding, UT 84511-0788.

From Blanding, drive a few miles south on US-191 and turn right on scenic UT-95 toward Natural Bridges National Monument, 31 miles away. Take the turnoff on the right at mile 10.5 for **Butler Wash Ruins.** A short, easy loop trail of under 1 mile round trip leads to an overlook of a cliff dwelling, perched in an alcove across the canyon. The ruin contains four kivas: one done in the square Kayenta style and three of the round, Mesa Verdean variety. Walk about 50 yards to the left of the overlook to see a natural bridge near the main ruin. The petroglyph panels for which Butler Wash is renowned are located at its confluence with the San Juan River, between Bluff and Mexican Hat.

About 2.5 miles farther on, UT-95 cuts through the tremendous **Comb Ridge** monocline, which extends for some 80 miles from the Abajo foothills through Monument Valley. Nine miles west of the roadcut is a spur road to **Mule Canyon Ruins,** a 700-year-old complex with twelve rooms, a restored kiva, and the remains of a tower.

Continue west for 11 more miles to Natural Bridges National Monument, where you will spend the next 3 nights. Be warned that the small campground fills quickly. If no vacancies exist, ask at the entrance station for information on overflow camping.

Day 2: NATURAL BRIDGES

- **Communing with three wondrous spans**
- **Searching for ruins and pictographs**
- **Camping at Natural Bridges**

Natural Bridges National Monument contains three spectacular bridges: Kachina (referring to ancestor spirits in the Hopi religion), Sipapu (named for a legendary opening to the underworld from which traditional Hopis believe their ancestors emerged), and Owachomo

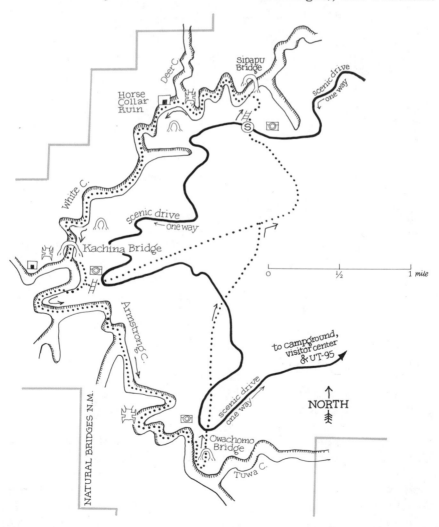

Cottonwood shimmers against the cliffs of White Canyon.

(meaning "rock mound" in Hopi). Since natural bridges are relatively rare, the proximity of these beauties to each other is just short of miraculous. No matter how their size is calculated, all rank among the largest in the world. Hewn from Cedar Mesa Sandstone, they were "discovered" by prospector Cass Hite in the 1880s, though the area was long known to local Indians such as the Paiutes (whose word for natural bridge translates to "under the horse's belly"). Even earlier, the Anasazi inhabited these canyons, and the national monument protects numerous artifacts from their culture.

An 8.75-mile loop through White and Armstrong Canyons connects the bridges and returns over the mesa top, but you can also see and visit them from overlooks along the scenic drive. Each bridge is accessible from the road by a short trail; of these, the one to Owachomo is easiest.

The loop trail through the canyons is highly recommended. You can either day-hike the whole route or a segment of it (the section between Sipapu and Kachina Bridge is especially picturesque) or plan on an overnight trip. Backcountry camping is forbidden in the national monument, so you must walk an extra 1.5 miles past Kachina Bridge down White Canyon, crossing into BLM land, to spend the night. During the late summer rainy season, camping in White Canyon is not recommended due to flash flood danger. Overnight parking along the scenic drive is always prohibited.

For further information, write to the Superintendent, Natural Bridges National Monument, Box 1, Lake Powell, UT 84533.

Day Hike: Natural Bridges Loop

> **Distance: 8.75 miles round trip**
> **Time: 1 day**
> **Maps: topos for Natural Bridges and Bears Ears**
> **Difficulty: easy**

Start at the parking lot near Sipapu Bridge, 2.75 miles past the visitor center (see map, p. 130). In the course of a steep 0.5-mile, 500-foot descent, aided by stairs and ladders, you pass a small ruin just before a spur to an overlook. Then you drop down to the floor of White Canyon. Turn left here and walk under **Sipapu Bridge,** the biggest of the three, with a span of 270 feet. Past Sipapu, look for handprint pictographs at the junction with Deer Canyon and a cliff dwelling named **Horse Collar Ruin** opposite a small arch.

About 2.25 miles past Sipapu, **Kachina Bridge,** the youngest of the trio, spans the idyllic spot where White and Armstrong Canyons meet. Look for pictographs on both abutments; more rock art and small ruins are located a short distance beyond the bridge. To proceed, turn left up Armstrong Canyon. The trail ascends the left bank of the streambed temporarily and then intersects with the trail up to the Kachina parking lot. Continue straight ahead here, dropping back into Armstrong Canyon after passing a section of narrows. In about 1.5 miles, the wash makes a big bend below a prominent, undercut formation shaped like an anvil. Look for a pictograph panel around the bend, on the right.

The trail soon goes up onto the left bank, about 50 feet above the canyon floor. About 2.75 miles past Kachina, **Owachomo Bridge—** the oldest, smallest, and most eroded in the monument—comes into view. Owachomo is actually adjacent to Armstrong Canyon, having been cut by a different stream. Go beneath the bridge and climb to the overlook in the next 0.25 mile. Cross the park road to join the easy, pleasant mesa trail, which winds through a pinyon and juniper forest for about 3 miles, back to the Sipapu parking lot.

Day 3: MULE CANYON

- **Discovering cliff dwellings**
- **Camping at Natural Bridges**
- **Gas, groceries, showers, and laundry available in Blanding**

Retain your campsite in Natural Bridges while you complete the following day hike. The trip provides a good introduction to wilderness travel: it is short and not terribly challenging. To reach the mouth of **Mule Canyon,** backtrack about 15 miles on UT-95 toward Blanding. Continue for 0.5 mile past the sign for the BLM roadside ruin, and turn left onto the good dirt road to Texas Flat. Pull off to park where this road crosses the south fork of Mule Canyon, in about another 0.5 mile.

After your hike, drive to Blanding and purchase supplies for 3 more days, 2 of which you will spend backpacking. Then return to Natural Bridges for the night.

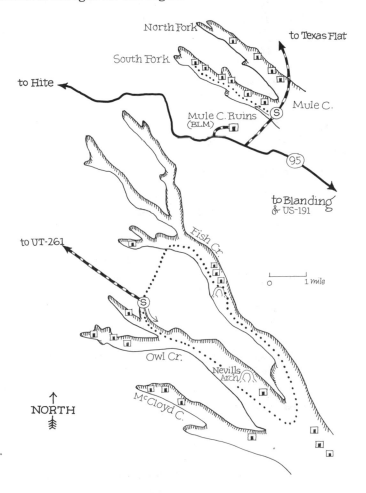

Day Hike: South Fork, Mule Canyon

Distance: 6 miles or more, round trip
Time: 4 hours
Maps: topos for Bears Ears and Brushy Basin Wash
Difficulty: moderate

Mule is a shallow, unremarkable canyon cut into Cedar Mesa Sandstone. Though it gets prettier toward the upper end, the principal reason to explore it is to see the unusually well-preserved ruins bejeweling both of its forks. As you visit these ancient dwellings, remember that disturbing archaeological sites is illegal. Please leave everything as you found it for others to enjoy.

You can hike up the 7-mile-long South Fork as far as you wish. Since no trail exists and you must walk in or frequently cross the creekbed, old sneakers are the recommended footwear. For the first 0.5 mile, and occasionally thereafter, you must fight through brush. During the monsoon season, pools and quicksand can slow you down, as well. The six cliff dwellings all occupy the south-facing wall of the canyon, beginning about a mile in (see map, p. 133). A particularly extensive ruin is nestled into the cliff, 3 miles from the trailhead.

Days 4 and 5: FISH AND OWL CREEKS

- **Strolling through remote canyons**
- **Spying ruins along the cliffs**
- **Camping near the confluence and in Valley of the Gods**
- **Gas, groceries, showers, and laundry available in Mexican Hat**

The next 2 days include an overnight backpack in deep sandstone canyons boasting numerous ruins, unusual rock formations, and a large arch, as well as a visit to the Valley of the Gods.

Before starting the hike in Fish and Owl Creeks, register and check on water availability at the Kane Gulch Ranger Station, 4.5 miles down UT-261 from its junction with UT-95, just east of Natural Bridges. Normally, these canyons contain pools and running springs, but remember to purify all drinking water.

Prior reservations are required for backpacking permits. Contact the Bureau of Land Management, 284 South First West, P.O. Box 7, Monticello, UT 84535 (435-587-2141).

Backpack: Fish and Owl Creeks

Distance: 15.5 miles round trip
Time: 2 days
Maps: topos for Cedar Mesa and Bluff
Difficulty: moderate, with strenuous ascent at end

To reach the trailhead, go south on UT-261 about a mile past Kane Gulch. Turn left onto a graded dirt road, and follow it for 5 miles through a pinyon and juniper forest to its end at a parking lot.

The recommended direction for this hike is to descend into Owl and return via the west arm of Fish. From the parking area, follow the roadbed on the right for about 50 yards to a wash, which leads to **Owl Creek's** rim (see map, p. 133). A short distance below the rim is the first ruin, on the right, near a dryfall. The cairned trail passes another ruin and pour-off before dropping into Owl Creek by means of a small side-canyon at mile 1.5. At the bottom, look for a spring at ground level. There may be pools of water over the next few miles.

Follow the wash downstream, passing large **Nevills Arch** high in a Cedar Mesa Sandstone fin on the left at mile 4.25. Owl Creek empties into Fish at mile 6.75. The confluence makes a good place to camp; you may find more pools in the vicinity. McCloyd Canyon, about a mile below the confluence, also contains ruins.

Turn left at the confluence and walk up **Fish Creek,** which is even more attractive than Owl. It boasts more archaeological sites as well, though you have to look sharp to find them. An intriguing area 2 or 3 miles from the confluence is open and grassy and ringed by oddly shaped monoliths.

Six miles above the confluence, Fish Creek forks. Go left here and continue about 0.5 mile to a pour-off and a spring gushing out of the canyon wall, on the left. The canyon narrows considerably past the fork, and heavy brush and boulders make walking more difficult. If you have another night to spare, consider camping opposite the spring on a slickrock terrace.

Immediately past the spring, look for a large cairn, which indicates the start of the nearly vertical 0.25-mile climb out of Fish Creek. Although no developed trail exists, there are occasional cairns along the 600-foot ascent. The top rewards you with great views of both canyons as well as the **Bears Ears** buttes. Pick up a 2-mile trail through the pygmy forest back to your car.

After the hike, drive south 27.5 miles on UT-261 through rolling country. The road executes a series of no-nonsense, hairpin bends down Cedar Mesa's 1100-foot cliff-face. This thrilling, unpaved stretch of road is called the **Moki Dugway:** "Moki" for the early Mormon name for the Anasazi and "dugway" to indicate a route carved from solid rock. Near the bottom, look for a sign on the right to **Goosenecks Overlook.** An 8-mile round-trip drive (paved) leads to a picnic spot 1000 feet above the twisty meanders of the San Juan River.

Where UT-261 intersects US-163, turn right and drive 4 miles to the hamlet of Mexican Hat, where you can resupply. Just north of Mexican Hat take a very short dirt road to the east, leading to the unusual rock that gave the town its name; it resembles a man sporting a sombrero. Behind it looms dramatic **Raplee Ridge,** a steeply tilted monocline through which the San Juan River has cut a deep canyon.

This formation, with its gray, rust, and purple bands, is known locally as the Navajo Rug.

Mexican Hat is a base for companies that offer white-water rafting adventures. Short trips commence at Sand Island Recreation Area south of Bluff and end in Mexican Hat (see Chapter 5, Anasazi Loop, Day 3), while longer trips continue all the way to Clay Hills Crossing, on the edge of Lake Powell. Another option for readers with extra time is an auto tour of Monument Valley, a few miles south of town.

When your business concludes in Mexican Hat, go northeast on US-163 for about 8 miles. Turn left onto a well-marked 16.5-mile-long dirt and gravel road that loops through **Valley of the Gods.** Take a right where the dirt road forks just past the highway, to ford a shallow wash. The broad, open valley, situated at the lower end of Lime Creek (into which Fish, McCloyd, and Road Canyons empty), contains a series of reddish brown monoliths—many of them pyramidal formations capped by round knobs. Among the most prominent are the Setting Hen, the Seven Sailors, and Scotchman Butte. It's a great place for photography and primitive camping—pull off onto a spur road and flop down your sleeping bag—but there are no trails.

Day 6: VALLEY OF THE GODS TO GOBLIN VALLEY

- **Visiting another vertiginous overlook**
- **Swimming in Lake Powell**
- **Camping and showers at Goblin Valley State Park**
- **Gas, groceries, showers, and laundry available in Hanksville**

This morning, complete the scenic drive through Valley of the Gods. At UT-261, turn right and proceed back up the Moki Dugway. At the crest, you can take a good dirt road on the left that parallels Johns Canyon and leads in a few miles to **Muley Point,** another San Juan River aerie, more than 1000 feet higher than Goosenecks Overlook.

Continue north on UT-261 to its end and turn left on UT-95 toward Hanksville, about 90 miles distant. The highway gives access to a number of wild and wonderful places not discussed between these covers, such as Dark Canyon Primitive Area. West of Natural Bridges, UT-95 hugs the edge of White Canyon, bestowing heart-stopping views. Cheese Box and Jacobs Chair Buttes appear on the right; between them, on the other side of the road, is Fry Canyon Store, which sells gasoline and basic grocery items.

After the highway dramatically crosses the Colorado and Dirty Devil Rivers near **Hite Marina,** it hugs the shoreline of Lake Powell's northernmost arm for a few miles before climbing quickly to the badlands to the west. Hite derives its name from a prospector who owned a store in this vicinity during the late nineteenth-century uranium boom and ran a ferry that transported people and stock across the river.

Utah's San Juan River has carved a serpentine canyon.

Past Hite, UT-95 follows North Wash on its way toward Hanksville. Attractions here include **Hog Springs** (where the BLM has established a picnic area and short trail; a small Fremont pictograph panel is across North Wash in an alcove 50 yards down the road), **Little Egypt** (a badlands area), and **Dirty Devil Overlook** (11 miles off the highway). The **Henry Mountains** on the horizon provide a refreshing contrast to this dry, desolate landscape.

In Hanksville, resupply, and travel north on UT-24 for 19.5 miles to the turnoff for **Goblin Valley State Park,** your camping spot. Consult Day 1 of Chapter 2, Desert Rivers Loop, for trail information.

Day 7: GOBLIN VALLEY TO CAPITOL REEF

- **Jaunts to Fremont River Overlook and Hickman Bridge**
- **Camping at Capitol Reef National Park**
- **Gas, groceries, showers, and laundry available in Hanksville**

After additional exploration of Goblin Valley in the morning, return to Hanksville and buy provisions for 2 nights. Continue west on UT-24 for 37 miles to Capitol Reef National Park, making camp here. In the afternoon, visit Hickman Bridge and examine Fremont petroglyphs along the riverbank. After dinner, ascend to the Fremont River Overlook.

Day 8: DAY HIKES ALONG THE SCENIC DRIVE

- **Hiking to Cassidy Arch and Cohab Canyon**
- **Strolling through Grand Wash**
- **Camping at Capitol Reef**
- **Gas, groceries, showers, and laundry available in Torrey**

This morning, organize a day pack and canteen and head south from the campground along the park's scenic drive, 25 miles round trip. Get an early start on the Frying Pan Trail, which visits Cassidy Arch and Cohab Canyon. Enjoy a picnic lunch in Capitol Gorge, and hike Grand Wash in late afternoon. For descriptions, see Days 3 and 4 in Chapter 2, Desert Rivers Loop.

Day 9: CAPITOL REEF AND BULLFROG MARINA

- **Morning blood-warmer to Chimney Rock**
- **Optional boat tour (or rental) on Lake Powell**
- **Camping at Natural Bridges or at Grand Gulch trailhead**
- **Gas, groceries, showers, and laundry available in Hanksville; some services in Bullfrog and Halls Crossing**

How you organize this day depends on whether you prefer to take a morning hike in Capitol Reef or a boat trip on Lake Powell. Whichever you choose, allow time for shopping, laundry, and showers, for tomorrow you begin a multiday backpacking expedition in Grand Gulch Primitive

Hikers examine a roadside ruin under vaulting cliffs.

Area. The drive to Grand Gulch includes a half-hour ferry crossing of Lake Powell. Call ahead, either to Bullfrog (435-684-2233) or Halls Crossing (435-684 2261) Marina, to learn the ferry schedule.

A good hiking option is the **Chimney Rock Trail** (see Chapter 2, Desert Rivers Loop, Day 4). Afterward, take UT-24 east to Hanksville and prepare for the upcoming backpack trip. If you would rather opt for the boat ride, proceed directly to Hanksville.

From Hanksville, go southeast 27 miles on UT-95. Turn right on UT-276, and travel 38 miles to **Bullfrog Marina.** There you can join a boat tour of Defiance House Ruin in Forgotten Canyon, 12 miles up Lake Powell. Those with extra time can cruise tomorrow to Rainbow Bridge National Monument. Boats can be rented from both marinas; reservations are recommended.

Take the ferry from Bullfrog to **Halls Crossing.** Make sure all available canteens are full. Continue east on UT-276, passing a seven-room Anasazi cliff dwelling on the left at milepost 68. Tonight's final destination will depend on which Grand Gulch hiking option you select. For each, a shuttle is necessary. Permits, required for all hikers, can be obtained at Kane Gulch Ranger Station. Plan to camp at or near your chosen trailhead, saving the shuttle for the morning.

The Collins Spring turnoff, marked by a sign, is about 40 miles up UT-276 past Halls Crossing, near milepost 85. Travel east on a dirt road for about 6.5 miles to the trailhead. Without a high-clearance vehicle, you may have to walk the last 2 or 3 miles.

To reach Bullet Canyon, take UT-276 to the junction of UT-95. Turn right here, and then right again onto UT-261. From this junction it is 4 miles to Kane Gulch Ranger Station and 7 more to the Bullet Canyon turnoff. The parking area is 1 mile down a dirt road to the right of the highway.

Days 10–12: GRAND GULCH

- **Surveying ancient cliff dwellings**
- **Walking between towering canyon walls**
- **Camping in Grand Gulch**

Few canyons house as many unspoiled Anasazi ruins and pictographs as this lovely tributary of the San Juan River. From the upper reaches of Grand Gulch to its confluence with the San Juan is 51.75 miles. Most hikers select a shorter alternative, of which two are given below. When you register, check with rangers about water availability and quality. Maximum group size is 12; reservations are accepted.

When you emerge from the canyons, you may stay either at Natural Bridges or at a private campground near Blanding.

Prior reservations for permits are required. For more information, contact the BLM, 284 South First West, Box 7, Monticello, UT 84535 (435-587-2141).

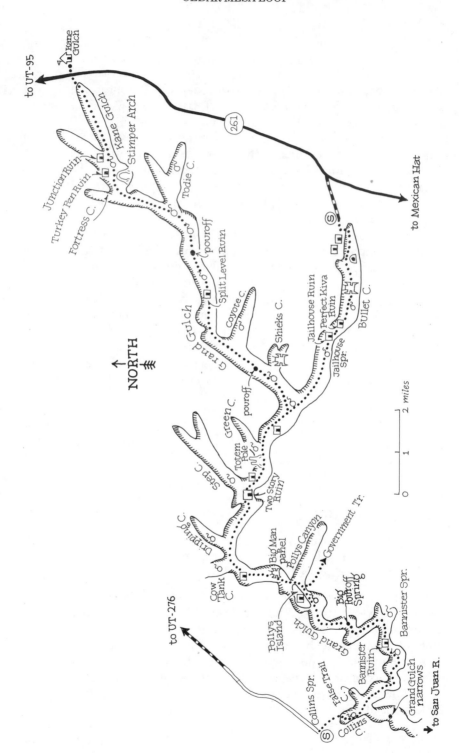

Backpack 1: Bullet Canyon to Kane Gulch

Distance: 23 miles one way
Time: 3 days
Maps: topos for Cedar Mesa North, Pollys Pasture,
    and Kane Gulch
Difficulty: moderate

The Bullet Canyon trail starts to the right of the parking area. (See map, p. 140, and Day 9 for driving directions.) Follow the rim a short distance. At a large cairn, descend to the canyon floor on a steep trail, turning right at the bottom. Within 0.25 mile, look up to the right as you round a bend to see a square masonry tower. You can reach this site easily from the large cairn on the rim.

Less than a mile from the trailhead, pass a large, shallow cave to your left. Another mile brings you to a long slickrock ramp, below which hiking becomes tougher as the canyon narrows. Where the route begins to flatten and a side-canyon enters from the left, there may be a spring. The trail remains brushy for the next mile, but walking improves as the canyon widens out.

Jailhouse and Perfect Kiva Ruins are on the right side of the canyon about 4.75 miles from the trailhead. **Jailhouse Ruin,** with its small, barred window and striking white circular pictographs (perhaps representing ghost faces), is much easier to spot. **Perfect Kiva Ruin** contains a kiva with a reconstructed roof and a ladder leading down to its interior. This is the only site on Cedar Mesa in which visitors are allowed to walk on a roof and enter a kiva. When the controversial explorer Richard Wetherill visited the canyon in the 1890s, his party excavated this and many other ruins.

Across the wash from Jailhouse Ruin is a good camping place amid cottonwoods. Just past the trees flows Jailhouse Spring at mile 5. About 2.5 miles of rather effortless walking brings you to the confluence with **Grand Gulch,** where there is another, more heavily used campsite. Turn right here and proceed upstream. Be alert for ruins in alcoves throughout this area, especially on the south-facing side of the canyon.

Shieks Canyon at mile 8.5, the first side-canyon on the right, is rich in rock art and may contain a spring about 0.25 mile from its mouth. **Split Level,** one of Grand Gulch's major houses, is on the left at mile 12.75. Todie Canyon, 3 miles farther, boasts many archaeological treasures. Past Stimper Arch are the significant pueblos of **Turkey Pen** (at mile 18.25) and **Junction Ruin** (at mile 19), both on the left. The latter, situated in a football field-sized alcove, bears John Wetherill's inscription. It marks the confluence of Grand Gulch with **Kane Gulch** (originally known as Wetherill Canyon), the 4-mile-long tributary from which you exit the primitive area. After a 500-foot ascent, the trail ends at the Kane Gulch parking lot.

Pictographs in Grand Gulch recall modern pointillist techniques.

Backpack 2: Collins Spring to Bullet Canyon

> **Distance: 30 miles (or 38 to Kane Gulch) one way**
> **Time: 4 days (or 5 to Kane Gulch)**
> **Maps: topos for Red House Spring, Pollys Pasture,**
>   **Cedar Mesa North, and Kane Gulch**
> **Difficulty: moderate**

Especially if you opt for the longer trip to Kane Gulch, this ambitious hike introduces you to the best of what Cedar Mesa has to offer. Not only do you cover more ground and view more dwellings, but you also enjoy more solitude here than on the popular Bullet-to-Kane route. Register at Kane Gulch Ranger Station before setting out.

The trailhead is marked by a large sign. (See map, p. 140, and Day 9 for driving directions.) Follow the trail 2 miles down Collins Canyon to its intersection with Grand Gulch. Careful map reading will prevent your being confused by False Trail Canyon, which joins Collins Canyon in the vicinity of Grand Gulch. If you want to detour to see the Grand Gulch narrows, you can drop your pack at the intersection and turn right, walking 0.25 mile downstream; otherwise, go straight ahead and amble up the canyon past a large slickrock platform. There may be shallow pools here.

In about 2.5 more miles, you come to Bannister Spring, just 0.25 mile below **Bannister Ruin** on the left. This two-tiered ruin contains an exposed horizontal beam and an intact but fragile kiva, which should not be disturbed. Big Pour-off Spring is at mile 8.75. About 0.25 mile before you reach it is another slickrock terrace that offers ideal camping.

The trail skirts Big Pour-off on the left. Your next landmark is the junction with the Government Trail at mile 11.75. A campsite, sometimes complete with springwater, is located between this trail junction and Pollys Island, formed by a "rincon" or abandoned meander of Grand Gulch; notice the ruin nestled up in the cliff on the left.

Look for the **Big Man** pictograph panel 1.5 miles past Pollys Island, about 200 feet above the canyon floor on the right. Shortly before the viewpoint for this panel, examine a shady undercut ledge on the left, which also shelters rock art. Water may be available up Cow Tank Canyon, at mile 15.25, and Dripping Canyon, 0.5 mile farther.

Just past Dripping Canyon is another terrace that could provide a pleasant campsite. Few other spots for camping exist between here and the Totem Pole. In fact, these next 4.25 miles, because they involve a lot of bushwhacking, may be the most tedious of the trip. Step Canyon, at mile 18.5, has a small clearing that you can use as a base of explorations. The entire tributary deserves study, if time permits. Anasazi sites abound, and you should persist until you locate **Two Story Ruin,** concealed by thick brush on the bank of the main canyon. Like Green Canyon farther on, Step may contain water.

The **Totem Pole,** an unmistakable pillar on the left at mile 20, signals the end of the difficult stretch. Relax among cottonwoods on the high ground past the Totem Pole before continuing to the Bullet Canyon junction, 2.5 miles beyond. Although this section of trail has continual ups and downs, you probably will be relieved to be done with the willows. Keep your eyes peeled for small Anasazi sites on both sides of the trail.

Day 13: GRAND GULCH TO CANYONLANDS

- **Deciphering the messages on Newspaper Rock**
- **Camping in Canyonlands National Park**
- **Gas, groceries, showers, and laundry available in Blanding or Monticello**

Today, take UT-95 east to Blanding, and then drive north 21 miles on US-191 to Monticello in the Abajo foothills, stopping in either town to buy supplies for 4 days. Then proceed north on US-191 for 15 miles, turning left on UT-211 to the Needles District of Canyonlands National Park. This road and its scenic attractions are described under Day 10 of Chapter 3, Redrock Loop; remember to stop at **Newspaper Rock** to inspect its fascinating multicultural inscriptions.

Camp at Squaw Flat (see Chesler Park backpack described under Day 11 of Chapter 3, Redrock Loop) and take scenic drives and nature walks. At the visitor center, secure a permit (fees are charged) for a 4-day backpacking trip in Salt Creek Canyon. Also inquire about the water situation. Reservations for backpacking or 4-wheel-driving up Salt Creek or Horse Canyon are recommended.

For more information, contact the Superintendent, Canyonlands National Park, 2282 S. West Resource Boulevard, Moab, UT 84532, or call (435) 259-3911.

Days 14–17: SALT CREEK CANYON

- **Ruins, arches, and pictographs**
- **Camping beneath golden cliffs**
- **The road home**

Salt Creek Canyon begins in the Abajo foothills and extends deep into the Needles District. The middle third of this verdant canyon is narrow and twisty, and worth a trip for that reason alone, but the main attraction for visitors is discovering ruins, arches, and Fremont Indian pictographs. The hike terminates at Cave Spring (or Squaw Flat; see below).

At the conclusion of your backpack trip, camp at Squaw Flat prior to your drive home.

Backpack: Salt Creek Canyon

> **Distance: 27.5 miles one way, including side trip to Angel Arch**
> **Time: 3 or 4 days**
> **Map: topo for Canyonlands National Park**
> **Difficulty: moderate**

To get to the trailhead, drive out of the Needles District on UT-211. Just before historic Dugout Ranch, turn south onto County Road 104 toward Beef Basin (see map, page 145). Take this unpaved road for approximately 12.5 miles, bearing right at mile 3.5. The road follows the North Cottonwood Creek drainage, climbing to Salt Creek Mesa. Your hiking route into the East Fork of Salt Creek begins 0.25 mile past prominent **Cathedral Butte,** off a short spur road on the right. This spur, not to be confused with a jeep road immediately before it, dead-ends after 100 yards. Park at the end of the spur, and follow a cairned route to the rim. You may need to scout around to find the place where the trail drops nearly 1000 feet into the white and pink canyon system.

Salt Creek in its upper stretches is brushy, requiring some bush-whacking. You'll be in the streambed practically the whole way, and there should be water both in the wash itself and in springs.

Aside from the park boundary sign at mile 2, your first landmark is the confluence with the main fork of Salt Creek at mile 3.5. Kirk Cabin, built by a Mormon pioneer, is close by, as are two natural arches. The route levels out in this area. Look for Anasazi ruins here. The first major side-canyon on the right, **Big Pocket** at mile 5.5, also contains ruins. Past Big Pocket, visit **Wedding Ring Arch** on the right. A mile or so farther on is an interesting joint cave on the left, formed by the meeting of several large slabs of rock. Across the canyon is a cliff dwelling.

Soon the canyon narrows, and a fair amount of water may be in the wash. There are more Anasazi sites on the left just before Upper

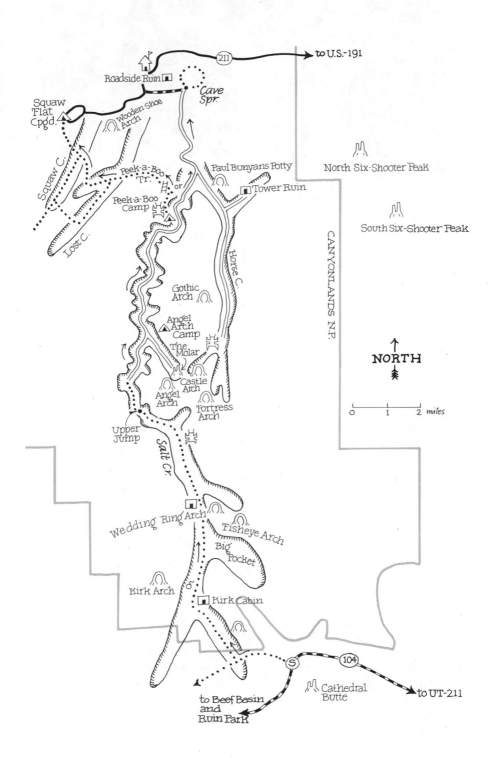

to U.S.-191

211

Roadside Ruin

Cave Spr.

Squaw Flat Cpgd.

Wooden Shoe Arch

Peek-a-Boo Tr.

or

Peek-a-Boo Camp

Squaw C.

Lost C.

Paul Bunyans Potty

Tower Ruin

North Six-Shooter Peak

South Six-Shooter Peak

CANYONLANDS N.P.

Horse C.

Gothic Arch

Angel Arch Camp

The Molar

Castle Arch

Angel Arch

Fortress Arch

NORTH

0   1   2 miles

Upper Jump

Salt Cr.

Wedding Ring Arch

Fisheye Arch

Big Pocket

Kirk Arch

Kirk Cabin

S

104

to UT-211

Cathedral Butte

to Beef Basin and Ruin Park

Salt Canyon's tributaries are studded with aboriginal ruins.

Jump, a pour-off, at about mile 11. The walls close in and rise, and the creek adopts a more serpentine course.

At mile 13.5, you join the Salt Creek 4-wheel-drive road. Go right into a side-canyon, ascending gradually, to spectacular **Angel Arch** (2 miles round trip), a Cedar Mesa Sandstone span whose right pillar resembles an angel in profile. Short of the arch is a formation called the Molar. Return to the main canyon.

From the junction of the trail and jeep road, it is a twisty 8.5 miles to **Peek-a-Boo Spring,** the casualty of a rockslide. At the primitive camp here, under the partially collapsed cliff on the left, look for a trail ascending about 50 feet to a Fremont pictograph of figures with shieldlike bodies.

Drop back down to Salt Creek. You are now 3.5 miles from the parking area. Less than a mile below Peek-a-Boo Spring, **Horse Canyon** enters from the right. Popular among 4-wheel-drive aficionados, this beautiful tributary contains several major arches and archaeological sites. Past here, Salt Creek is wide and dusty. Slog along through deep sand, swatting deerflies when in season. The trail ends near **Cave Spring,** where an easy 0.5-mile loop visits a cowboy camp.

An alternate way to finish the trip, one that leads to Squaw Flat Campground, 5 miles distant, is to pick up the **Peek-a-Boo Trail,** which begins just a few feet below the Peek-a-Boo petroglyphs. This option adds about 2.5 miles to the hike. After mimicking Salt Creek's big bend on a sandy bench, the trail ascends through a narrow cleft to the slickrock above by means of a ladder. It remains on sandstone rimlands all the way to Lost Canyon, about 2.5 miles from Peek-a-Boo Camp. One of the most scenic and imaginatively designed in the park, this trail heads numerous side-canyons, passing through a window in a fin near a small jug-handle arch. In Lost Canyon, where the Peek-a-Boo Trail ends, turn right and head toward Squaw Flat, about 2.5 miles away. This trail follows the washbed for a short time and then climbs a slickrock pass and drops into the Squaw Canyon drainage on the way to the campground.

Chapter 5

ANASAZI LOOP

New Mexico, Colorado, Utah, Arizona

Short in days but long in miles, this loop will appeal especially to people interested in the ancient artifacts and modern cultures of Native Americans. Day hikes are showcased, and backpacking is minimized. The circuit, while concentrating on New Mexico, is the only one to cross into all the Four Corners states. Though not available at every destination, creature comforts beckon in the Rio Grande Valley from Los Alamos and Taos to Albuquerque.

Day 1: ALBUQUERQUE TO EL MORRO

- **Getting acquainted with Albuquerque**
- **Puzzling over petroglyphs**
- **Visiting the Sky City**
- **Camping at El Morro National Monument**
- **Gas, groceries, showers, and laundry in Albuquerque**

With over 400,000 residents, Albuquerque is by far the largest city in the high desert region (see map, p. 148). This metropolis on the Rio Grande offers so much to keep visitors busy that it is tempting to spend half one's vacation there. Attractions include the restored Old Town section, with its shady plaza bordered by gift shops and New Mexican eateries; the Mountain Road district, home to the Museum of Natural History and the Albuquerque Museum of Art; the nearby Rio Grande Nature Center State Park and Indian Pueblo Cultural Center; and the sky-scraping Sandia Mountain range (meaning "watermelon" in Spanish) just outside the city limits, whose crest can be reached by either car or aerial tram.

High on the list of interesting places to visit is **Petroglyph National Monument** in the northwestern part of the city, which features short walks along the base of a 17-mile-long talus cliff. The estimated 15,000 petroglyphs laboriously pecked into huge igneous boulders here many centuries ago depict birds, reptiles, mammals, and anthropomorphic figures. Unfortunately, the petroglyphs are threatened by encroaching development. To see them, turn north at the Unser Road exit off I-40, and continue on for 2 miles to the entrance station. The Mesa Trail ascends about 100 feet to a tableland, winding

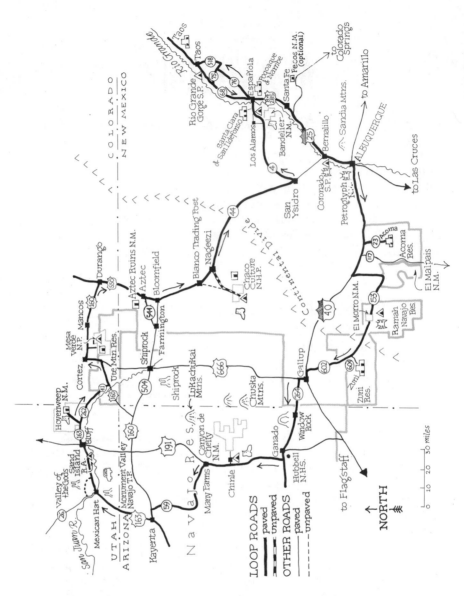

its way through a rock garden rich with primitive art. The Macaw and Cliff Base Trails, near the picnic area, are easy and take only 5 and 15 minutes, respectively, to complete. In the Upper Park, a few hundred yards farther up Unser Boulevard, is the start of the steep, poorly marked Canyon Trail. One of the petroglyphs here is of Kokopelli, the hunchbacked, priapic flute-player who symbolizes hunting, rain, and fertility.

For more information, contact the Superintendent, Petroglyph National Monument, National Park Service, 4735 Unser Boulevard NW, Albuquerque, NM 87102.

Buy food and ice for tonight before heading west on I-40 to the first of several pueblos on this loop: dramatic **Acoma,** the Sky City. This is one of nineteen politically independent communities in New Mexico inhabited by descendants of the Anasazi. Taken together, the communities, concentrated in the Rio Grande Valley, are home to 40,000 people. They welcome visitors, charging modest entrance fees in most cases; photography and sketching permits cost extra. Several times a year, they sponsor sacred dances and hold feasts on saints' days. (Spanish colonial efforts to Christianize these Native Americans succeeded only superficially, with the Indians fusing Catholic beliefs with their more traditional ones. Persecution led the residents of many villages to rise up in the Pueblo Revolt of 1680.)

To reach Acoma, drive 52 miles west of Albuquerque on I-40 until you come to exit 108. Turn south on NM-23 and proceed 12 miles to the visitor center. Acoma, celebrated for its pottery, seems in many ways representative of contemporary Pueblo life. Poor by U.S. standards, but picturesque, it is positioned 360 feet above the surrounding countryside on a forlorn, sheer-sided mesa. Only a few people currently inhabit the mesa year-round; most tribal members reside in the valley, where electricity and running water are available. The one-hour guided tour includes a visit to San Esteban del Rey mission church, constructed in the early seventeenth century. According to folklore, some Indians once starved to death on nearby Enchanted Mesa (Katzimo) when a storm-caused rockslide prevented them from descending the cliffs.

From Acoma, return to I-40. Drive west 26 miles to the Grants exit, and turn south on NM-53. On its way to El Morro, where you will camp, the road swings through **El Malpais National Monument,** a volcanic badlands area complete with caves, lava tubes, cinder cones, and sandstone bluffs. Nearby, on NM-117, is **La Ventana Arch.** Nature trails provide access to these wonders. Ambitious, seasoned hikers may enjoy the strenuous Zuni-Acoma Trail, 7.5 miles one way, which follows an old Anasazi route, crossing four major lava flows. To extend your visit to El Malpais, drive 10 miles down Route 42 (a high-clearance road) to the Big Lava Tubes area. A cairned trail leads to Big Skylight and Four Windows. The lava tube system measures 17 miles in length. Guides or very detailed directions, available at El Malpais Information Center 23 miles southwest of Grants on NM-53, are necessary.

Both El Malpais and neighboring **El Morro National Monument** contain prehistoric ruins. From the visitor center at El Morro ("the bluff"), the beautiful Mesa Top Trail ascends to Atsinna, a partially excavated Anasazi pueblo with 850 rooms; allow about 1.5 hours for this easy-to-moderate 2-mile hike. El Morro is better known, however, for **Inscription Rock,** a sandstone cliff face into which aboriginal peoples, Spaniards, and Anglo-Americans engraved their names and messages. The very easy 0.5-mile **Inscription Trail** (30 minutes) to the cliff face passes the freshwater pool that made the area a mecca for so many groups.

Since time immemorial, travelers have recorded their passage at El Morro.

For further information contact the Superintendent, El Morro National Monument, National Park Service, Route 2, Box 43, Ramah, NM 87321; and El Malpais National Monument, National Park Service, Box 939, Grants, NM 87020.

Day 2: EL MORRO TO CANYON DE CHELLY

- **Ancient ruins and modern craft shops in Zuni**
- **A trading post and a rock window on the Navajo Reservation**
- **Touring and camping at Canyon de Chelly National Monument**
- **Gas, groceries, and laundry available in Gallup**

Just west of El Morro on NM-53 is **Zuni,** a large reservation dotted with lakes. Historians believe the ancient Zuni town of Hawikuh, now in ruins, to have been the first pueblo encountered by the Spanish in the sixteenth century. Another site here is the Village of the Great Kivas, a Chaco outlier with impressive pictographs. Inquire locally about hiring a guide if you wish to tour these ruins. Zuni's silversmiths craft high-quality jewelry inlaid with turquoise, coral, and other semiprecious stones.

Leaving Zuni, go north on NM-604 and NM-602 to Gallup, on the periphery of the Navajo Reservation. This border town is a good place to refuel and buy supplies for tonight. Your next stop, reached by driving north on US-666 for 7.5 miles and west onto Route 264 for 16.5 miles, is **Window Rock,** capital of the Navajo nation. The town derives its name from a large natural arch, or "window," which can be reached by a short trail.

Past Window Rock, stop at **Hubbell National Historic Site** in Ganado. The Park Service runs tours of the beautifully appointed home of John Lorenzo Hubbell, who established a trading post in 1878 that still operates today. Top-quality Navajo rugs and other craft items are sold here. For further information, contact the Superintendent, Hubbell National Historic Site, Box 150, Ganado, AZ 86505.

Head east 6 miles on AZ-264 to hit US-191, and then drive north on US-191 to the turnoff for **Canyon de Chelly National Monument** (see map, below), setting up camp upon arrival. The national monument, containing over 100 ruins, lies on the windward side of the Lukachukai and Chuska Mountains (sometimes called the "Navajo Alps"). It is drained by Chinle Wash, which empties into the San Juan River.

Canyon de Chelly (pronounced de-SHAY; a Spanish/Anglo corruption of "tsegi," the Navajo word for rock canyon) is a gem, but unless you arrange to join a guided tour, your access is restricted to what you can see from overlooks along the rim or on the trail to White House Ruin. Freelance travel is strictly prohibited, in part because the deep canyon of De Chelly Sandstone provides a summer home to about 30 Navajo families.

All of the observation points along the scenic drives are worth visiting. On South Rim Drive, don't miss the 800-foot needle called **Spider Rock,** legendary home of Spider Woman, who taught the

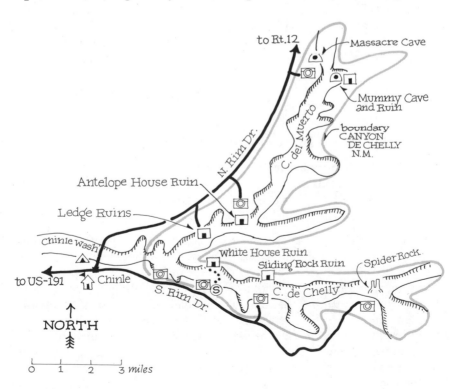

Spider Rock, a setting for Navajo tales

Navajo people weaving. On North Rim Drive, stop at the overlooks for Massacre and Mummy Caves. In 1805, Spanish soldiers—trying to punish and deter raids on their settlements—slaughtered 115 Navajos who were hiding in what came to be called **Massacre Cave.** At nearby **Mummy Cave,** prehistoric burial remains were found in a 50-room ruin. The 1849 expedition that explored Mummy Cave named the tributary in which it is located Canyon del Muerto, or "canyon of the dead."

For more information, write to the Superintendent, Canyon de Chelly National Monument, Box 588, Chinle, AZ 86503.

Day Hike: White House Ruin

> **Distance: 2.5 miles round trip**
> **Time: 2 hours**
> **Map: topo for Canyon del Muerto**
> **Difficulty: moderate**

This trail, which starts from a spur road 6 miles past monument headquarters along the South Rim Drive, switchbacks 600 feet to the canyon floor (see map, p. 151). At the bottom, turn left and proceed to the ruin, crossing a small bridge over the lushly foliaged creek. White House Ruin, so named because of the color of some of its adobe, is straight ahead on the right. Once home to nearly 100 people, it has two tiers. The canyon walls are streaked with "desert varnish," dark mineral traces that rains have leached from the rock and washed down in long stripes from the rim. A pleasant picnic area is here amid the cottonwoods.

Day 3: CANYON DE CHELLY TO SAND ISLAND

- **Driving through incomparable Monument Valley**
- **And nearby Valley of the Gods**
- **Visiting San Juan River overlooks**
- **Optional river trip**
- **Camping at Sand Island or in Valley of the Gods**
- **Gas and groceries available in Kayenta; showers and laundry in Mexican Hat**

Today you leave the Navajo Reservation and cross into Utah, driving through spectacular country drained by the San Juan River and its tributaries. From Canyon de Chelly, go north 14 miles on US-191 to Many Farms. Take a left at the fork onto Route 59. Follow this road 44.5 miles over remote mesas to its end, turning left onto US-160. Drive 8 miles to Kayenta. In Kayenta, head north 23.5 miles on US-163 to Monument Valley.

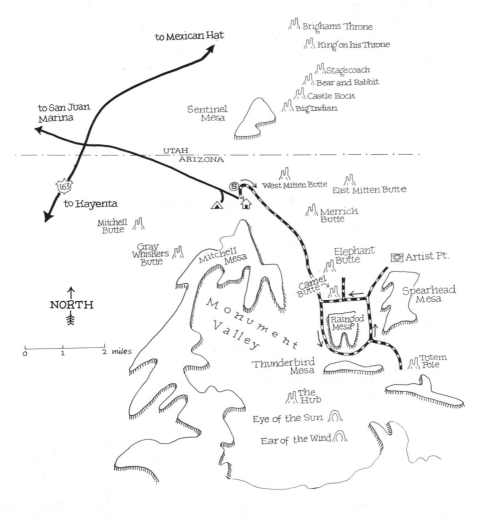

Scenic Drive: Monument Valley

Distance: 14 miles
Time: 2 hours

Monument Valley Tribal Park is not only a tourist destination but also the setting for countless car commercials and a favorite backdrop for Westerns and Bible films (see map, p. 153). For a small fee, you can take the 14-mile round-trip scenic drive. The road snakes down a few hundred feet to the valley floor and then circles mammoth Cutler Formation spires and buttes. Coming in all shapes and sizes, and looking fresh from each new angle, these formations are all that remain of a high plateau subjected to millions of years of erosion. Unfortunately, the road does not offer a glimpse of the valley's many arches. For that, you must take a tour, which typically includes a stop at a "hogan," or traditional one-room earthen dwelling. No hiking is allowed without an official guide.

From Monument Valley, continue north 19 miles on US-163 to Mexican Hat, on the San Juan River. Visit Goosenecks Overlook and Valley of the Gods (see Chapter 4, Cedar Mesa Loop, Day 5). About 22 miles farther north on US-163, just short of Bluff, is **Sand Island Recreation Area.** A few hundred yards downstream from the campsites is a wall of pictographs from the Basket Maker and Pueblo phases of Anasazi history.

You can camp tonight at Sand Island, which has pit toilets but no drinking water. During the mosquito season, however, it would be prudent to stay instead in Valley of the Gods (which has no amenities).

Optional Float Trip: Rafting the San Juan River

Distance: 28 (or 84) miles
Time: 2 to 8 days

Many float trips originate at Sand Island Recreation Area, concluding either at the Mexican Hat Bridge (28 miles) or Clay Hills Crossing, at the tip of Lake Powell (84 miles). This delightful run passes through the Monument Upwarp, giving access to rock art, ruins, and magical side-canyons. Especially memorable between Bluff and Mexican Hat are River House pueblo and the Butler Wash petroglyphs. Past Mexican Hat are the tortuous **Goosenecks,** a bowknot bend. Slickhorn Canyon and Grand Gulch, both studded with Anasazi sites, join the river between here and Clay Hills Crossing. There are moderate rapids as well as "sand waves," which boil up from the bottom at higher water levels.

The stretch from Sand Island to Mexican Hat makes an excellent 1- or 2-day trip for experienced rafters. From Sand Island to Clay Hills allow 5 to 8 days, plus 5 hours on each end for shuttling. Permits, which are required, can be obtained at the BLM office, P.O. Box 7, Monticello, UT 84535. Alternatively, you can float the San Juan with an organized group. Companies based in Mexican Hat sponsor trips and provide shuttle services.

Day 4: SAND ISLAND TO HOVENWEEP

- **Locating a seldom-visited cliff dwelling**
- **Camping and hiking at Hovenweep National Monument**
- **Gas and groceries available in Bluff**

Buy 2 days' supplies before leaving Bluff. To reach **Hovenweep National Monument,** your destination today, travel east for 23 miles on US-163, passing through the town of Montezuma Creek on the way to Aneth. In Montezuma Creek the route number changes to UT-262. Just short of Aneth, turn left along the bank of McElmo Creek and follow signs to Hovenweep, 20 miles distant.

Situated in pinyon and juniper country in the shadow of **Sleeping Ute Mountain,** Hovenweep—meaning "deserted valley" in Ute—consists of six prehistoric Anasazi complexes, "discovered" by white settlers in 1854 (see map, p. 157). The Hovenweep Anasazi, closely related to the residents of Mesa Verde, excelled in constructing stone and mud towers. Two complexes are in Utah (Square Tower and Cajon Mesa); the others (Holly, Horseshoe/Hackberry, Cutthroat Castle, and the unexcavated Goodman Point) are just across the border in Colorado. The campground and visitor center are near the Square Tower Complex, the most extensive and interesting of the six groups.

Select a spot in the campground, and then proceed to the visitor center and begin the short hike in the Square Tower Complex. Afterwards, you may want to visit the Cajon site, about 9 miles to the southeast; ask the ranger for directions. One of the buildings there served as an astronomical observatory.

For more information, contact the Superintendent, Hovenweep National Monument, McElmo Route, Cortez, CO 81321.

Day Hike: Square Tower Complex

> **Distance: 2 miles round trip**
> **Time: 2 hours**
> **Difficulty: easy**

Two short trails, originating at the visitor center (see map, p. 158), explore the masonry structures of shallow Little Ruin Canyon, formed of Dakota Sandstone. These trails can be combined for a distance of 2 miles, round trip. The **Tower Point Loop** stays atop the mesa, providing views of many buildings and doubling as a nature trail that introduces visitors to local flora. The somewhat more challenging **Twin Towers Loop,** 1.5 miles long, affords a closer look at more archaeological sites.

Day 5: HOVENWEEP TO MESA VERDE

- **Holly Ruins day hike**
- **Camping, showers, and laundry available at Mesa Verde National Park**
- **Gas and groceries available in Cortez**

Take advantage of the cool morning temperatures to complete the Holly Ruins Trail in Hovenweep before setting off for Mesa Verde.

Day Hike: Holly Ruins Trail

Distance: 4 miles one way
Time: 2 hours
Map: topo for Cajon Mesa
Difficulty: easy

This trail begins at the lower end of Hovenweep Campground and leads up Keeley Canyon to the mesa top occupied by Holly Ruins (see map, p. 159). To make this a one-way hike, set up a car shuttle.

The trail descends to the canyon floor through a small joint, which may be a bit tricky to find. The otherwise well-marked route sometimes follows the wash and sometimes goes up onto the bank in its gentle progress toward the head of the canyon. In about 3 miles, you come to a small ruin located on private land. Soon the trail ascends to the left, passing through another slot on its way to the mesa top. Once it levels out, it turns right and proceeds directly to **Holly Ruins,** whose major buildings include Great House, Boulder House, and Tilted Tower. Notice how the Anasazi, without alcoves to build in, made creative use of boulders to anchor their structures.

To reach Mesa Verde, return to UT-262 and drive southeast on this road, which becomes CO-41 at the border, for 19.5 miles. Intersecting US-160, go left, reaching US-666 in 13 miles. Turn left onto US-666 and proceed 19.5 miles to Cortez. In the distance, watch for **Shiprock** across the New Mexico border—a black volcanic plug almost 1700 feet high that is known to Navajos as the "rock with wings." According to folklore, Shiprock guided the tribe southward to their present homeland.

Poised on the cusp where deserts meet mountains, Cortez (population 7500) provides all the services you will need in preparation for your trip to Mesa Verde National Park. Buy provisions for today and tomorrow.

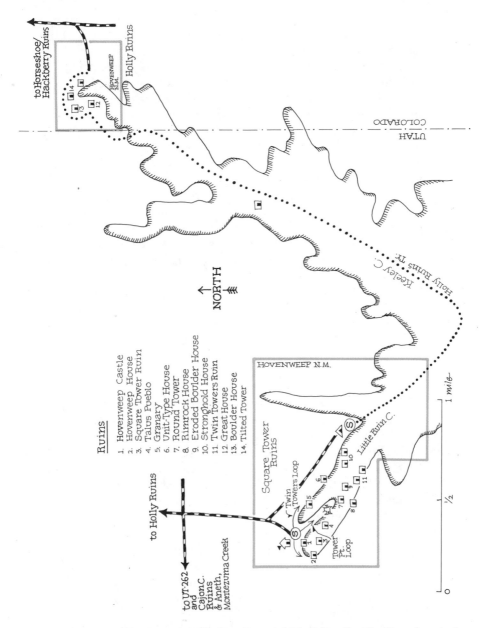

Mesa Verde ("green table" in Spanish) is 9.5 miles farther, located about halfway between Cortez and Mancos off US-160. Turn right to the park entrance and begin the climb to the undulating, forested country 2000 feet above the valley. Make selecting a campsite your first priority.

In spite of the crowds it attracts, this internationally celebrated park is a treat to visit, for concentrated within its 52,000 acres are many of the largest, best preserved, and most thoroughly excavated cliff dwellings in the United States. The dominant rock stratum is Cliff House Sandstone, which weathered to produce the alcoves that the Anasazi, or Ancestral Pueblan peoples (to use the term preferred here), found so suitable for home-building. To date, almost 600 cliff dwellings have been identified on these mesas. Because of the large number of visitors and the fragile nature of the sites, you can expect considerable regimentation here. At the cliff dwellings, everyone must be accompanied by a ranger, and tickets are required for some tours.

The sites are clustered on two mesas (see map, p. 161). Chapin Mesa stays open year-round, with curtailed services from mid-October to mid-May, while Wetherill Mesa is open only in the summer months.

Although Mesa Verde is not a hiker's park, a few short trails are open to visitors. Two of these—the Petroglyph Point and Spruce Canyon Trails—start near Spruce Tree House on Chapin Mesa; hiking either of them requires official permission. Three others—Knife Edge, Prater Ridge, and Point Lookout—commence at the campground and are unrestricted.

Compared to Hovenweep, Chaco, and other dwelling complexes that you will visit in this circuit, Mesa Verde—inhabited beginning about A.D. 500 and abandoned (for reasons that probably included drought, overuse of resources, and other environmental problems) before 1300—is a bustling tourist center, complete with snack bars, showers, church services, a museum, shuttle buses, and a colossal campground. In addition to the thirteenth-century cliff dwellings for which the park is renowned, there are two other types of structures here: earthen pit houses, dating back to the Basket Maker culture that prevailed prior to the mid-eighth century, and mesa top masonry dwellings. During most of their period of occupancy, the Mesa Verde people lived on the mesa tops, utilizing alcoves below the rim only very early and very late in their residency. Probably, construction of the cliff dwellings was not a defensive measure taken against actual enemies, since no evidence suggests that warfare occurred during the time when Mesa Verde was inhabited. (Indeed, the modern Hopi— who, with the Rio Grande Pueblo, are the closest living relatives of the Anasazi—are such a pacific people that their language doesn't even contain a word for war.) Anthropologists have also established fairly conclusively that erecting the cliff dwellings was a community effort involving men, women, and children.

To learn more about these structures and the people who built them, plan to spend some time at the visitor center and also the park museum near Spruce Tree House. Tour **Spruce Tree House** today, saving other sites for tomorrow, and hike the Petroglyph Point Trail (see below). Of the cliff dwellings in the park, Spruce Tree House is the most accessible, reached by a paved, switchbacking trail from the museum. Visitors to this crescent-shaped, 115-room site can enter a reconstructed kiva.

Mesa Verde's undercliff cities date from the thirteenth century.

For further information, write to the Superintendent, Mesa Verde National Park, Mesa Verde CO 81330. Guided tours of spectacular sites on the Ute Mountain Ute Reservation, adjacent to the park, can be arranged. For information, call (970) 565-4684 in Towaoc, CO, weekdays.

Day Hike: Petroglyph Point Trail

Distance: 2.75 miles round trip
Time: 2 hours
Difficulty: moderate

You must register for this pleasant and varied hike at the Chief Ranger's Office, next to the Chapin Mesa museum. A booklet with text corresponding to numbers along the route can be purchased for a modest sum. The well-marked trail begins at one of the switchbacks down to Spruce Tree House (see map, p. 161). Go right here, and when the trail splits almost immediately, take the left fork. The first half of the trail stays one level below the canyon rim, arriving at an excellent rock art panel. It then climbs stairs to the mesa top—a good rest or lunch place. From an overlook on the way up, search for **Echo House,** a cliff dwelling in an alcove across the canyon. The trail follows the rim of Chapin Mesa, passing directly above Spruce Tree House before looping back to the museum.

Day 6: MESA VERDE

- **Admiring America's finest cliff dwellings**
- **Ridgetop day hiking**
- **Camping, gas, groceries, showers, and laundry available at Mesa Verde**

Today's recommended itinerary includes stops at ruin sites on Chapin Mesa and, if it is open to the public, Wetherill Mesa as well.

Begin your tour at Chapin Mesa's spectacular **Cliff Palace,** in the southeastern sector of the park. This site—found and named in 1888 by two local ranchers, Richard Wetherill and Charles Mason, while they were looking for stray cattle during a snowstorm—contains 217 rooms and 23 kivas and is believed to have accommodated between 200 and 250 people. Access to the site is gained by steps and ladders. Near the far end of the alcove, where you exit, look for wall paintings inside one of the rooms.

Farther along on the same loop road is the unusual **Balcony House,** visitable by guided tour only. This small cliff dwelling may once have served as a nursery. Reaching it requires you to ascend a 32-foot ladder and crawl through a 12-foot tunnel.

Adjacent to the loop road off which Cliff Palace and Balcony House are situated is another loop enabling visitors to view Square Tower House and Sun Temple and to examine pit house sites.

Your next destination is **Wetherill Mesa.** To drive there, return to the Far View area and turn left at a junction before reaching the visitor center. The parking lot is 12 miles down this road. Near the parking lot, a trail descends the cliff to **Step House,** named for a set of stairs built to connect the pueblo to the mesa top. Some pit houses are next to the cliff dwelling.

A minibus ride from the parking lot takes visitors to the **Long House** trailhead, from which guided tours depart. This beautiful

Wetherill Mesa features both cliff dwellings and pit houses.

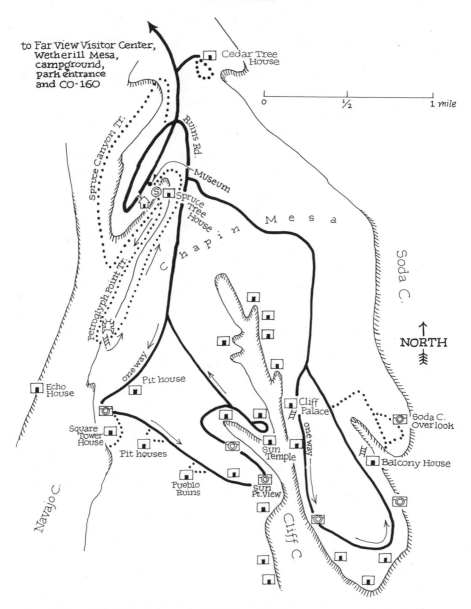

to Far View Visitor Center, Wetherill Mesa, campground, park entrance and CO-160

Cedar Tree House

Museum

Spruce Tree House

Chapin Mesa

Soda C.

Spruce Canyon Tr.

Ruins Rd.

Petroglyph Point Tr.

NORTH

Echo House

one way

Pit house

Square Tower House

Pit houses

Pueblo Ruins

Sun Temple

Sun Pt. View

Cliff Palace

one way

Soda C. Overlook

Balcony House

Navajo C.

Cliff C.

0   ½   1 mile

dwelling, with 150 rooms and 21 kivas, features an exceptionally large plaza. The minibus also stops at a 0.75-mile trail to the **Badger House Community** and other pit house complexes.

When finished on Wetherill Mesa, return to the Far View area. If time allows, turn right at the intersection with the main park road and drive 1.25 miles back toward Chapin Mesa, stopping at **Far View Ruin.** Like many pueblos here, Far View is a surface apartment, located on the mesa top rather than on the canyon cliffs. In fact, most of the ancient inhabitants of the area lived on the mesas, which they farmed (in contrast to other Ancestral Pueblo communities, where the general

practice was to grow corn, beans, and squash in the canyon bottoms).
Back at the campground, take a walk up the Knife Edge Trail.

Day Hike: Knife Edge Trail

> **Distance: 2 miles round trip**
> **Time: 1 hour**
> **Difficulty: very easy**

Originating at the north end of the campground, near the Lone Cone Formation, this well-trod trail follows the bed of the original road through the park. Level nearly all the way, it hugs the rim of a cliff for its entire route, offering gorgeous, unobstructed vistas of Sleeping Ute Mountain and the snow peaks of the southern Rockies as well as of the Knife Edge itself. Erosion has eaten away at the old roadbed, closing the last section of the trail, which used to terminate at the Montezuma Valley Overlook. Unless the route is repaired, hikers must double back when they reach a sign warning that it is dangerous to proceed.

Day 7: MESA VERDE TO CHACO

- **Viewing Aztec Ruins**
- **Camping at Chaco Canyon**
- **Gas, groceries, showers, and laundry available in Durango**

Leave Mesa Verde today and drive east 35 miles on US-160, crossing a pass and dropping into Durango. Located in the Animas River valley, conveniently close to the ski areas and hiking trails of the San Juan Mountains, this small city (population 14,000) is an all-season resort that proudly displays its history as a mining and railroad boomtown. Visitors can ride a narrow-gauge train through the mountains to Silverton, a daylong round trip, or tour the city's quaint Victorian neighborhoods. Buy gas, ice, and groceries here for the next 2 days.

US-550 follows the Animas valley south 35 miles to the town of Aztec, New Mexico, the location of **Aztec Ruins National Monument.** The complex is near the junction of US-550 and NM-544. Turn north onto Ruins Road, following signs to the national monument. The names of both the monument and the town derive from the belief of early settlers that the ruins were Mesoamerican in origin.

In the twelfth and thirteenth centuries, Aztec was one of the major Anasazi communities of the Southwest, possibly housing up to 700 people. A very easy 0.25-mile trail acquaints you with this 500-room complex. Because building and pottery styles identified with both Chaco and Mesa Verde were replicated here in consecutive historical periods, archaeologists think that the pueblo may have been occupied first by Chacoan Anasazi and then abandoned and later reoccupied by people influenced culturally by Mesa Verde. Of special interest is an enormous, lovingly reconstructed kiva, into which native music is piped. The kiva occupies a portion of the plaza once used for various communal activities.

For additional information, write to the Superintendent, Aztec Ruins National Monument, P.O. Box 640, Aztec, NM 87410.

To drive to Chaco Culture National Historical Park, go south 8.5 miles on NM-544 to Bloomfield, an oil and gas refining center, where you pick up NM-44 south. Follow NM-44 for 29.5 miles until it intersects County Road 7900, 3 miles beyond Nageezi Trading Post. Turn right here and follow signs to the park. In all, it is 30 miles amid scenic badlands from NM-44 to the Chaco Visitor Center; only the last 7 miles are paved. Find a spot in Gallo Campground at the east end of the park.

Day 8: CHACO CANYON

- **Inspecting pueblos on the canyon floor**
- **Day hikes to mesa-top sites**
- **Camping at Chaco Culture National Historical Park**

Once the center of a thriving civilization, **Chaco Culture National Historical Park** contains 12 major Anasazi sites (see map, p. 164). The canyon is low and wide, and the Anasazi built confidently out in the open here instead of hugging the cliffs, as others would later do.

Chaco Canyon was the metropolis of the Anasazi world.

The masonry work at Chaco is arguably the finest in all the Southwest. Residents of the canyon—which may have supported a population as large as 5000 in its heyday—established over 70 outlying pueblos throughout the San Juan basin, whether to ease population pressure or as insurance against drought. Seven wide, poker-straight roads led from Chaco to its various "colonies" (including the Aztec and Salmon

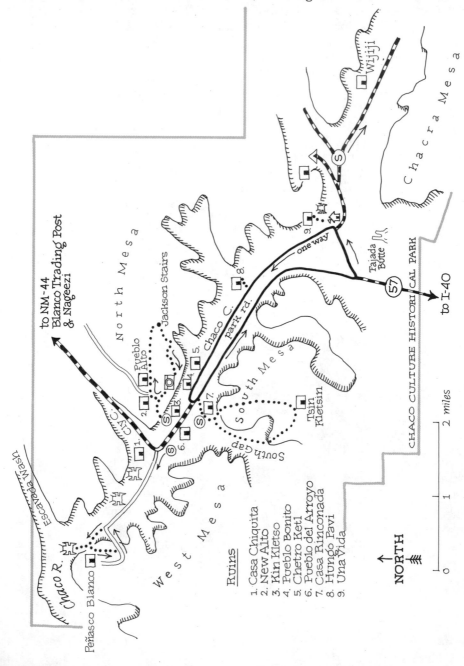

Ruins
1. Casa Chiquita
2. New Alto
3. Kin Kletso
4. Pueblo Bonito
5. Chetro Ketl
6. Pueblo del Arroyo
7. Casa Rinconada
8. Hungo Pavi
9. Una Vida

NORTH

ruin complexes to the north). These roads, over 250 miles of them, are visible from the air, and may have been used by traders, laborers, and pilgrims. Water control systems, including irrigation, enabled the communities of the Chaco Plateau to wrest a living from an often harsh environment. The construction of roads, water systems, and large masonry buildings required a rather elaborate social structure, complete with a bureaucracy to collect information, make decisions, and respond to contingencies. In fact, one of the "great houses" here—Pueblo Bonito—may have evolved into an administrative and religious center for the civilization, with Pueblo Alto above it serving as a commercial entrepôt. The nature of the relationship between center and periphery is controversial, but it seems that when Chaco Canyon was depopulated in the twelfth and thirteenth centuries, linkages among the outlying communities collapsed, yielding more local autonomy as well as more insecurity.

Although rangers conduct tours daily between Memorial Day and Labor Day, most visitors opt for self-guided walks through the sites. Pueblo Bonito, Chetro Ketl, and Casa Rinconada, which have 0.5-mile trails winding through or around them, should not be missed. Allow approximately an hour at each of them. All trails and ruins are closed between sunset and sunrise.

Pueblo Bonito (meaning "beautiful town" in Spanish) is the largest and most illustrious of the sites, with between 600 and 800 rooms and 33 kivas. Completed in the mid-eleventh century, this D-shaped complex housed up to 1000 people. **Chetro Ketl,** a 500-room structure adjacent to Pueblo Bonito, is noteworthy for its uplifted platform plaza. In ancient times, Pueblo Bonito and Chetro Ketl were connected to the mesa top by a set of foot- and handholds, or Moki steps. The 280-room **Pueblo del Arroyo,** across the canyon from Pueblo Bonito, also contains a large plaza. **Casa Rinconada** ("house in a box canyon") is located among a number of small ruins on the south side of Chaco Wash. Built in about A.D. 1100, it is a restored "great kiva" that visitors may enter. The size and location of the ceremonial chamber suggest that it serviced the community as a whole rather than belonging to any particular clan. Finally, **Una Vida** ("a life"), behind the visitor center, is a smaller, older, partially excavated dwelling of about 150 rooms. The remains of a hogan and corral here indicate subsequent Navajo occupation. From the number 5 marker on the 0.25-mile loop trail, a steep path leads to an astonishing petroglyph panel near the canyon rim.

After you have viewed the major sites, hike one of the trails described below. Required permits are available at the visitor center. Each of the backcountry trails is well-designed and popular, despite lacking shade and water. In hot weather, the trails are best hiked in early morning or late afternoon. Remember, when you visit backcountry sites, not to touch, climb, or lean on fragile walls or collect any cultural or natural specimens.

For more information, write to the Superintendent, Chaco Culture National Historical Park, Star Route 4, Box 6500, Bloomfield, NM 87413.

Day Hike 1: South Mesa Loop

Distance: 4 miles round trip
Time: 3 hours
Difficulty: moderate

Tsin Kletsin, a site on South Mesa, commanded a panoramic view of six other major buildings from the second story of one of its kivas and thus may have served as a communications center or relay station. Reach the trailhead from marker number 9 of the Casa Rinconada loop, near the great kiva (see map, p. 164). After ascending on switchbacks to a point just below the rim, the trail climbs through a short chimney, swings widely to the left, and levels out. It bends to the right and then heads straight for the ruin, visible from afar. From the windswept mesa top, 450 feet above the valley, Pueblo Bonito, Chetro Ketl, Casa Rinconada, and Pueblo del Arroyo are clearly discernible; this may be the best view in the park. Near the ruin, the trail turns west and descends into South Gap. It follows the wash downstream toward Pueblo del Arroyo. Turn right before reaching this pueblo to get back to your car.

Masonry wall detail, Chaco Canyon

Day Hike 2: Wijiji Trail

Distance: 3 miles round trip
Time: 2 hours
Difficulty: very easy

Of the backcountry sites in Chaco Canyon that are open to the public, **Wijiji** is the best preserved and most easily reached. Driving from the campgound, turn left at the first fork in the road and proceed about 100 yards to the parking area (see map, p. 164). The route, which bicyclists can also use, follows a level service road. Wijiji, up against the left wall of the canyon, contained 100 rooms and rose three stories. Built early in the twelfth century, it was one of the last of the "great houses." Look for a panel of rock art on the bluffs.

On the return trip, you face **Fajada Butte,** where an ancient astronomical marker known as a "sun dagger" was discovered in the late 1970s. In conjunction with three carefully positioned rock slabs, this petroglyph enabled the Chacoans to determine the exact dates of solstices and equinoxes—information that must have been invaluable to their society for both agricultural and religious reasons. The fragility of the marker led the Park Service to close Fajada Butte to tourists, but a 1-hour film shown at the visitor center focuses on its role in indigenous culture.

Day 9: CHACO TO BANDELIER

- **Another Chaco day hike**
- **Driving through the Jemez Mountains**
- **Camping at Bandelier National Monument**
- **Gas, groceries, showers, and laundry available in Los Alamos**

Today's itinerary includes day-hike options in Chaco (see below) before setting out on a long but beautiful car ride to Bandelier National Monument.

Day Hike 1: Pueblo Alto Loop

Distance: 4.75 miles round trip
Time: 3 hours
Difficulty: moderate

This wonderful hike allows you to visit two major sites and to attain excellent vantage points on several others. Beginning at Kin Kletso, the trail ascends improbably through a sort of couloir in the Cliff House Sandstone (see map, p. 164). At the top, the cairned trail veers to the right, hugging the rim. About 0.75 mile of walking over slickrock brings you to the Pueblo Bonito Overlook. Here the trail forks. Turn left, climbing slowly and steadily for 0.5 mile through the Lewis Shale

Formation and onto the Pictured Cliffs Sandstone, reaching Pueblo Alto ("high town") and New Alto atop North Mesa. The elevation gain to North Mesa from the valley floor is 350 feet. Of the two structures here, the 35-room New Alto site, on the left, is better preserved, though the partially excavated Pueblo Alto is much larger, with 135 rooms.

The trail continues on in front of Pueblo Alto, marked by a sign. From here it is 2.75 miles back to Pueblo Bonito Overlook to close the loop. The trail heads a side-canyon, revealing the so-called **Jackson Stairs,** a set of Moki steps by which inhabitants of the mesa top gained access to the farming terraces below. Don't worry—the trail doesn't use these steps; instead, it continues on the slickrock bench, eventually descending through another crack, which returns you to the level of Pueblo Bonito Overlook. As the loop closes, it offers outstanding views of Chetro Ketl directly below and Pueblo del Arroyo across the canyon.

Day Hike 2: Peñasco Blanco Trail

> **Distance: 6.5 miles round trip**
> **Time: 4 hours**
> **Difficulty: easy**

Handsome **Peñasco Blanco** ("white rock") perches atop West Mesa (see map, p. 164). The trail winds through a section of Chaco Wash that abounds in rock art, most notably a pictograph archaeologists believe represents the supernova of A.D. 1054. Start this hike at Pueblo del Arroyo. Shortly, you will pass Kin Kletso and Casa Chiquita on your right. Look for petroglyphs along the cliffs, especially at the mouth of the first significant side-canyon on the right beyond Casa Chiquita. Opposite the second side-canyon, the trail veers to the left. Before long, the signed spur to the supernova pictograph takes off to the right. Crossing the wash, the spur heads toward the base of the cliff of West Mesa, following it for several hundred yards to the pictograph panel.

Backtrack a short distance to rejoin the main trail, which ascends about 150 feet to Peñasco Blanco. Overlooking the confluence of the Chaco River and Escavada Wash, Peñasco Blanco is a very extensive building that originally had three stories. When you finish exploring the site, return the way you came.

To reach Bandelier National Monument, return to NM-44 and go south. Between here and San Ysidro, 92 miles away, colorful breaks give way to distant mesas and buttes and finally to the mountainous highlands of central New Mexico.

At San Ysidro, on the Jemez Indian Reservation, go left on NM-4, an equally spectacular road. From here it is 55 miles to Bandelier. The highway passes near **Jemez Pueblo** as it follows the narrow Jemez River Valley to its head in the mountains and crosses a divide into the Rio Grande drainage. Jemez Falls Campground has a 0.25-mile trail to the 50-foot waterfall. A 1.5 mile trail (#137) in Battleship Rock

Campground leads to an 80-foot waterfall and McCauley Warm Springs. On the other side of the divide, you enter **Valle Grande,** a seemingly endless meadow in the caldera of ancient Jemez Volcano.

Before long, Bandelier's Ponderosa Campground (intended for large groups) appears on the right. A sign a few miles farther on directs you to the Bandelier entrance station. Just beyond the booth, a spur to the right leads to Juniper Campground, where you should choose a campsite. In White Rock, 10 miles east on NM-4, purchase supplies for 3 nights. Or you can backtrack on NM-4 west to the turnoff for equidistant Los Alamos, where there are excellent supermarkets and restaurants, plus shower and laundry facilities. Many tourists rave about Los Alamos's science and history museums, focusing on nuclear and other high technologies.

Day 10: BANDELIER

- **Peering into cave dwellings**
- **Hiking past waterfalls to the Rio Grande**
- **Camping at Bandelier**
- **Gas, groceries, showers, and laundry available in Los Alamos**

Bandelier National Monument is located on the forested Pajarito ("little bird") Plateau. Its 50 square miles are geographically diverse, ranging from 5300-foot elevation near the Rio Grande to over 10,000 feet in the Jemez Mountains. Important to the park's natural history was the eruption, over a million years ago, of Jemez Volcano, which blanketed the area with white volcanic ash, or "tuff." Subsequently, streams cut deep canyons through this material, exposing the underlying basalt—a dark, dense rock left over from previous volcanic activity. After the volcano expelled huge quantities of gas, ash, and lava, its center collapsed, producing the caldera you drove through earlier. Pyramidal formations called "tent rocks," composed of tuff that hardened as hot gases escaped from the volcano, are a geological curiosity of the area.

Another legacy of vulcanism was enhanced soil fertility. This helps to explain why Bandelier contains the greatest aggregation of prehistoric dwellings in our national park system. Members of the large Anasazi (Ancestral Pueblo) farming community, which flourished here until about A.D. 1550, built multistory apartments along the base of cliffs, enlarging preexisting caves in the soft volcanic rock with the aid of stone implements. The excavated sites are concentrated in Frijoles Canyon, which is honeycombed with trails.

Forests in and around the national monument were ravaged by fire in 1996. Although the fire was advantageous from an ecological standpoint, the area may be less aesthetically pleasing than normal for several years.

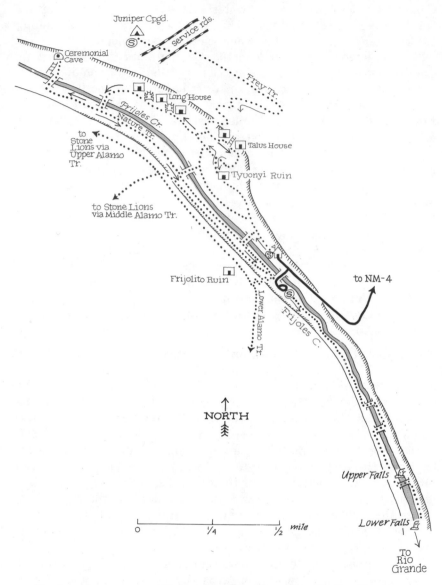

Juniper Cpgd.

service rds.

Ceremonial Cave

Frey Tr.

Long House

Frijoles Cr.

Nature Tr.

to Stone Lions via Upper Alamo Tr.

Talus House

Tyuonyi Ruin

to Stone Lions via Middle Alamo Tr.

to NM-4

Frijolito Ruin

Lower Alamo Tr.

Frijoles C.

NORTH

0   ¼   ½   *mile*

Upper Falls

Lower Falls

To Rio Grande

Backpackers can explore over 70 miles of trails leading to mesa tops with panoramic vistas and canyons boasting aboriginal artifacts. Today's recommended itinerary, however, focuses on three of the shorter, more heavily used trails, which can be combined into a loop beginning at the campground. At the visitor center, obtain a brochure about the Frijoles Canyon sites and make arrangements for the upcoming overnight backpacking trip (see Days 11 and 12), securing a permit to camp in Capulin Canyon for tomorrow night.

For further information, contact the Superintendent, Bandelier National Monument, Los Alamos, NM 87544.

Day Hike 1: Frey Trail

>**Distance: 1.5 miles one way**
>**Time: 1 hour**
>**Map: topo for Bandelier**
>**Difficulty: moderate**

This well-designed trail, once the sole route into Frijoles Canyon, starts near the amphitheater in Juniper Campground (see map, p. 170). After a short distance the trail crosses two service roads. At the second road, turn left and walk about 50 feet to rejoin the trail proper. As you reach the canyon rim, sweeping views greet you. The trail contours to the

The Frey Trail overlooks circular Tyuonyi pueblo.

right and abruptly descends 400 feet on switchbacks, passing tent rocks on its way to the canyon floor. Tyuonyi, a large, circular apartment house, is visible en route. At the base of the cliff, the trail intersects with the Frijoles Canyon loop near Talus House, on your left.

Day Hike 2: Frijoles Canyon Loop

Distance: 2 miles round trip
Time: 1.5 hours
Map: topo for Bandelier
Difficulty: easy

This walk is a must for all visitors to Bandelier, for it loops around the cave, cliff, and surface dwellings of lovely **Frijoles Canyon,** inhabited between the eleventh and sixteenth centuries. For much of its length, the trail is shady, and therefore fairly cool even in midsummer.

Assuming you have just descended the Frey Trail from the campground (see map, p. 170), turn left at the first trail junction to examine **Talus House,** a restored cliff dwelling, and the nearby caves that the area's ancient inhabitants enlarged out of soft, volcanic tuff. Beyond Talus House, stop to visit **Tyuonyi** (possibly meaning "place of treaty" in the Keres tongue). The nearby kiva is fully excavated.

Continuing up the canyon, away from the visitor center, you soon come to a second set of foundations and cave dwellings, collectively known as **Long House,** set against the cliff. There are petroglyphs

Natural caves in Frijoles Canyon tuff, remodeled as dwellings

and a pictograph here, as well as a cave housing 15,000 bats. Notice the branching cholla plants that favor this location. Take the bridge across Frijoles Creek, and turn right, into the woods. Another half mile, with several stream crossings, brings you to **Ceremonial Cave,** 150 feet above the canyon floor. Reached by a series of ladders, it sports a reconstructed kiva.

Backtracking, walk downstream to the visitor center.

Day Hike 3: Falls Trail

> **Distance: 5 miles round trip**
> **Time: 3 hours**
> **Map: topo for Bandelier**
> **Difficulty: easy to Upper Falls, moderate thereafter**

Because of its suitability for family outings, this delightful trail can be congested all the way to the Rio Grande, but at least as far as Upper and Lower Falls (see map, p. 170). In summer the hike is often hot, especially at the top and bottom where little shade is available. Be sure to carry water.

Beginning downstream from the visitor center, near the picnic area, the trail crosses Frijoles Creek twice on wooden bridges, descending gradually. It stays somewhat above the creekbed as the stream becomes entrenched, diving deeply into the earth. Soon it reaches an overlook of 140-foot-high **Upper Falls,** 1.25 miles from the trailhead.

Now the trail gets rougher. Descending on switchbacks, it recrosses the creek on a bridge above some small pools before swinging down to a viewpoint for the (less dramatic) **Lower Falls,** 80 feet high. Crossing the stream three more times on stones and logs, the trail enters open, scrubby country, where it meets the **Rio Grande.** The banks are littered with dead cottonwoods, a bleak legacy of a flood that backed up Cochiti Reservoir 80 feet above its normal level.

The river, at mile 2.5, is 700 feet lower in elevation than the visitor center. The Cerros del Rio mesas are visible on the other side. The trail past this point is not maintained, so you must double back.

Days 11 and 12: CAPULIN CANYON

> • **Stunning views of mountains and canyons**
> • **Visiting Ancestral Pueblo (Anasazi) sites**
> • **Camping at Capulin and Juniper Campgrounds**

The route described below gives the hiker a good feel for Bandelier's backcountry, particularly Capulin Canyon. It does require a short car shuttle or some equivalent, however. One nonshuttle option is to return to your car from the visitor center via Frijoles Creek, which adds 7.75 miles (an extra day) to the trip.

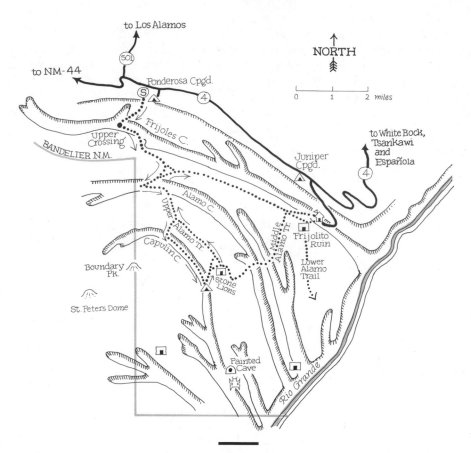

Backpack: Capulin Canyon

Distance: 18.75 miles one way
Time: 2 days
Map: topo for Bandelier
Difficulty: moderate

To reach the trailhead, drive to the entrance station and then go left on NM-4, reaching the turnoff for Ponderosa Campground on the left in about 5.5 miles (see map, above). Park here and pick up a jeep road to the right of the campground. In under a mile, the jeep road turns into an excellent trail that descends 400 feet into Frijoles Canyon. The trail leads to **Upper Crossing** at mile 1.75. Cross the stream on a log bridge, and climb 400 feet to a windswept mesa top. Magnificent 360-degree views of the surrounding peaks can be enjoyed from this aerie.

At about mile 3, your trail will intersect first the trail to lower Frijoles Canyon and then the trail into **Alamo Canyon.** Go right at each of these Y intersections, heading south and dropping 400 feet into narrow Alamo Canyon at mile 4. Follow Alamo Canyon downstream for a short distance before gradually climbing out past some tent rocks to reach another plateau at mile 5. Turning right at a trail junction, you soon reach the lip of the **Capulin** ("chokecherry") **Canyon,** where you begin your third and most precipitous descent (600 feet). The trail deteriorates here, but views of the mountains on the other side provide ample compensation. You attain the floor of Capulin Canyon at mile 6. Turn left and proceed down the canyon through heavy timber for 2 miles until you reach the backcountry ranger's cabin and your designated camping zone. Those with extra time will find it worthwhile to hike down Capulin Canyon to **Painted Cave** (5 miles round trip), with its reddish pictographs. The shallow cave is nestled 50 feet above the canyon floor but the drawings are visible from below.

Back at the camping area, locate the junction with the Middle Alamo Trail. Go north on that trail and climb out of Capulin Canyon. In less than 1.5 miles you reach a set of Y-type trail junctions. Turn right at the first junction; immediately to the right of the second, don't miss the **Stone Lions,** two figures of crouching mountain lions carved from volcanic rock and ringed by antlers. After visiting this ancient shrine, head northwest and climb back to the mesa top between Capulin and Alamo Canyons. In about 2 miles you arrive at another intersection. Turn right here onto the same trail you hiked yesterday for the 1.5-mile drop into Alamo Canyon, and then climb to the mesa on the other side. A mile past the floor of Alamo Canyon you come to the familiar Y where your trail joins the ones to Upper Crossing/Ponderosa Campground and Lower Frijoles Canyon. Turn right at these intersections to head toward the visitor center.

Pueblo Indians still visit the ancient Stone Lions shrine.

The next 4 miles are easy and beautiful, paralleling the lip of Frijoles Canyon. After about 3 miles, you arrive at a trail junction; the left fork drops directly down to Frijoles Creek, while the right (the Middle Alamo Trail) returns to Alamo Canyon. Continue straight ahead along the rim here. Near the end, as you undertake a rapid 500-foot (in 0.75 mile) descent on switchbacks into Frijoles Canyon, you command a bird's-eye view of the sites in the canyon itself. After some refreshments at the snack bar, pick up your vehicle and claim a spot in Juniper Campground.

Day 13: BANDELIER TO TAOS

- **Day-hiking to Tsankawi Pueblo**
- **Camping and showers available at Rio Grande Gorge State Park**
- **Gas, groceries, and laundry available in Española**

Your first stop today is **Tsankawi** (san-kuh-WEE), a detached unit of Bandelier, located 11 miles to the northeast on NM-4. The unobtrusive entrance gate stands directly opposite the start of the truck route to Los Alamos. Park here and prepare yourself for an interesting early-morning hike.

─────

Day Hike: Tsankawi

> **Distance: 2 miles round trip**
> **Time: 2 hours**
> **Map: topo for Bandelier**
> **Difficulty: easy**

The ostensible attraction here is an unexcavated 350-room pueblo, built in the fifteenth century, that looks like a mound of rubble to the untrained eye. Nevertheless, this section of the park (its name derived from a Tewa phrase meaning "village between two canyons at the clump of sharp, round cacti") deserves a visit, both for its panoramic views of the surrounding canyons and high country and for other points of interest along the way.

The trail starts near the ranger station a level below the mesa top where the dwelling, once two or three stories tall, is situated (see map, p. 177). It soon forks; go left, proceeding to the top with the aid of a ladder. Notice petroglyphs here at marker number 6. After visiting Tsankawi, a masonry surface site, the trail drops back to the lower level by means of another ladder. Petroglyphs and cave dwellings abound in this area; scout for rock art especially around marker 18. The trail follows for some distance an ancient path worn nearly a foot deep into the tuff. It then rejoins the other section of the trail, closing the loop and heading back to the parking area.

ABOVE: Inaccessible upper tier of White House Ruin, Canyon de Chelly

LEFT: All-American Man pictograph, bedecked in Fourth of July garb.

OVERLEAF: Many Anasazi dwellings feature T-shaped doorways.

Soft morning light flatters The Castle, Capitol Reef.

Mechanical weathering of cliffs can produce mini-arches.

Intense orange pigments vivify Bryce Canyon spires.

Marching Men descend a sunlit cliff, Arches National Park.

LEFT: Cloud shadows create a dramatic chiaroscuro in Grand Canyon.

BELOW: Tracks on a sand hill, Arches National Park

FACING PAGE: Double Arch Alcove graces Zion's Kolob section.

Delicate Arch commands a slickrock bowl, Arches National Park.
Color saturates the sky at twilight.

Devote the rest of the day to visiting inhabited pueblos. Several interesting ones lie north and east of Bandelier, near Española, which can be reached via either NM-30 or NM-502 and US-84/285. **San Ildefonso,** a left turn off NM-502, is an attractive village set dramatically under pink mesas and blue mountains. Famous for matte on black pottery, it also takes pride in its impressive aboveground kiva, located in the plaza. The residents here, like those at Cochiti Pueblo, believe that their forebears inhabited Tsankawi and other sites in Bandelier. An exact replica of the original Spanish colonial mission was completed in 1968. **Santa Clara Pueblo** nearby, a left turn on NM-30, is a black-on-black pottery center; on this reservation you can visit Puyé Cliff Dwellings, which the Santa Clarans regard as another ancestral home. **Nambe Pueblo,** also near Española, boasts sacred Nambe Falls, one of only a few large cascades in New Mexico. If Nambe is the oldest of the northern Rio Grande pueblos, tiny **Pojoaque** (a right turn off US-84/285) is the youngest, constructed in the 1940s by the members of a tribe whose ancestors were devastated by smallpox.

For information, contact the Eight Northern Pueblos Council, Box 969, San Juan Pueblo, NM 87566.

Driving north from Española on NM-68, find a campsite in **Rio Grande Gorge State Park** near Pilar. If all sites are taken, more campgrounds are close by on NM-567 along the river and in the mountains above Taos.

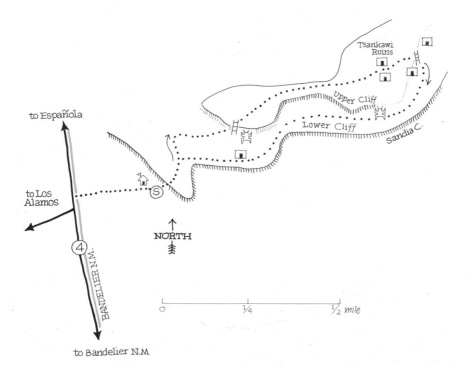

Approximately 47 miles north of Española on NM-68 is **Taos Pueblo** ("place of the red willows") on the outskirts of the Hispanic and Anglo town of the same name. Tucked comfortably between the Rio Grande Gorge and the Sangre de Cristo Mountains, Taos's charming adobe dwellings—all interconnected, Anasazi style—house 1800 Tiwa-speaking residents. Take special note of the traditional beehive ovens, or "hornos," in which bread is baked, and the plaza's handsome Catholic church, dating from the mid-nineteenth century.

The town of Taos, cool in summer because of its high elevation, has been a haven for writers and artists at least since the time of D. H. Lawrence and Georgia O'Keeffe. Indeed, its plaza district appears to support even more art galleries, craft shops, and bookstores per capita than its larger counterpart, Santa Fe. And it contains fine restaurants and hotels, as well as historic attractions like the Kit Carson Home, just off the plaza. Only a few miles south of here in Ranchos de Taos is the St. Francis of Assisi Mission, an enduring subject for painters.

By now you may be ready to return to your campsite on the Rio Grande Gorge. The impressive 1000-foot-deep gorge, with its dark volcanic walls, offers challenging white-water rafting opportunities, such as the Taos Box. Look for petroglyphs along the riverbank.

Day 14: TAOS TO ALBUQUERQUE

- **Taking the High Road through Spanish Rio Grande country**
- **Romancing elegant, cultured Santa Fe**
- **Optional side trip to Pecos National Monument**
- **Camping and showers at Coronado State Park**
- **Gas, groceries, and laundry available in Española or Santa Fe**

From Taos, return to Española via NM-518, -75, and -76, the so-called "High Road" through the pine and aspen uplands of the Carson National Forest. This 52-mile route connects a series of Hispanic villages celebrated for their weaving, their fiery red chiles, and their piety. The **Spanish Rio Grande** region, with its exquisite mission churches, such as the ones at Chimayo and Las Trampas, is the center of the waning Penitente movement, a sect whose members practice rites of self-mortification, particularly during Lent.

In Española, pick up US-84/285, the expressway to historic **Santa Fe,** which ranks among America's most beautiful cities. It owes its charm to its unique amalgamation of three cultures: Pueblo, Hispanic, and Anglo. An ordinance issued decades ago stipulated that all new buildings be faced with adobe or some look-alike material, and as a result the city exhibits a wonderful unity of style. The state

Spanish padres built Rio Grande missions to last.

capital, Santa Fe is renowned for its fashionable shops and restaurants, its opera and symphony orchestra, its Canyon Road galleries, its Wheelwright and Finc Arts museums, and its Palace of Governors.

When finished in Santa Fe, take US-84/285 south 5.5 miles to I-25. From here it is 35.5 miles to Bernalillo, near Albuquerque, or—in the opposite direction on I-25—25 miles to Pecos National Monument, if you opt for the side trip (below). Along the way to Bernalillo, you pass more pueblos, including **Santo Domingo** on the Rio Grande, noted for its jewelry, and **Tesuque,** which contains a curiously shaped butte, Camel Rock.

Exiting at Bernalillo, follow signs to **Coronado State Park.** Located on the west bank of the Rio Grande, on the site of the ancient community of Kuaua (meaning "evergreen" in Tiwa), it offers commanding views of the Sandia Mountains. It has extensive low-walled ruins and a museum filled with artifacts from the colonial period, which began with Coronado's failed 1540 expedition in search of the Seven Cities of Cibola. But the star attraction here is the restored kiva in which archaeologists found several layers of colorful murals, dating from the fourteenth to sixteenth centuries. Although the originals were

Pecos mission church exhibits a stark geometry.

removed to the museum for their protection, exact reproductions line the kiva interior. Camp tonight at the state park in preparation for tomorrow's trip home.

Optional Side Trip: Pecos National Monument

To reach Pecos, travel east on I-25 from Santa Fe for about 17 miles to Glorieta. Exit here, taking Alt. 84/85 to the national monument, 8 miles distant. Pecos is the site of a 600-room community constructed around a courtyard. With the coming of Spanish conquistadors and Franciscan missionaries, centuries of intercultural conflict ensued. The very easy **Ruins Trail** (1.25 miles; 1 hour) allows visitors to inspect the mission church, a kiva, and the remains of many other ancient buildings, and to soak up the area's dramatic mountain scenery.

Chapter 6

PAINTED DESERT LOOP

Arizona, Utah

Focusing on northeastern Arizona, this diverse loop roughly circumscribes the Navajo Reservation. It features day trips to prehistoric and modern pueblos, short walks along canyon streams or on mesas covered with petrified wood, and two rugged backpacking opportunities: one to Rainbow Bridge on the shoulder of Navajo Mountain and the other to the floor of the Grand Canyon. Alternatives are suggested for readers preferring less strenuous activities.

Day 1: FLAGSTAFF AND SEDONA

- **Walking up Oak Creek Canyon**
- **Touring Sinagua ruins at Tuzigoot**
- **Camping at Dead Horse Ranch State Park**
- **Gas, groceries, showers, and laundry available in Flagstaff**

Flagstaff (population 46,000), one of the biggest cities in the high desert region, is positioned on the slope of the San Francisco Peaks, volcanic mountains sacred to the Hopis and Navajos. Its 7000-foot altitude makes it quite comfortable even in summer, and its **Museum of Northern Arizona,** dedicated to the perpetuation and promotion of local Native American cultures, should not be missed. Purchase a day's worth of gas, food, and ice in the city, and then drive to the museum, 2 miles north of town on US-89.

After visiting the museum, return to Flagstaff and pick up US-89A going south. The 29-mile drive through the national forest to the resort town and New Age mecca of Sedona is a knock-out, following the main drainage of **Oak Creek** for much of the way. This 16-mile-long stream, adjacent to the Secret Mountain Wilderness, cuts a watery canyon up to 2500 feet deep through the dramatic cliffs of the Coconino Plateau. Coconino Sandstone is the dominant stratum here. The route described below is just one of many excellent hiking possibilities along the West Fork of Oak Creek.

To reach the confluence of Oak Creek and West Fork, where the hike begins, drive about 18.5 miles south of Flagstaff on US-89A, or

0.75 mile south of Cave Springs Campground, to Call of the Canyon Picnic Area, where you park. Fees apply. Be prepared for some rock-hopping, but don't attempt the trip during high-water periods, such as the spring runoff, or when flooding threatens from upstream storms.

Day Hike: West Fork of Oak Creek

> **Distance: 6.75 miles round trip**
> **Time: 4 hours**
> **Maps: topos for Munds Park and Wilson Mountain**
> **Difficulty: easy**

From the parking area, walk to the stream. Turn left and then right to locate the trailhead, marked by an iron sign. The trail first crosses Oak Creek, on a small footbridge, and then crosses the **West Fork** near a shallow pool. Here you enter the narrow, orange and white gorge lined with evergreens and deciduous trees.

The trail is easy, with frequent stream crossings but little elevation

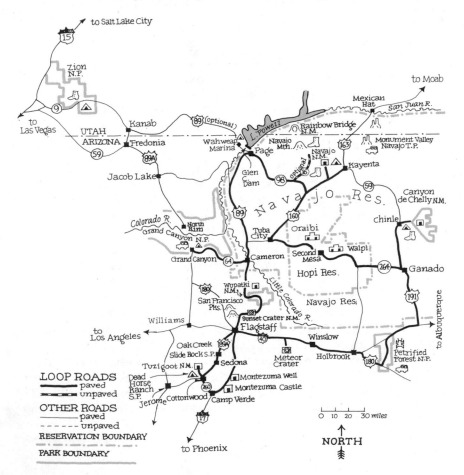

gain. Many exotic bird species, including the painted redstart and the red-faced warbler, make their home in the canyon. In about 2.25 miles, a rock ledge overhangs the creek's right bank. This makes a good rest stop. The trail continues for about another 1.25 miles to the point where the canyon walls close in. Backtrack to your car.

For additional information, contact the Sedona Ranger District, P.O. Box 300, Sedona, AZ 86336.

———

Down US-89A just south of the trailhead, about 8 miles north of Sedona, watch for **Slide Rock State Park** on the right. Small, erosion-sculpted chutes make delightful waterslides for those interested in swimming. Also visit Sedona, with its fashionable shops and restaurants and the spectacular setting that's made it a favorite film location. Try to identify some of the local monoliths, such as Coffee Pot, Bell, Castle, and Court House Rocks. Although the drive from Flagstaff to Sedona along Oak Creek is famous for its scenic beauty, the redrock country south of Sedona is equally remarkable, presenting views into Sycamore Canyon.

Near Clarkdale and Cottonwood, farther south on US-89A, is **Tuzigoot National Monument** (from the Apache word meaning "crooked water"), located just past Dead Horse Ranch State Park, where you will camp. Tuzigoot ruin and six other structures here were erected around A.D. 1200 by the Sinagua culture. In pre-Columbian times, the Sinagua and Hohokam tribes coexisted peacefully in the fertile Verde Valley, the Sinaguas sharing masonry skills and the Hohokams teaching their neighbors irrigation. Take a short, self-guided tour of this impressive structure, which housed over 200 people. Don't miss the outstanding exhibits inside the visitor center.

For more information, contact the Superintendent, Tuzigoot National Monument, P.O. Box 219, Camp Verde, AZ 86322.

Day 2: SINAGUA COUNTRY TO
THE PETRIFIED FOREST

- **Visiting Montezuma Castle**
- **Gazing into a gigantic meteor crater**
- **Camping in the Petrified Forest backcountry**
- **Gas, groceries, showers, and laundry available in Winslow and Holbrook**

In Cottonwood, pick up AZ-260 south, which intersects I-17 in 12.5 miles. Follow signs to another Sinagua site, **Montezuma Castle,** just north of Camp Verde. Early settlers believed the well-preserved dwelling was erected by Aztecs from Mexico. One of the Southwest's most amazing archaeological treasures, Montezuma Castle was fashioned of limestone blocks and river stones in the twelfth century. Fifty people inhabited this five-story, twenty-room structure, which is set like a jewel in the cliff. Too fragile to enter, it can be admired from a viewpoint behind the visitor center. Past the viewpoint, the very easy 0.25-mile trail visits another ruin before returning to the parking lot along the banks of Beaver Creek, which the Indians farmed.

North of Montezuma Castle off I-17, a few miles' drive down a dirt road from the McGuireville exit, is **Montezuma Well.** An easy, 0.5-mile loop trail begins at the parking lot. The well, formed when the roof of a limestone cavern collapsed, is fed by perennial springs. Both the Hohokam and Sinagua tribes utilized this reliable water source in their irrigation systems. Ruins of ancient dwellings ring the well.

For additional information, contact the Superintendent, Montezuma Castle National Monument, P.O. Box 219, Camp Verde, AZ 86322.

Montezuma Castle guards the valley of Beaver Creek.

Continue north on I-17 for 40.5 miles to I-40 and turn east. About 35 miles past Flagstaff is an exit for **Meteor Crater,** a privately run national landmark 5 miles to the south. This impact site, 560 feet deep and almost a mile across, is one of the world's largest. Films and exhibits at the Astrogeological Museum on the rim detail how and why the collision occurred nearly 50,000 years ago, while the Astronaut Hall of Fame demonstrates the crater's use as a mock moon surface for Apollo mission training. A 3.5-mile Rim Trail encircles the crater, but entry into the depression is forbidden.

For more information, write to Meteor Crater Enterprises, 603 North Beaver Street, Flagstaff, AZ 86001.

Go eastward on I-40 through Winslow and Holbrook. Both towns contain campgrounds with shower and laundry facilities. Backcountry camping is available at Petrified Forest National Park. The Painted Desert Wilderness north of I-40 and the smaller Rainbow Forest Wilderness in the south part of the park offer opportunities to explore unique areas. Information and permits are obtainable at the Painted Desert Visitor Center, Painted Desert Inn Museum, and Rainbow Forest Museum.

Day 3: PETRIFIED FOREST TO
CANYON DE CHELLY

- **Seeing petrified logs and Anasazi rock art**
- **Admiring handicrafts at Hubbell Trading Post**
- **Camping at Canyon de Chelly National Monument**
- **Gas and groceries available in Ganado and Chinle**

The **Petrified Forest** and **Painted Desert**, combined in one national park, straddle I-40 east of Holbrook (see map, p. 186). Although the main attraction is petrified wood, prehistoric Indian ruins and rock art are also scattered through these gray, pink, and orange Chinle Formation badlands. Petrified wood develops when dead trees saved from normal processes of decay are invaded by mineral-bearing waters that gradually replace the trees' cellular material with cryptocrystalline structures, such as those found in agate or jasper. Please don't take pieces of petrified wood as souvenirs; the Park Service estimates that over ten tons of it are pilfered annually.

Scenic Drive: Petrified Forest/Painted Desert

Distance: 28 miles one way
Time: 4 hours or more, with stops

Numerous short trails, all easy or very easy, branch off from the scenic drive. At the southern end, where the petrified wood is concentrated, the Rainbow Forest Museum has exhibits on the geologic and

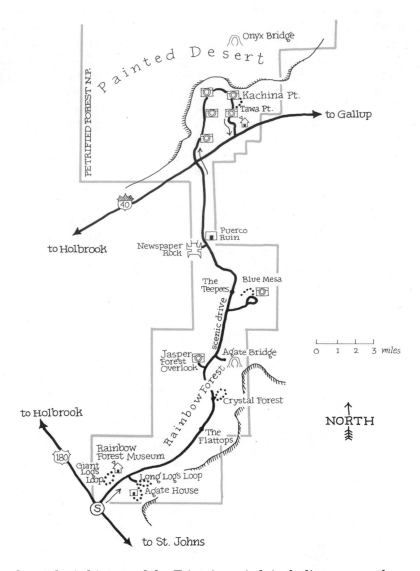

paleontologic history of the Triassic period, including one on the evolution of dinosaurs. The **Giant Logs Loop** (0.5 mile), which originates here, displays some outstanding specimens, including Old Faithful Log. Up the road, the paved **Long Logs Loop** (0.5 mile) visits the park's largest collection of petrified logs; from the same parking lot a 1-mile round-trip trail departs for **Agate House,** an Anasazi dwelling constructed of petrified wood. This area is open midday to vehicles and by foot from the Rainbow Forest Museum parking lot at other times.

Farther north, past the Flattops—low mesas that yield views of the Rainbow Forest—is the **Crystal Forest,** where a 0.75-mile loop trail traverses an area of petrified logs filled with amethyst quartz crystals. From the **Jasper Forest Overlook,** the next stop along the scenic drive, visitors can observe huge numbers of petrified logs strewn throughout the valley below. The next stop on the right is **Agate Bridge,** created when both ends of a petrified log became embedded in sandstone. Off a spur road to **Blue Mesa,** a 1-mile loop trail descends steeply into erosion-scoured, sedimentary badlands. Closer to the highway, opposite each other, are **Newspaper Rock** and **Puerco Pueblo.** An overlook provides views of Newspaper Rock, with its array of fascinating petroglyphs, probably left by peoples who later migrated east to Zuni and west to the Hopi mesas. Puerco Pueblo, near the river of the same name, is a largely unexcavated 75-room community with more petroglyphs below it.

North of I-40, the loop road through the Painted Desert leads to numerous overlooks. A very easy 1.25-mile trail connects Kachina and Tawa Points. Past Kachina Point is the visitor center. **Kachina Point** is a favorite departure place for backpackers. Although no wilderness hiking trails exist in the park, limitless cross-country opportunities beckon. Destinations include the dark petrified stumps of the Black Forest, including a standing stump; Pilot Rock, a volcanic butte; and Wildhorse Wash. Backcountry permits are available at the Painted Desert Visitor Center.

For further information, write to the Superintendent, Petrified Forest National Park, P.O. Box 2217, AZ 86028.

When your tour of the park is over, travel east on I-40 for 23 miles to Chambers. Turning north on US-191, drive 73.5 miles to Chinle, on the outskirts of Canyon de Chelly, and pitch your tent at Cottonwood Campground. Along the way, make a stop at **Hubbell National Historic Site** in Ganado; for details, see Chapter 5, the Anasazi Loop, Day 2.

Day 4: CANYON DE CHELLY TO
NAVAJO NATIONAL MONUMENT

- **Anasazi cliff dwellings**
- **Hopi villages**
- **Camping at Navajo National Monument**
- **Gas, groceries, showers, and laundry available in Tuba City**

Devote this morning to **Canyon de Chelly,** stopping at overlooks and hiking 2.5 miles round trip to **White House Ruin.** See Day 2 of Chapter 5, the Anasazi Loop, for a full description.

After Canyon de Chelly, proceed to the Hopi Reservation by backtracking 30 miles on US-191 to AZ-264 and heading west toward Tuba City. The Hopi population of about 10,000 is concentrated on three fingers of Black Mesa. First Mesa is considered the reservation's pottery-making capital. A cultural center on Second Mesa (57.25 miles down AZ-264) acquaints visitors with Hopi history and crafts. There is a small admission charge.

The Hopis, a very traditional people, do not normally charge admission fees, but neither do they normally allow photography or sketching in their villages. Third Mesa's Shungopavi and some of the other twelve Hopi towns discourage contacts with outsiders; in fact, the ancient pueblo of Oraibi—the oldest continuously inhabited settlement in the United States (dating back to A.D. 1150)—was once declared off-limits to visitors. Most villages do allow people who register at the village office to walk their grounds, provided they behave respectfully and follow the rules. Currently, outsiders are not permitted to attend the tribe's sacred dances.

One particularly interesting Hopi community is First Mesa's Walpi, situated on a ridge so narrow that it will accommodate just two rows of buildings. Walpi is the only Hopi settlement offering guided walks. The walks, which last 20 to 30 minutes, run on a regular schedule from 9:00 A.M. to 5:30 P.M. in season. Check at the village information booth for details.

For more information, contact the Hopi Cultural Center, P.O. Box 67, Second Mesa, AZ 86043.

Tuba City, one of the larger communities on the Navajo lands surrounding the Hopi Reservation, is a good place to purchase 3 days' worth of food before turning right (north) on US-160. At tiny Black Mesa, a coal-mining center 51.5 miles distant, go left onto AZ-564, winding through a slickrock wilderness for 9.5 miles to Navajo National Monument. Camp here.

Day 5: BETATAKIN

- **Day-hiking to a marvelously well-preserved ruin**
- **Camping at Navajo National Monument**
- **Gas, groceries, and laundry available at Black Mesa**

If you want to visit cliff dwellings but the crowds at Mesa Verde leave you cold, **Navajo National Monument** may be your kind of place. In addition to countless smaller sites, it protects Keet Seel (the largest in Arizona) and Betatakin. As mentioned previously, the Navajos are culturally and genetically unrelated to the Anasazi; the national monument's name refers only to the surrounding reservation.

Be at the visitor center when it opens at 8:00 A.M. to register for today's hike to Betatakin and tomorrow's backpack trip to Keet Seel. Since only a limited number of permits to tour Keet Seel are available, call for reservations (520-672-2366) 2 months in advance, reconfirming

Steps leading to unforgettable Betatakin Ruin

a week before your visit. You can always go to the visitor center on the morning you wish to hike, hoping to replace someone who fails to appear. Keet Seel is open between Memorial Day and Labor Day.

For more information, write to the Superintendent, Navajo National Monument, HC 71, Box 3, Tonalea, AZ 86044-9704.

———

Day Hike: Betatakin Ruin (ranger-led only)

> **Distance: 5 miles round trip**
> **Time: 5 to 6 hours**
> **Difficulty: moderate**

During the summer months, ranger-guided tours, filled on a first-come, first-served basis, leave twice daily for **Betatakin** (Navajo for "ledge house"). Obtain a ticket at the visitor center at 8:00 A.M. After walking to the rim of Tsegi Canyon, you descend about 700 feet to the 135-room apartment building, located in the forest in a magnificent, vaulting amphitheater. Erected in the late thirteenth century, this multilevel dwelling was first seen by non-Indians (John Wetherill's party) in 1909.

Take note of the rock art to the right of the ruin. Betatakin is also visible from an overlook at the end of the very easy **Sandal Trail** (1 mile round trip) that originates at the visitor center.

Days 6 and 7: KEET SEEL

- **Hiking past waterfalls in deep desert canyons**
- **Admiring a superlative ruin**
- **Camping at Keet Seel and Monument Valley**
- **Gas, groceries, showers, and laundry available in Kayenta**

Unlike the Betatakin trip, the 8.5-mile hike to Keet Seel is unguided (though some people hire horses and local Navajo escorts through the monument headquarters). A ranger is stationed at Keet Seel, however, to accompany visitors inside the ruin. At the visitor center, obtain a required hiking permit, a trail map, and instructions for finding the trailhead. The proximity of the ruin to a usually reliable spring enables you to carry just 2 or 3 quarts of water apiece on the trip.

At the conclusion of this hike, drive back to US-160, the main road through the northern part of the Navajo Reservation, and turn left toward Kayenta. The highway snakes through a dramatic desert landscape. In Kayenta, head north on US-163 past **Owl Rock** on the left and **Agathla Peak** (aka El Capitan), a volcanic plug, on the right. Your destination will be Monument Valley, which straddles the Utah-Arizona border. Turn right into this Navajo Tribal Park and set up camp on Day 7.

Backpack: Keet Seel Ruin

> **Distance: 17 miles round trip**
> **Time: 2 days**
> **Difficulty: moderate**

At the start of the trail is a steep, 1000-foot descent into a canyon over rock and sand. On the canyon floor, you follow a stream course most of the way, passing four small waterfalls as well as some intriguing rock formations and climbing about 400 feet in the last 5.5 miles. The stream has cut an arroyo whose sides restrict your views. The wash bottom is mostly sand, with possible pockets of quicksand. Don't drink water from the wash, which has been polluted by grazing livestock; wait to replenish your supply at the spring, near the ruin.

Drop your gear at the camping area and approach the ranger's cabin for an extensive tour of **Keet Seel,** situated under a cavernous Navajo Sandstone overhang where the canyon opens up. This unforgettable site, with its 165 rooms, was "discovered" by Richard Wetherill; its name is from the Navajo word for "broken pottery." To prevent damage to the fragile cliff-dwelling, ranger-guided tours—which last about an hour—are limited to five people. The ranger will also direct you to the spring. Rise early tomorrow for the return to your car.

Day 8: MONUMENT VALLEY

- **Touring spectacular desert landscape**
- **Setting up a boat or backpack trip**
- **Camping near Navajo Mountain or Lake Powell**
- **Gas, groceries, showers, and laundry available in Kayenta**

Today's uncrowded itinerary allows you to enjoy a leisurely swing through **Monument Valley** (see Chapter 5, Anasazi Loop, Day 3) before preparing for the trip to Rainbow Bridge. You will have to decide whether to visit Rainbow Bridge on foot or by boat so that you can make the necessary arrangements. At the conclusion of your Monument Valley tour, backtrack to Kayenta. If you are planning to hike to Rainbow Bridge, buy groceries here for 4 nights and fill all available canteens.

In Kayenta, go west on US-160 for 31.5 miles, until you come to AZ-98. Turn right onto this spectacular road, which crosses a high plateau before dropping down to Lake Powell.

Those who are taking the boat trip to Rainbow Bridge should continue on AZ-98 all the way to Page. Arrange for tomorrow's full-day excursion at the lodge at **Wahweap Marina,** northwest of town on US-89, where it may also be convenient to camp both tonight and

Monument Valley road winds past East and West Mitten Buttes.

tomorrow. All services are available in Page. On Day 10, plan to drive 110 miles from Wahweap to Zion National Park on US-89 West and UT-9. Consult Chapter 7, Canyons Loop, Days 1 through 3, for hiking suggestions. Return to Page on the morning of Day 13, and head as directed to the South Rim of the Grand Canyon.

Those who are backpacking to Rainbow Bridge should drive about 12.25 miles northwest on AZ-98 from the US-160 junction. Turn right onto the unpaved Navajo Mountain Road (Route 16), whose condition varies from year to year and even day to day. Continue on this road for about 35 miles, past Inscription House Trading Post. The road will then fork.

Which way you should go at the fork depends on whether you prefer to combine the North and South Rainbow Trails or to hike to the bridge on one or the other of them and double back. (The North Rainbow Trail is 28.5 miles round trip, while the South is 26.5.) Combining the trails requires a car shuttle, but hikers without two cars may be able to arrange a ride at a local trading post (see below). For the combination hike, it is wise to start on the South Rainbow Trail and end on the North.

To reach the South Rainbow Trail, turn left at the big fork mentioned above. Drive for about 5 miles, passing a barn to the left and a house on the right. Turn right just before a large sandstone dome. The road gets very rough, and it might be advisable to walk these last 2.5 miles to the trailhead at Rainbow Lodge ruin.

To get to the North Rainbow Trail, turn right at the fork mentioned above and proceed to the Navajo Mountain School and Trading Post, 6 miles away. About 4 miles past the trading post is a T intersection with another dirt road near a butte named Navajo Begay. There are several buildings at this junction. Continue straight ahead for about 3 miles to a Y in the road. Bear left here. Where the road descends a slope, it deteriorates badly and should be attempted only in a 4-wheel-drive vehicle. The small Cha Canyon parking lot, 2 miles from the Y, is where the North Rainbow Trail begins.

Camp tonight near your chosen trailhead.

Days 9–12: RAINBOW BRIDGE

- **Unexcelled desert scenery**
- **A world-famous natural span**
- **Camping in watery canyons along the trail**

This backpack trip would be well worth the effort even without the opportunity to savor Rainbow Bridge, 275 feet across. Together, the South and North Rainbow Trails nearly encircle 10,400-foot-high Navajo Mountain, considered sacred and referred to as "head of the earth" by traditional Indians. At the base of this isolated peak lies some of the most rugged and magnificent redrock wilderness in the Southwest.

Because this hike is on the Navajo Reservation, a permit is required. Fees are charged. Obtain permits from the Navajo Tourism Office, P.O. Box 308, Window Rock, AZ 86515. Bring along enough canteens (at least a 1-gallon capacity per person) and some way to purify water, since this is grazing country.

When your hike is over, drive to Page on US-98 for supplies, and camp at Wahweap Marina, where showers are available.

For more information, contact the Superintendent, Glen Canyon National Recreation Area, P.O. Box 1507, Page, AZ 86040.

Backpack: South and North Rainbow Trails

> **Distance: 27.5 miles one way**
> **Time: 4 days**
> **Map: topo for Navajo Mountain**
> **Difficulty: very strenuous**

The **South Rainbow Trail** begins at a group of dilapidated stone buildings called Rainbow Lodge, once a dude operation owned by the Goldwater family (see map, p. 194). A large cairn indicates the trailhead, and red mileposts mark the entire route. In the first 5 miles, expect many tiring ups and downs as you cross the arms of First and Horse Canyons. Be careful not to lose the trail as you approach Sunset (aka Yabut) Pass at mile 5, which offers astounding views into **Cliff Canyon,**

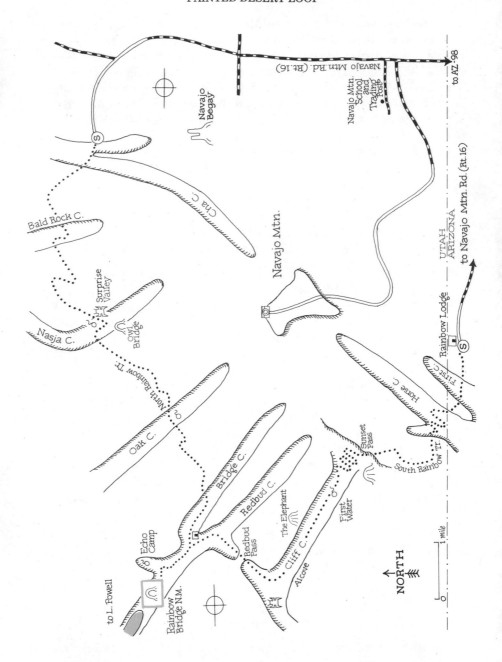

1600 feet below. The 2-mile descent into Cliff is steep and rocky, but the canyon's incredibly lovely lower reaches make up for it. First Water Campsite, at mile 8, has flowing springs, and sometimes even small pools. The more scenic campsites, however, are a mile farther on, near the junction with Redbud Pass Canyon, where deep alcoves provide shelter.

You can't miss the junction at mile 9 with the first sizable side-canyon to the right, opposite a massive alcove and not far past a slickrock dome called the Elephant. Hunt for Anasazi rock art 50 yards to the left of the junction. Turn right up this side-canyon, which gets progressively narrower as it climbs toward **Redbud Pass,** at mile 9.5. The pass was blasted out in 1922 by John Wetherill, who led the first party of white men to visit Rainbow Bridge. The trail goes through a narrow cleft to extraordinary Redbud Canyon at mile 10. Turn left and walk downstream. Near a small ruin at mile 11, Redbud Canyon meets Bridge Canyon; the South Rainbow Trail forks left, heading downstream. After a while, Bridge Canyon dives deeply into the earth. Here the trail ascends slightly up to the right bank of the arroyo and remains on this shoulder the rest of the way. In about 0.25 mile you can see the bridge down the canyon. Immediately thereafter, a spur trail to the right leads to Echo Camp at mile 13—a grotto marred by the remains of a horse camp. Some good springs are here.

From this point, it's a flat, easy walk down the main trail to **Rainbow Bridge.** Composed of Navajo Sandstone, this is among the largest formations of its kind in the world. At high-water levels, Lake Powell backs up under the span. Other tourists come to within 0.25 mile of the bridge by boat. Nearby is a plaque honoring Nasja, the

Navajo Mountain's slopes provide a backdrop for Rainbow Bridge.

Paiute guide who assisted Wetherill. Although no camping is allowed in the postage-stamp-sized national monument, you can pitch your tent within a short distance of the bridge and springs.

To return via the **North Rainbow Trail,** backtrack up Bridge Canyon and take the left fork at the Redbud Canyon junction. Although the next 2 miles are steeper than the section near the bridge, good campsites do exist in this area. Be careful not to lose the trail here. It goes up a side-canyon to the left and onto the slickrock rim. You may find a fair amount of water in upper Bridge Canyon as well as in some or all of the systems to the east: Oak, Nasja, Bald Rock, and Cha. Between these drainages you're usually walking on benchlands, enjoying phenomenal views.

The trail to Oak Canyon (5 miles from Rainbow Bridge) is faint and often difficult to follow. This V-shaped canyon offers cool mountain water to refresh thirsty hikers. Three miles farther is Nasja Canyon, the biggest and most beautiful on the North Rainbow Trail. Plentiful water makes camping excellent here. There is a picnic table close to **Owl Bridge,** a natural span. Climbing out of Nasja Canyon toward Surprise Valley, look for a Navajo drawing of a horse on the wall just above the trail.

Bald Rock Canyon, 2.5 miles past Nasja, has a small, unnamed arch to your right and some good places to camp. After Bald Rock, cross two arms of Cha Canyon in the next 3 miles. When the trail forks, about a mile before the end, go right. The second arm of Cha Canyon is shallow where you cross it. Immediately beyond, a large rockpile marks the parking lot.

Day 13: PAGE TO SOUTH RIM, GRAND CANYON

- **Gazing into the abyss**
- **Easy day-hiking on nature trails**
- **Camping at Grand Canyon National Park**
- **Gas, groceries, showers, and laundry are available in Page**

From Page, take US-89 south 82 miles through the Navajo Reservation to Cameron. Turn west on AZ-64, a road that follows the Little Colorado River to Desert View, where you enjoy your first dizzying peek into that wonder of wonders, the **Grand Canyon.**

Carved by the Colorado River over millennia as the plateau was uplifted, this 277-mile-long gash in the earth defies description. Nothing can ready you for how it feels to stand on the rim and contemplate the awesome gorge, with its magnificent side-canyons, high desert mountains flanking the river, and play of light and shadow on layered cliffs. As its explorer, Major John Wesley Powell, put it, the Grand Canyon is "a land of music" that "cannot be adequately represented by speech."

Found by the Spanish in the mid-sixteenth century, the canyon remained uncharted by white men until Powell's party made its historic boat trips down the Green and Colorado Rivers in 1869 and 1872. But Native American artifacts (including split-twig figurines of mule deer and bighorn sheep dating back to between 1600 and 2000 B.C.) have been found at certain of its 1000 archaeological sites, and the Havasupai Indians—whose ancestors constructed a number of trails from the rim to the river—still farm in the Supai area, west of the main park corridor.

Both the North and South Rims are developed, offering stores, restaurants, lodges, showers, gas stations, hotels, and campgrounds. The South Rim in particular has the feel of a miniature city, and a very cosmopolitan one, drawing visitors from every corner of the earth. In summer, the Park Service provides free bus service several times an hour to viewpoints between Bright Angel Lodge and Hermits Rest; you can disembark at any stop and catch a later bus to resume your tour. By contrast, the North Rim is more remote and consequently much less crowded, though perhaps no less regulated. But both rims offer what you came for: awe-inspiring overlooks, rewarding nature trails, and the chance to descend thousands of feet into the canyon, reading the earth's history as you go.

Because Mather Campground at Grand Canyon Village fills up very early in the day, either make advance reservations (a new reservation system should be functioning by the spring of 1999) or proceed to the campground immediately upon your arrival. If Mather Camp-ground is full, sites may still be open at Desert View or in the Kaibab National Forest off AZ-64 South. Rooms can be rented on either rim, though they generally must be booked well ahead.

Stop along South Rim Drive at places such as Tusayan Ruins and Museum and Lipan, Moran, Grandview, Yaki, and Yavapai Points. If you wish to backpack into the canyon, secure a required permit from the ranger station. The Park Service recommends making reservations months in advance for popular trails, but you might luck into a cancellation.

Two other options also require advance planning. The first is riding on muleback to Phantom Ranch, the rustic lodge near the floor of the canyon, and spending a night or two there before returning to the rim. Young children and persons weighing over 200 pounds are ineligible for mule trips. The second is taking a commercial, multiday white-water rafting trip down the river, beginning at Lees Ferry, Arizona.

For further information, write to Trip Planner, Grand Canyon National Park, P.O. Box 129, Grand Canyon, AZ 86023, or Grand Canyon National Park Lodges, c/o Amfac Parks and Resorts, 14001 East Iliff, Aurora, CO 80014 (call 303-279-2757 for reservations). The phone number of the Backcountry Reservation Office is (520) 638-2473, weekdays from 1:00 P.M. to 5:00 P.M. only; phone reservations are not accepted.

Day Hike: Rim Trail

Distance: up to 9 miles one way
Time: up to 1 day
Map: topo for Grand Canyon National Park
Difficulty: very easy

The **Rim Trail,** from Hermits Rest at the farthest west end of development to Yavapai Point where the park museum is located, has multiple accesses during the summer months, courtesy of the West Rim shuttle bus. You can therefore sample this incredibly scenic route in small portions. Since the bus does not run east of Yavapai Point, you'll have to walk back if you follow the trail beyond it. Probably the best sections are from Yavapai Point to the El Tovar Hotel (paved), Bright Angel Lodge to Maricopa Point (also paved), and the Abyss to Pima Point or Hermits Rest (unpaved); in all of these sections, the road is relatively far from the rim.

Days 14–17: INNER CANYON ADVENTURE

- **Selecting from various backpacking options**
- **Or riding a mule to Phantom Ranch**
- **Camping in the canyon**
- **Gas, groceries, showers, and laundry available in Grand Canyon Village**

The park's backcountry trails vary tremendously in length and difficulty and can be either maintained or unmaintained. Visitors should hike a maintained trail (either the Bright Angel or the Kaibab) before attempting any other routes; rangers question permit-seekers about prior experience and check for canteens and other essential gear.

Before venturing into the canyon, familiarize yourself with major rock strata through which you will be passing. In the vicinity of Grand Canyon Village, those layers are, from top to bottom: Kaibab Limestone (gray); the Toroweap Formation (very narrow, gray); Coconino Sandstone (white and sheer); the Hermit Shale and Supai Group (red and sloping); Redwall Limestone (red or light gray, thick and sheer); Bright Angel Shale (greenish gray, narrow and sloping); Tapeats Sandstone (brown and vertical, below the Tonto Rim); and the Vishnu Group (the black, jumbled rock of the Inner Gorge).

To journey into the Grand Canyon is to journey through geologic time. But it is also to journey toward the equator, because every 1000 feet of descent is equivalent to 300 miles of southward travel in regard to flora and fauna. This change is especially evident in the descent from the North Rim, which passes through the Canadian, Transition, Upper Sonoran, and Lower Sonoran life zones. Ecologically speaking,

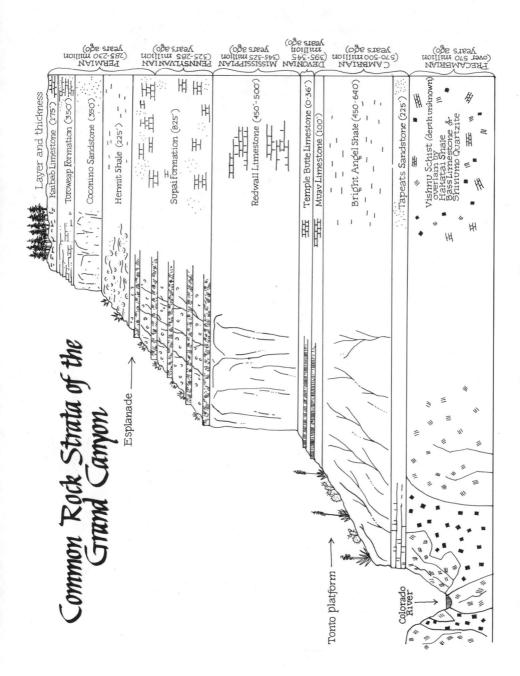

Common Rock Strata of the Grand Canyon

Layer and thickness

PERMIAN (285-230 million years ago)
Kaibab Limestone (175')
Toroweap Formation (350')
Coconino Sandstone (350')
Hermit Shale (225')

PENNSYLVANIAN (325-285 million years ago)
Supai formation (825')

MISSISSIPPIAN (345-325 million years ago)
Redwall Limestone (450'-500')

DEVONIAN (395-345 million years ago)
Temple Butte Limestone (0-36')

CAMBRIAN (570-500 million years ago)
Muav Limestone (100')
Bright Angel Shale (450-640')
Tapeats Sandstone (225')

PRECAMBRIAN (over 570 million years ago)
Vishnu Schist (depth unknown) overlain by Hakatai Shale Bass Limestone & Shinumo Quartzite

Esplanade

Tonto platform

Colorado River

the Grand Canyon hiker has gone from Canada to Mexico in only 14 miles! The change is less dramatic in descents from the South Rim, where the Upper Sonoran zone predominates.

But the most important thing about hiking the Grand Canyon is carrying enough water. This basic rule of all desert travel is even more imperative here, because of the often extreme heat and fatiguing hiking conditions (particularly on the ascent, which normally takes at least twice as long as the descent). A minimum of a gallon per person per day is essential, and it is sometimes advisable to exceed

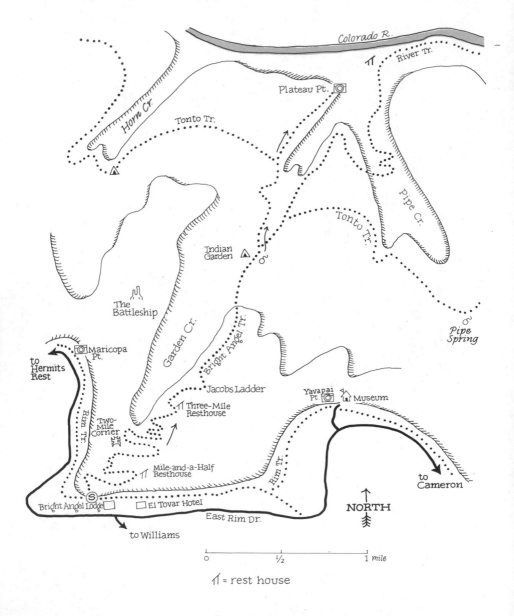

⩔ = rest house

this requirement, even to double it in the summer months when hiking completely dry trails.

Whatever you might choose to do, plan to camp on the South Rim on Day 17.

Backpack 1: Bright Angel Trail

> **Distance: 11.5 miles, round trip, to Plateau Point**
> **Time: 2 days**
> **Map: topo for Grand Canyon National Park**
> **Difficulty: strenuous**

The Bright Angel Trail, from Bright Angel Lodge on the South Rim down to Indian Garden Campground and the Colorado River (see map, p. 200), is the "easiest" and most popular inner canyon trail in the park. It receives heavy use not only from hikers but from mule parties going to or from Phantom Ranch, on the north side of the river. Expect your senses to be assaulted by equine droppings along the way, and when you encounter mule trains, quietly step aside (standing above the trail) to let them pass. From May through September, water is available at shelters erected by the Park Service. A year-round water source is 4.75 miles down the trail at **Indian Garden,** a creekside oasis shaded by cottonwoods, where the Havasupai once farmed. **Plateau Point,** a gently rolling mile past Indian Garden on the edge of the Inner Gorge, offers excellent river views.

Since the other hike outlined below finishes with an ascent of the Bright Angel, this trip will be described from the bottom up. Along the steep, wide trail from Indian Garden, you can look forward to two huts, complete with shade, emergency telephones, and (during the summer months) water. But, huts or no huts, even this easiest of Grand Canyon ascents can be exhausting, and in hot weather you should start before dawn. Your pack should be as light as possible for the climb, which usually takes 3 hours for a hiker in good condition, if begun early enough. Although higher means cooler in the Grand Canyon, the sun's increased strength as the morning wears on more than offsets any advantage gained from elevation.

The trail stays to the east side of the Garden Creek drainage for most of its route. Prominent formations visible on the ascent include Cheops Pyramid, the Battleship, Brahma Temple, and the Tower of Ra. Through the vertical Redwall, the trail consists of 500 feet of switchbacks called Jacobs Ladder. Three-Mile Resthouse beckons at the top of these switchbacks, where the Redwall meets the Supai Group. At Two-Mile Corner, look up at some light-colored rocks above the trail after a series of long switchbacks in the Supai; you may be able to spot a panel of Havasupai pictographs. Past here is Mile-and-a-Half Resthouse, in the Hermit Shale, and some tight switchbacks through the Coconino Sandstone layer. Near the end of the ascent, the trail

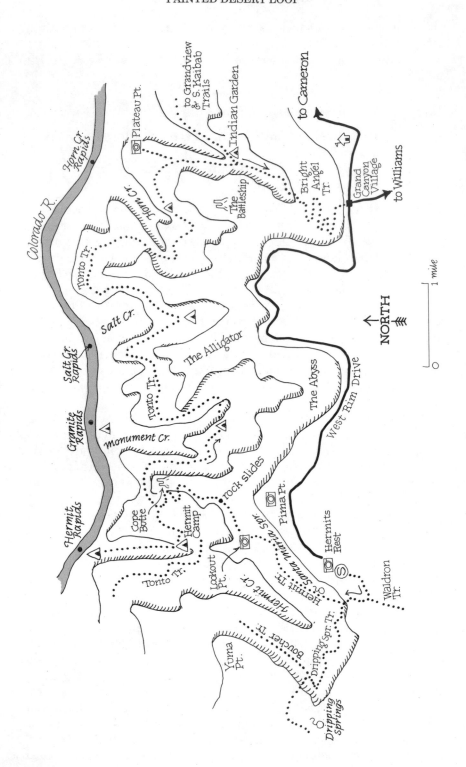

passes through Second Tunnel, in the Toroweap Formation, and First Tunnel, in the Kaibab Limestone stratum. Just below is more ancient rock art. At the top is the Bright Angel Lodge, where food and drink are sold.

An alternative to the double-back hike to Plateau Point is a 13-mile trip from Yaki Point, down the **South Kaibab Trail,** across the Tonto Platform and up the Bright Angel Trail. (That is the preferred direction, since the South Kaibab is waterless, and water sources are not as vital on the descent.) To make it a 3-day, 16.5-mile walk, spend the first night at Bright Angel Campground on the north side of the river and the second at Indian Garden. Reservations are needed for both.

———

Backpack 2: Hermit Trail to Grand Canyon Village

> **Distance: 26 miles, one way, including side trip to river**
> **Time: 4 days**
> **Map: topo for Grand Canyon National Park**
> **Difficulty: very strenuous**

The **Hermit Trail,** built for tourists by the Santa Fe Railroad Company early in this century, is by far the easiest of the nonmaintained routes from the rim to the river and also one of the most beautiful. The hike is a popular one and permits, obtainable in advance from the backcountry office, are required. Be sure to ask about water availability when you pick up your permit.

To begin the trip, park your car behind Bright Angel Lodge and catch the free shuttle bus to the trailhead at **Hermits Rest,** the westernmost stop on the run (see map, p. 202). Take either the first bus in the morning—a hikers' express—or one in the late afternoon, to avoid hiking in the midday sun. You might want to stop at Pima Point to gawk at most of your route into the canyon.

At Hermits Rest, walk less than 0.25 mile down a short service road toward the rim. Look for the trailhead sign. It is a 7.25-mile hike from here to Hermit Camp, and then another 1.5 miles to the river. Switchback through rocky terrain, bearing right at the intersections with the Waldron Trail and the trail to the bird-lover's paradise of **Dripping Springs** (at mile 1.75). The latter connects with a difficult, unmaintained route down to the river via Boucher Creek. (Louis Boucher was the hermit for whom the trail was named; headquartered at Dripping Springs, this French Canadian prospected in the canyon for over 15 years.)

After the trail junctions, descend to Santa Maria Spring, which has water and a small shelter. The trail skirts the eastern edge of Hermit Creek gorge. By now you have entered the Supai Group. Fourmile Spring, noted on the topo map, ran dry many years ago.

A hiker enjoys solitude and unmatched beauty along the Tonto Trail.

The trail switchbacks down to Lookout Point, which offers splendid views of the temples and canyons across the river. Around a bend is a long, gently sloping section of trail. Soon you come to a potentially hazardous area, where rock slides have damaged the trail; follow a cairned route through the rubble. A short distance from the rock slides is the big Redwall descent at mile 5. The steep switchbacks here, on the west side of Cope Butte, are called the Cathedral Stairs. At the bottom of yet another set of switchbacks is the **Tonto Rim** (mile 6) and the junction with the Tonto Trail. Bear left and continue for 1.25 miles until you drop into the creekbed and arrive at **Hermit Camp,** a pleasant, "improved" campground with water and a toilet.

The 1.5-mile hike from Hermit Camp to the Colorado River is delightful and unchallenging. This route starts a short distance back up the Hermit Trail and follows the bed of Hermit Creek down to the river. Unless the year has been particularly dry, you may find pools along the way. The beach at the river is extremely rocky and not good for swimming, but it's fun to watch rafts negotiate the fierce Hermit Rapids formed by a boulder fan at the creek's mouth.

From Hermit Camp, backtrack to the junction with the Tonto Trail and turn left (east), heading up Cope Butte rather precipitously. The trail follows the lip of **Monument Canyon** for some distance before dropping into the drainage about 3.5 miles past Hermit Camp. The scenic beauty of this part of the trip is unexcelled, affording haunting views of the Inner Gorge. Monument Creek is named for a tall spire that dominates its upper reaches. Good campsites are in the main canyon just past this spire, as well as a probable water supply and a (rather exposed) outhouse. With care, you can reach the river from here and watch boats shoot Granite Rapids.

The Tonto Trail goes past a Sphinx-like formation and out the east arm of Monument Creek. Back on the Tonto Rim, it swings around a formation called the Alligator. Above is the Abyss, a beautiful red amphitheater. Salt Creek, the next major drainage, 3.5 miles past Monument, is a hydra-headed monster that takes a while to circumambulate. Four miles later comes the similar Horn Creek system. Reaching the river from either canyon is difficult, but sometimes nearby springs are flowing; check with the ranger. About 1.5 miles past Horn Creek the trail forks. Drop your pack and hike down the trail to the left to appreciate the outstanding vistas from Plateau Point.

Back at the fork, turn the other way and within a mile or so reach the campground at **Indian Garden**, where you'll find cottonwoods, fireplaces, toilets, and crowds of people. Most hikers reserve a campsite here in anticipation of the arduous ascent to the rim. Travelers able to afford the accommodations at Phantom Ranch may wish to arrange to stay there. Others may prefer to walk across one of the two suspension bridges over the Inner Gorge and sleep at Bright Angel Camp. This excursion adds about 10 round-trip miles to the hike, and an extra day or two should be allotted for it. It involves joining the **River Trail** in the Inner Gorge, which connects with the North Kaibab on the other side of the Colorado.

Day 18: WUPATKI AND HOME

- **Contemplating Sinagua ruins**
- **Visiting Sunset Crater**
- **Optional climb of Humphreys Peak**
- **Gas, groceries, showers, and laundry available in Flagstaff**

To start this last day of the travel circuit, drive east 51.5 miles on AZ-64 to Cameron and turn south on US-89. Continue for 20.5 miles,

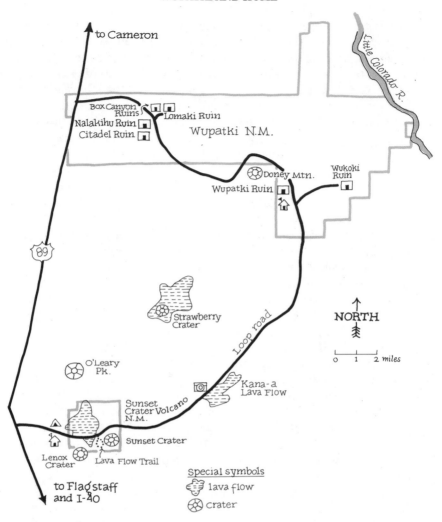

bearing left onto the 36-mile road connecting Wupatki and Sunset Crater National Monuments (see map, above).

The Wupatki–Sunset Crater area was once a cultural meeting-ground for the Sinagua, Anasazi, and Cohonina tribes. The national monuments protect close to 2700 Neolithic ruins, a few of which are open to the public. Because of the fragility and historical and scientific value of these sites, the backcountry is closed to hiking and camping without official permission.

The first attraction along the northern end of the scenic drive is **Lomaki** (meaning "beautiful house" in Hopi), a multistory apartment building at the end of a 0.5-mile spur road. Box Canyon Ruins are nearby. A short distance farther down the main loop road, on the right, one can visit **Citadel Ruin,** a relatively large, unexcavated complex.

Monument Canyon derives its name from a tall spire.

Positioned on a knoll composed of volcanic rock, it grants fine views of the lofty San Francisco Peaks and surrounding countryside. Adjacent to Citadel Ruin is the Nalakihu site ("house standing alone"). At the visitor center, near the southern end of the monument, is the most extensive and interesting cluster, **Wupatki** ("tall house"). This magnificent, well-preserved surface site features a large outdoor amphitheater and a smaller, elliptical structure thought to have been a ball court. Ball courts were widely used by Mesoamerican indigenous peoples like the Mayas and Toltecs; the presence of a ball court here attests to the vast reach of those peoples' cultural influence. About 0.25 mile from the visitor center, a 3-mile spur road on the left leads to **Wukoki** ("wide house"). All the above buildings were constructed in the early thirteenth century.

Leaving Wupatki National Monument, the loop road skirts the Kana-a Lava Flow before entering Sunset Crater Volcano National Monument. **Sunset Crater,** a black and red cinder cone, was formed almost 1000 years ago. Ash deposited during the eruption made for improved farming for the area's native peoples and may have attracted additional immigrants. Although tourists are not allowed to scale the 1000-foot-high cone, they can hike to its base on the very easy, mile-long **Lava Flow Trail,** which includes a stop at a lava tube. For further information, write to the Superintendent, Flagstaff Areas National Park Service, 2717 North Steves Boulevard, Suite 3, Flagstaff, AZ 86004.

From Sunset Crater, proceed south on US-89 for 12.25 miles to Flagstaff and the road home. If you can spare another day, consider climbing **Humphreys Peak,** a member of the San Francisco chain and the highest mountain in the state, at 12,625 feet. The strenuous, 9-mile round trip, involving a 3150-foot ascent, begins near the Fairfield Snow Bowl northwest of Flagstaff, off US-180. Dress warmly. Close to the top, the trail forks; Humphreys Peak is on the left, with Agassiz Peak (closed much of the year for ecological reasons) on the right. Alternatively, you can opt to backpack an 18-mile circuit on the Humphreys, Weatherford, and Kachina Peak trails. Check with the Coconino National Forest at (520) 556-7400 about camping restrictions.

Chapter 7

CANYONS LOOP

Utah, Arizona

Backpackers seeking memorable wilderness adventures will find this loop especially appealing. But it contains enough day-hiking and car exploring to keep everyone else busy, too. Its star attractions are the "big three" of the western Colorado Plateau: Zion, Bryce, and Grand Canyon National Parks. The ready availability of services and facilities also recommends this loop.

Day 1: ST. GEORGE TO ZION

- **Easy day hikes to pools, springs, and narrows**
- **Camping at Zion National Park**
- **Gas, groceries, showers, and laundry available in St. George**

St. George, population 40,000, makes a good jumping-off point for this loop. Located on I-15, in the extreme southwestern corner of Utah, this gateway community offers numerous services to the visitor. It is an attractive resort town where Brigham Young, the early Mormon leader, preferred to spend his winters. (Not his summers, though; at under 3000 feet elevation, St. George can get uncomfortably hot in July and August.)

St. George is about 39 miles from Zion's South Entrance (see map, p. 210). Go north on I-15 to the exit for Hurricane on UT-9, a road that continues through the park. Just past the entrance station, pull into one of the two large campgrounds and find a spot to spend the night—preferably a sheltered spot, to avoid being sandblasted by gusty canyon winds that blow up like clockwork in late afternoon. Once this chore is completed, begin your tour of the park.

Zion National Park is Yosemite painted red, a crowded but otherwise unblemished paradise that lives up to its name. The dominant rock strata in this 147,000-acre preserve are Navajo Sandstone and the Kayenta Formation. The park's main road snakes through the bottom of the lush, spectacular canyon carved into the Markagunt Plateau by the North Fork of the **Virgin River,** a tributary of the Colorado. Over 150 miles of trails branch off in every direction, leading to desert waterfalls, hanging gardens, narrow canyons, cool pools and grottoes, and dazzling overlooks. Wildlife is varied: Zion's larger mammals include the cougar, mule deer, elk, desert bighorn, and fox. Only a portion of the Virgin's East Fork, called **Parunuweap** ("raging waters" in Ute), is protected within the park; this canyon is now set aside as a "research natural area" and closed to the public.

Visitors who enter the park from the south should drive around to the East Entrance, at almost 6000 feet, just for the scenery. UT-9 switchbacks up Pine Creek past the **Great Arch** (really an alcove) from the floor to the rim of the canyon. It braves a dark, mile-long tunnel constructed in the 1920s and winds among cross-bedded sandstone domes. Of these, **Checkerboard Mesa** is the best known.

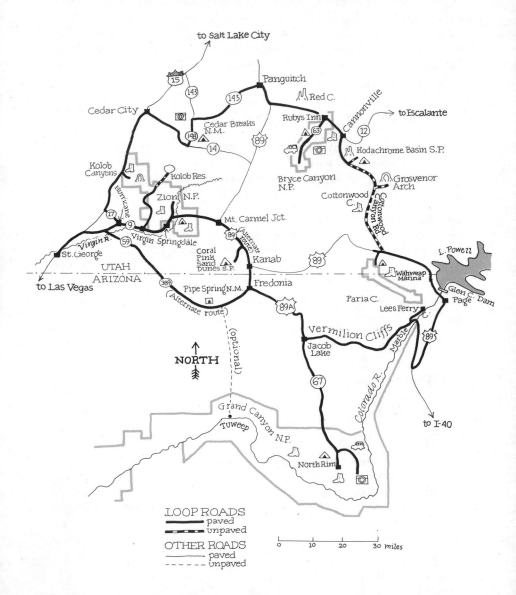

Rim-walking Zion's canyons yields spectacular vistas.

From the parking lot beyond the tunnel departs the easy **Canyon Overlook Trail** (1 mile round trip); this nature trail, which is rather exposed despite protective guardrails, ends at a perch above the Great Arch, with exciting views of the western part of Zion Canyon.

The Park Service plans to close Zion Canyon to private automobiles beginning in the year 2000. Shuttle buses running from Springdale and from Watchman Campground will transport visitors to trailheads and scenic attractions.

Today's recommended itinerary involves travel on the scenic drive through Zion Canyon (12 miles round trip), with hikes to Weeping Rock, Emerald Pools, and the Virgin River gorge—all very popular destinations. Before the day is through, obtain a camping permit for one of tomorrow's backpacking options, the East or West Rim hikes. Both require a car shuttle or some equivalent; inquire at Zion Lodge.

For more information, write to the Superintendent, Zion National Park, Springdale, UT 84767.

———

Day Hike 1: Emerald Pools

> **Distance: 2.5 miles round trip**
> **Time: 2 hours**
> **Map: topo for Zion National Park**
> **Difficulty: very easy to Lower Pool; moderate**
>   **thereafter**

Trails originating at both Zion Lodge and the Grotto Picnic Area lead to two idyllic pools (see map, p. 212). **Lower Pool** is only 0.5 mile

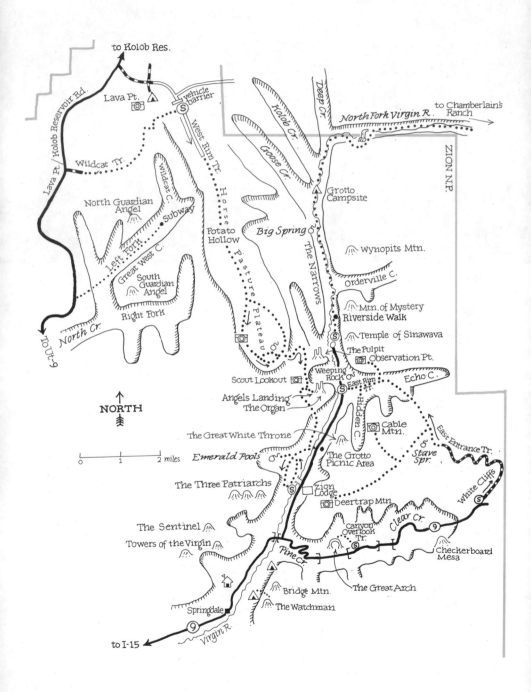

from the lodge. Cross a footbridge over the river and turn right, following a paved path. At Lower Pool, you will pass under some gossamer waterfalls. **Upper Pool,** reached by a picturesque but rocky and steep 350-foot ascent, lies 0.5 mile farther on. There is a small beach where you can relax; take care on the uneven, slippery terrain. On the descent, locate an alternate 1-mile trail beginning 0.25 mile below Upper Pool on the right, for the return to the lodge.

Day Hike 2: Weeping Rock

> **Distance: 0.5 mile round trip**
> **Time: 0.5 hour or less**
> **Map: topo for Zion National Park**
> **Difficulty: easy**

This paved trail to a "raining" spring surrounded by hanging gardens begins about 2 miles up the road from Zion Lodge, on the right (see map, p. 212). Initially, the route coincides with the East Rim Trail, but it immediately veers off to the left just across the bridge and wends its way over to the cliffs, climbing steadily. The spring water has been filtered through hundreds of feet of sandstone.

Day Hike 3: Riverside Walk

> **Distance: 2 miles round trip**
> **Time: 1.5 hours**
> **Map: topo for Zion National Park**
> **Difficulty: very easy**

The walk on this paved, level trail—formerly called "Gateway to the Narrows"—begins at the Temple of Sinawava parking lot, at the end of the scenic drive (see map, p. 212). It follows the right bank of the Virgin River, whose canyon walls progressively close in. This lush gorge teems with life: dark green ferns, babbling springs, and miniature gardens of wildflowers. Most people turn back at a rocky viewpoint beyond which the canyon is too constricted to accommodate a trail. But the intrepid continue upstream, wading through the rushing river over slippery rocks. This practice is safe only when water levels are low and no flash flood danger exists. Walking sticks are recommended.

Day Hike 4: Watchman Trail

> **Distance: 3 miles round trip**
> **Time: 2 hours**
> **Map: topo for Zion National Park**
> **Difficulty: easy to moderate**

To reach the trailhead, turn left at the trail sign just past the RV dump station in Watchman Campground, and follow the road a short distance.

The trail ascends 350 feet on well-engineered switchbacks to the top of a plateau. A short loop here provides views in all directions. Since this is a low-elevation trail offering little shade, during the summer months it is best attempted in early morning or evening. Return as you came.

Days 2 and 3: CANYON RIM BACKPACK

- **Hiking Zion's East or West Rim**
- **Camping near a canyon overlook**
- **Gas, groceries, showers, and laundry available in Springdale**

The low-mileage, overnight backpacking alternatives presented below start on high plateaus and end in Zion Canyon. Either is excellent preparation for more ambitious trips to come. You can day-hike portions of these trails from the canyon floor, but be warned that substantial elevation gains make that option quite demanding. By contrast, the backpacking routes are mainly downhill. Backpackers should carry about 1.5 gallons of water apiece in the summer months. Since water

Trees silhouetted against Zion's pale cliffs

availability from springs varies both annually and seasonally, make the appropriate inquiries at the visitor center when obtaining your permit. Arrange for a shuttle, if necessary, at Zion Lodge. Plan to stay in one of the park's campgrounds at the conclusion of the hike. A day trip to the Subway, in the Left Fork of North Creek, is also described below for people seeking a rugged, off-trail experience.

Backpack 1: West Rim Trail

> **Distance: 15.25 miles, one way, including side trip to Angels Landing**
> **Time: 2 days**
> **Map: topo for Zion National Park**
> **Difficulty: moderate, with strenuous, exposed climb to Angels Landing**

This magnificent and varied hike to the rim and then the floor of Zion Canyon—a 3000-foot descent—begins near Lava Point, about an hour's drive north of Zion Lodge (see map, p. 212). If you are shuttling cars, leave one at the Grotto Picnic Area, where the hike concludes.

To reach the trailhead, drive west through Springdale on UT-9 to the town of Virgin. Turn right (north) onto a spectacularly scenic road, which climbs into heavy timber toward Kolob Reservoir. At mile 21, turn right onto a dirt road in the direction of the Lava Point Campground and fire tower. Within a mile, you reach a Y intersection. First veer left here, and then soon go right, descending a hill. This narrow, steep, often rutted road leads in 1.25 miles to the trailhead, which is marked by a parking area and vehicle barrier.

On foot, cross the vehicle barrier and follow the jeep track for several miles through the cool, semiwooded uplands of **Horse Pasture Plateau.** This is fast, easy walking over level terrain, and before long the trail veers to the edge of the plateau for a tantalizing glimpse of Wildcat Canyon. The trail descends into Potato Hollow at mile 5, a rather humid, boggy valley that teems with aspens, flowers, and wildlife. Then it climbs several hundred feet, heading once again toward the plateau rim, which it hugs for the next few miles. Peering into **Great West Canyon** (North Creek) is unforgettable, especially at dawn and sunset. Camp here, at least 0.25 mile off the trail (camping is prohibited within 0.25 mile of the rim), to wake up to that view: enormous mesas of muscular pink and white rock, often cross-bedded, separated by deep canyons and blanketed on top with tall conifers.

At the loop trail near the end of the plateau, bear right and continue skirting the rim. Where the trail begins its long descent to the floor of the main canyon, at mile 9.5, look for a pit toilet and a sign indicating a spring. From the overlook to the Grotto Picnic Area is 4.75 miles, all downhill (except for the highly recommended side trip to Angels

Landing). But because it offers little shade and no water, in hot weather you should begin this stretch in the morning hours. The scenery is breathtaking, especially after you cross a low slickrock pass into Zion Canyon itself.

Only 2 miles from the conclusion of the trail, Scout Lookout supplies a commanding vantage point on the whole area. But nothing rivals the vistas from **Angels Landing** (elevation 5785 feet). A rather hair-raising spur trail—1 mile round trip and very strenuous—climbs steeply to the top of a tall fin that juts out into the middle of the canyon, nearly 1400 feet above the river. You can see the entire canyon at a glance. Although the spur has guardrails, its exposed, 500-foot climb can be frightening and is not recommended for children. Drop your pack before ascending to Angels Landing, bringing only your valuables, camera, water, and a snack.

Returning to the main trail, descend quickly on 21 switchbacks (called "Walters Wiggles," after the park's first superintendent) into cool, shady Refrigerator Canyon. At the base of the canyon, the trail emerges into hotter, more open country and parallels the Virgin River the rest of the way. Eventually it crosses a bridge and ends at a parking lot opposite the Grotto Picnic Area.

Backpack 2: East Rim

> **Distance: 10.5 miles one way, plus side trips**
> **Time: 2 days**
> **Map: topo for Zion National Park**
> **Difficulty: moderate**

This excellent hike, starting high above the gorge of the Virgin River and ending at Weeping Rock parking area (see map, p. 212), winds through forested country to the canyon rim and then drops to its floor far below. With an early start, it can be done as a long day trip. When you obtain your permit, check with rangers about water availability.

Drive to the east entrance station. Just before the station, turn left to reach the **East Entrance Trail.** On foot, follow the old road up Clear Creek in the White Cliffs region for a few miles, passing a series of massive pink and alabaster domes. The road climbs through woodlands, eventually turning into a regular footpath. At mile 5.5 is Stave Spring (usually the only water around, and sometimes dry in summer). From here, a level, clearly designated spur trail veers left to **Cable Mountain** (6 extra miles, round trip) and **Deertrap Mountain** (6.5 extra miles). Both offer outstanding views. At Cable Mountain, the remains of a cableworks operation built by a lumber company early in the century are still evident.

Zion's Navajo Sandstone erodes into massive walls and domes.

Back at the main trail, turn left. From here it is 5 miles to the canyon bottom, 2100 feet below. Pick up the **Echo Canyon Trail** to your left in about 0.25 mile and head northwest through timber toward the rim. Expect some gradual ups and downs. Before reaching the rim, descend rapidly alongside a neatly eroded wash. Views from the rim are panoramic, dominated by Angels Landing and the Organ, on the far side of a big U-turn made by the river.

The trail now plummets to the floor of Zion Canyon. Along the way are three spur trails. The first is a 3.5-mile round-trip detour, up 850 feet of switchbacks, to **Observation Point.** At this first junction, the Echo Canyon Trail merges with the **East Rim Trail.** The second goes to narrow **Hidden Canyon,** suspended almost 1000 feet above the valley. This exhilarating route, up to 3 miles round trip, clings to a cliff face initially and can be scary in spots, despite guardrails. The final spur is at trail's end and leads to Weeping Rock. Water and rest rooms beckon at the bottom.

Day Hike: The Subway

Distance: 8.75 miles round trip
Time: 8 hours
Map: topo for Zion National Park
Difficulty: strenuous

The Subway (see map, p. 212) is the star attraction of the Left Fork of North Creek. Here, Navajo Sandstone cliffs pinch together above a Kayenta Formation floor, and the resulting overhangs create a sensation of tunnel-like enclosure. The trip is off-trail and involves wading, boulderhopping, and bushwhacking. Check on weather and water levels when obtaining your required permit.

The route begins about 8 miles up the Kolob Reservoir Road from the hamlet of Virgin (see description of West Rim Trail for directions), just after a curve. Look for a parking lot on the right, 1.75 miles past the park boundary sign. Walk east along the rim for about 0.5 mile until you spot a large cairn, which marks the start of the steep descent over talus into the canyon. Exercise caution here, and make sure you can recognize the exit point on your return.

At the bottom of the dark, basalt cliffs (mile 1.25), go left. You can expect to do a fair amount of boulder-hopping, bushwhacking, and stream-crossing as you proceed up North Creek. Near mile 1.75, you pass the mouth of Pine Springs Wash, a small tributary carrying water, on the left. The canyon narrows, and there may be shallow pools in this vicinity. Be on the lookout for two slabs of light-colored mudstone on the left (north) side of the creek at mile 2.5; they are festooned with birdlike dinosaur tracks, over 70 in all.

Between here and the Subway, about 1.75 miles farther up the canyon, are cascades that you need to scale, which is easily done. **The Subway**, with its spectacular architecture, comes at a bend in the canyon. Beyond it, the number and difficulty of obstacles increase, and you would need rock-climbing equipment to continue up the canyon. Retrace your steps to the parking area.

Days 4 and 5: KOLOB CANYONS

- **Journeying to the world's largest arch**
- **Camping along luxuriant La Verkin Creek**
- **Gas, groceries, showers, and laundry available in Springdale and Cedar City**

The dazzling Kolob section of Zion National Park rivals the main Virgin River canyon for beauty, yet attracts far fewer visitors. After reprovisioning for 2 days in Springdale, take UT-9 west to its junction with UT-17. Turn north on UT-17 and follow that road through the small towns of La Verkin and Toquerville until it intersects I-15 in about 27 miles. Drive north for about 13 miles to the **Kolob Canyons** exit. A delightful overnight expedition to Kolob Arch begins at the Lee Pass trailhead, 4 miles up the Kolob Canyons Road. Obtain a back-country permit at the Kolob Visitor Center. Only about 2 quarts of

to Cedar City

Horse Ranch Mtn.

Finger Canyons

Double Arch Alcove

Taylor Cr.

Lee Pass

Timber Cr.

Willis Cr.

Bullpen Mtn.

Beartrap C.

Kolob Arch

Timbertop Mtn.

Gregory Butte

La Verkin Cr.

Langston Mtn.

ZION N.P.

Neagle Ridge

Hop V.

to St. George

Burnt Mtn.

NORTH

0   1 mile

to Lava Point Rd.

Virgin River Narrows near Orderville Canyon

water per person need to be carried (supplies en route are plentiful, but must be purified). The alternate suggestion is a day hike to Double Arch Alcove. Whatever you decide to do, don't neglect to drive to the end of the road, from which you enjoy enchanting views.

Because the Kolob region is well-watered, it attracts not only hikers but also rattlers, black widow spiders, deerflies, red ants, and other creepy crawlers. Long pants, heavy boots, and common sense are your best protection.

On the evening of Day 5, camp in Dixie National Forest east of

Cedar City, where you can resupply, or even at Cedar Breaks National Monument, since your trip should end fairly early. Drive north on I-15, and then turn right on UT-14 toward the uplands of the national forest. Cedar Breaks is to the north on UT-148.

Backpack: Kolob Arch

> **Distance: 14 miles round trip**
> **Time: 2 days**
> **Map: topo for Zion National Park**
> **Difficulty: moderate**

The trail starts with a rapid 500-foot, 1.25-mile descent to cottonwood-lined but sometimes dry Timber Creek (see map, p. 219). You enjoy sublime views of wild, narrow finger canyons along the way. After following the creek for a distance, the trail climbs to a low saddle. **La Verkin Creek,** a couple of hundred feet below, is a rushing stream with a small waterfall and many shallow pools. The trail meets the creek at mile 4.75. The prominent cliffs of Gregory Butte and Neagle Ridge loom on either side; composed of Navajo Sandstone, they sit atop the Kayenta Formation, through which the stream cuts its channel.

The trail gradually ascends the creek, crossing it several times in the next 1.75 miles. A small grotto to the left of the trail provides spring water. To reach Kolob Arch, turn into the first side-canyon on the left. After about 0.5 mile you enjoy your first distant view of this brick-red giant. The arch, perched high in a cliff, is actually located in an arm of the side-canyon. Go left into this arm and continue on for a better look. At 310 feet across, Kolob Arch is the world's largest span.

Return to La Verkin Creek and either retrace your steps to the parking lot or take a side trip first to Hop Valley overlook or Beartrap Canyon, which is farther up the creek, on the right.

Day Hike: Double Arch Alcove

> **Distance: 5 miles round trip**
> **Time: 4 hours**
> **Map: topo for Zion National Park**
> **Difficulty: easy**

This hike leads up the Middle Fork of Taylor Creek to a dramatic alcove with two "blind arches" above it. The trailhead is to the left of the park road, 2 miles beyond the Kolob Visitor Center (see map, 219). After about a mile of walking, you reach a pioneer cabin at the confluence of the North and Middle forks of Taylor Creek. Bear right here. Past this point, the canyon closes in, framed by steep red mountains of sandstone. The trail, sometimes in the creekbed and sometimes on benches, ascends slowly. The alcove dominates a sharp bend, past a second cabin and just before a dryfall. Colorful streaks of desert varnish and hanging gardens of columbine make this grotto a special place. To avoid hastening erosion, do not walk on the slope below the lower "arch." Return to your car the way you came.

Day 6: CEDAR BREAKS TO BRYCE CANYON

- **A car and foot tour of majestic Cedar Breaks**
- **A drive through the national forest**
- **Camping at Bryce Canyon National Park**
- **Gas, groceries, showers, and laundry available in Rubys Inn; some services at Bryce Canyon**

Begin this day in **Cedar Breaks National Monument,** located east off UT-14, 23 miles from Cedar City. Once called "the circle of painted cliffs" by indigenous peoples, Cedar Breaks sits high in the evergreens of the Markagunt Plateau at 10,000 feet, so you'll need a sweater here even in summer. The scenic road through the monument stays close to the lip of a 2500-foot-deep amphitheater, providing extravagant views of the pastel badlands (or "breaks") below. Very similar to lower-lying Bryce Canyon, Cedar Breaks features rows of tall Claron Formation spires marching down a limestone cliff.

Overlooks and short trails enable you to inspect at closer range the national monument's orange, pink, and white spires, alpine glades blanketed with wildflowers, and bristlecone pines, the oldest living trees (see map, p. 224). The very short, very easy **Bristlecone Pine Trail** extends from Chessmen Ridge Overlook to the canyon rim. The 2-mile round-trip (1.5-hour) **Alpine Pond Trail,** from Chessmen Ridge Overlook, parallels the highway, looping past a pond on upper Rattle Creek and back through forested country. The more scenic **Wasatch Rampart Trail** from the visitor center (4 miles round trip; allow 2 hours) follows the edge of the amphitheater to Spectra Point and beyond, with a 600-foot elevation change. These last two trails are rated easy and moderate, respectively.

For further information, write to the Superintendent, Cedar Breaks National Monument, P.O. Box 749, Cedar City, UT 84720.

Continue north on UT-148 to its junction with UT-143. Turn right (east) and proceed 26 miles, passing a fishing lake, to the town of Panguitch. Turn south on US-89 and continue driving for 7 miles until UT-12 comes in on the left. Take UT-12 east past incredible **Red Canyon,** another Bryce look-alike. Anywhere else in the United States, this would be a national park in its own right. It has a Forest Service campground (between mileposts 3 and 4) and several short, uncrowded trails winding through limestone spires and hoodoos. Unlike Bryce Canyon trails, these start on the floor rather than the

Bristlecone pines thrive on the rim of Cedar Breaks National Monument.

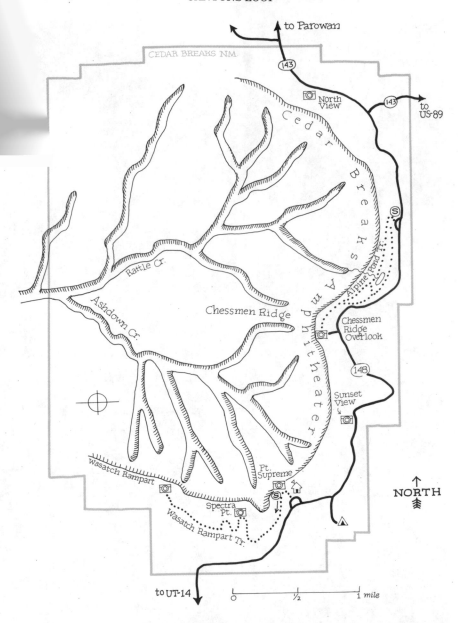

rim. Particularly recommended are the Buckhorn and Tunnel Trails, both rated moderately difficult. The 2-mile round-trip **Buckhorn Trail,** which takes off from site 23 in the campground, switchbacks about 500 feet to an exposed, knife-edge ridge (avoid it in windy or stormy weather). The 1.5-mile round-trip **Tunnel Trail,** starting just west of a tunnel between mileposts 4 and 5, crosses a wash and ascends to a low ridge amid bristlecone pines.

At Rubys Inn, 13 miles past Red Canyon, go south on UT-63 to arrive at the entrance station to **Bryce Canyon National Park.**

After securing a campsite, take the 17-mile scenic drive or hike the Navajo/Queens Garden Loop that begins at Sunset Point Overlook. This trail is described under Day 8 of Chapter 2, Desert Rivers Loop.

Days 7 and 8: DAY HIKER'S SPECIAL

- **Trails—your pick**
- **Camping at Bryce Canyon**
- **Gas, groceries, showers, and laundry available in Rubys Inn**

For these 2 days, follow the itinerary and various options given for Days 8 and 9 of Chapter 2, the Desert Rivers Loop.

Day 9: BRYCE CANYON TO PARIA RIVER

- **Sand pipes and a double arch**
- **Practical hassles**
- **Camping at a Paria Canyon trailhead**
- **Gas, groceries, showers, and laundry available in Page**

Today will be schizophrenic, with the morning devoted to sightseeing in Grand Staircase-Escalante National Monument and the afternoon to finalizing plans for a multiday hike in Paria Canyon. An early start is advisable, since car shuttling or some equivalent will probably be necessary. From Bryce Canyon, go right (southeast) on UT-12 to Cannonville. Then turn south on the beautiful 46.5-mile Cottonwood Canyon Road, which crosses the Paria River and extends to US-89. Inquire locally about the condition of this road, paved only as far as the turnoff for Kodachrome Basin State Park. If it is not in good shape, detour back through Red Canyon to US-89 south, which eventually passes the Paria entrance.

About 4.5 miles past the Paria River crossing on the Cottonwood Canyon Road is a spur to **Kodachrome Basin State Park** (see Day 10 of Chapter 2, the Desert Rivers Loop). Another 9.5 miles to the south is a spur to **Grosvenor Arch.** This heavenly white arch, with its unusual double opening, was (re-)named for the founder of the National Geographic Society. An outhouse, a covered picnic table, and a grill are here, but no water.

Continue on the Cottonwood Canyon Road in a southerly direction and approach the colorful **Cockscomb** monocline. If you wish, you can hike the sublime, 1.5-mile-long narrows of **Cottonwood Wash,** 3.25 miles south of the Grosvenor Arch turnoff. Where the road crosses a small bridge, park at the pullout, and then scramble down into the canyon any way you can. Explore the upstream narrows, which continue about 300 yards, before proceeding downstream for the bulk of the hike. Although the drainage is mostly level and easy to walk in, you do encounter obstacles at the end, near two small windows in the

Remote Grosvenor Arch resembles Paris's Arc de Triomphe.

Navajo Sandstone cliffs. Powerlines are strung overhead where the canyon rejoins the road; turn left on the road for the 20-minute trudge to your car.

Farther south, at the junction of Cottonwood Canyon Road with US-89, turn right. Descending a grade, watch for a sign for **Paria Canyon–Vermilion Cliffs Wilderness Area,** about 3 miles down on the left, between mileposts 20 and 21. After deciding which backpacking trip to take (options are described under Days 10–13, below), visit the ranger station, or check with the BLM office in Kanab, for information about shuttling cars or arranging rides.

Buy supplies in Page (population 4900), fill canteens, complete car shuttles, and camp at your trailhead: either White House, 2 miles past the Paria Ranger Station, or Wire Pass, near the head of Buckskin Gulch. Where you camp at the end of your trip—and where you leave your car—will depend on whether you exit Paria Canyon at Lees Ferry or White House. Convenient campgrounds exist at Lees Ferry and Wahweap Marina (which has showers and laundry facilities).

Because of the potentially life-endangering flash flood hazard, visitors must check the kiosk at the ranger station for an up-to-date weather report. For the same reason, you can hike the length of Paria Canyon only in the downstream direction. To see the entire canyon, you must either leave cars at both ends of the trip, White House and Lees Ferry, or arrange other transportation. Some people hike past the narrows, spend a night or two in the canyon, and then double back. Others commence at Buckskin Gulch, walk to the Paria confluence, and either turn upstream toward the White House trailhead (weather permitting) or downstream toward Lees Ferry.

To shuttle a car to Lees Ferry (a 150-mile round-trip drive from White House), cross the Colorado River just outside Page at Glen Canyon Dam. Pick up US-89A and recross the river on the Navajo Bridge over **Marble Canyon.** On the right, look for the turnoff to Lees Ferry, the outpost where Grand Canyon float trips originate. A pioneer, John Doyle Lee, ran a ferry service across the Colorado River here in the late nineteenth century. Lees Ferry (dubbed "Lonely Dell" by Lee himself) is located 6 miles off the main highway under the Vermilion Cliffs; it has a gas station, convenience store, and primitive campground. Park your car in the long-term lot between the Paria River bridge and the boat launch ramp.

If you decide on the Buckskin Gulch option, leave one car where your trip will end (either White House Campground or Lees Ferry). Then drive to the Wire Pass Trailhead, traveling west on US-89 past the Paria Ranger Station for 5 miles, where the road cuts through the Cockscomb. Immediately to the west of this monocline, the highway crosses a dry wash and bends to the right. On the far side of the wash, turn left onto House Rock Valley Road. Continue on this somewhat bumpy dirt road for 8 miles, paralleling the Cockscomb, which is to your left. A sign marks the parking area on the right, opposite Wire Pass, a point of entry into the Buckskin drainage.

Days 10–13: PARIA RIVER

- **Splashing through deep, narrow canyons**
- **Visiting major arches**
- **Camping along the riverbank**

The wild and spectacular canyon of the Paria (puh-REE-uh) River, a tributary of the Colorado, represents the ultimate in desert hiking. Except in its lower reaches, the canyon, whose name means "muddy water" in Paiute, is relatively shady and well watered. The terrain is either level or downhill. The cliffs loom up to 1600 feet high. And the scenery is splendid: enormous sandstone alcoves streaked with desert varnish, hanging gardens of orchids and ferns, deep pools, and two impressive arches.

Paria owes much of its renown to the narrows section, where canyon walls hundreds of feet high close in—and where it would be extremely hazardous to get caught in a flash flood. Late spring and early summer are the best times for undertaking the hike, though be warned that the canyon is very busy then, with some competition for campsites. Since you will be splashing around in ankle-deep water, wear old sneakers or boots and bring several pairs of socks.

For additional information, contact the Bureau of Land Management, Kanab Resource Area Office, 318 North 1st East, Kanab, UT 84741. An excellent guide to the canyon, including a detailed map, is available through the Arizona Strip Interpretive Association; call (435) 628-4491.

Backpack 1: Paria Canyon

> **Distance: 37.25 miles one way, plus side trips**
> **Time: 4 days**
> **Maps: topos for West Clark Bench, Bridger Point,**
>   **Wrather Arch, Water Pockets, Ferry Swale, Lees**
>   **Ferry**
> **Difficulty: moderate**

From the White House Campground, the route leads immediately into the **Paria Canyon,** remaining in its bed the next 28.25 miles (see map, p. 230). Except in very dry years, there should be ample water most of the way, but make sure you have a 1-gallon carrying capacity for the last 11.75 miles, where no springs exist.

About 1.5 miles downstream you pass a series of low "windows" in the Navajo Sandstone cliffs. The canyon walls quickly deepen and close in until you reach the narrows section about 4 miles from the trailhead. **Sliderock Arch** spans the canyon 2.5 miles past this point. The darkest narrows continue for 5 miles; don't camp here, except on benches high above the river, because of the flash flood danger. Some good high campsites are to the left, just before you enter the narrows; as the canyon slowly widens beyond the narrowest sections, you can camp on a sandbar on the left at mile 10, opposite a freshwater seep. Another campsite is located on a high bench to your right about 0.25 mile up the Paria's tributary, **Buckskin Gulch.** The confluence occurs 0.5 mile below Sliderock Arch, at mile 7.

A particularly beautiful portion of the main canyon begins 10 miles from the White House trailhead. The canyon widens somewhat and becomes lusher. You may find shallow pools to splash around in, and you can fill canteens at several reliable springs (at miles 12.25, 20.5, 22, and 25.5). Noteworthy physical features in this part of the canyon include the Hole, an intimate grotto with a keyhole-like opening at mile 19.25, and **Wrather Arch,** 0.75 mile up a short side-canyon to the right at mile 20.5 (look sharp, for the side-canyon's mouth is obscure). This enormous arch ranks among the Southwest's ten largest, at approximately 200 feet across.

The last spring is located on the left canyon wall at mile 25.5. Here

Soaring Navajo Sandstone cliffs dwarf backpackers in Paria Canyon.

you should stock up for the waterless 11.75-mile stretch to come. Check
with the ranger in advance to make sure this spring is flowing. From
here on, the trail touches base only occasionally with the river, which
by now has cut through many layers of sandstone in rapid succession:
the Navajo, Kayenta (starting below Wrather Canyon), Moenave, and
Chinle strata. About 2.5 miles beyond the last spring, you face some
tedious boulder-hopping in the streambed. Where the river takes a
sharp bend to the left, scramble up the slope on the right and pick up
a faint trail that will usually stay fairly high above the river. The canyon
becomes very wide for its last 10 miles as it crosses open desert. Since
there's not much shade here, plan to do this stretch very early in the

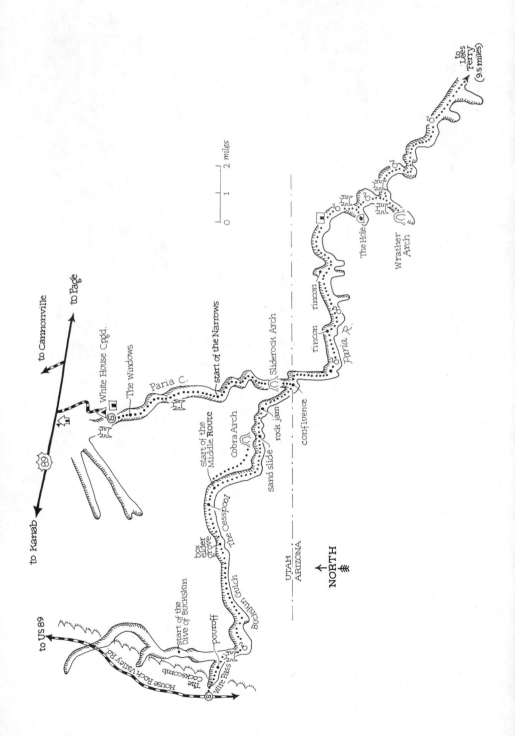

to Cannonville

to Page

to Kanab

to US 89

89

White House Cpgd.

The Windows

Paria C.

start of the Narrows

start of the
Middle Route

Cobra Arch

sand slide

rock jam

Sliderock Arch

confluence

The Cesspool

boxer
elder
grove

Buckskin Gulch

start of the
Dive of Buckskin

pouroff

The Cockscomb

Wire Pass

HOUSE ROCK VALLEY Rd.

UTAH
ARIZONA

NORTH

Paria R.

rincon

rincon

rincon

The Hole

Wrather
Arch

to
Lees
Ferry
(9.5 miles)

0   1   2 miles

morning or else split it between evening and morning. But the walking is fast and easy. At mile 35 you cross into **Glen Canyon National Recreation Area,** and before you know it you're within sight of Lees Ferry.

Backpack 2: Buckskin Gulch

> **Distance: 20 miles one way to White House; 43 miles one way to Lees Ferry**
> **Time: 3 to 5 days**
> **Maps: topos for West Clark Bench, Bridger Point, Wrather Arch, Water Pockets, Ferry Swale, Lees Ferry**
> **Difficulty: moderate**

To hike Buckskin Gulch (see map, p. 230), walk 1.75 miles down **Wire Pass** through a very narrow slot, doing some scrambling and possibly removing your pack once or twice to negotiate pour-offs. Turn right at the intersection with Buckskin, a canyon gouged out of Navajo Sandstone. From here it is 11.25 miles to the confluence with the Paria River.

    Buckskin Gulch is very narrow (only 3 feet wide in spots) and gothically spooky. Its silty water is not recommended for drinking. Near Buckskin's junction with Paria, the 400-foot-high canyon walls

Hikers rest in the "windows" of Paria Canyon.

come so close together that it is almost possible to touch both sides at once. Buckskin's height and extreme narrowness prevent much light from penetrating, creating a sort of natural refrigerator. Repeated flash floods have scoured and sculpted the smooth canyon walls into gargoyle-like shapes and have left piles of driftwood jammed between rocks.

About 8 miles down Buckskin from the Wire Pass junction is the hazardous **Middle Route** (not for inexperienced hikers) to the canyon rim near Cobra Arch. Sometimes there are stagnant pools just upstream from the start of this route. Farther on, you will need to execute a 15-foot scramble to descend a rock jam located about 9.75 miles below Wire Pass junction; roping packs is recommended. In another 1.5 miles Buckskin converges with the Paria River. You can turn left (north) and hike up Paria to the White House trailhead or take the main canyon southeast to Lees Ferry. In either case, safety dictates that you exit the narrows before establishing your next camp.

Day 14: PARIA TO NORTH RIM, GRAND CANYON

- **Swimming in Lake Powell**
- **Sightseeing and camping on the North Rim**
- **Gas, groceries, showers, and laundry available in Page or North Rim**

After reclaiming any vehicle left at your trailhead, a morning swim in Lake Powell near **Wahweap Marina** might hit the spot. Then leave Wahweap and cross Glen Canyon Dam at the mouth of Lake Powell. Detour into Page to stock up on supplies. Continue south on US-89 to its junction with US-89A and turn right, recrossing the river on the Navajo Bridge. For the next 45 miles or so, the Vermilion Cliffs will be on your right.

Past here, as the road climbs, you enter Kaibab National Forest and continue on for 11.5 miles to Jacob Lake. Here you pick up AZ-67 south, which crosses the Kaibab Plateau to **Grand Canyon National Park** (44 miles). The plateau, most of it in the 8000-foot range, is a heavily wooded region characterized by Ponderosa pines and quaking aspens, small lakes, and lupine-covered meadows. When you arrive at the **North Rim,** look for a campsite; if all sites are occupied, there may still be room in the national forest campgrounds to the north. Better still, to avoid disappointment, reserve a campsite in advance. The Park Service is currently establishing a new reservation system, which should be operational by the spring of 1999.

Dedicate the remainder of the day to overlooks and nature trails (such as the one to Bright Angel Point) around Grand Canyon Lodge, at the road's end. A general discussion of Grand Canyon National Park is in Chapter 6, the Painted Desert Loop, Days 13–17. The North Rim, however, differs significantly from the South. It receives only a tenth as many visitors; it ranges between 1000 feet and 1500 feet higher (and is therefore cooler and wetter); it is considerably farther away from the Colorado River; and it remains open only from mid-March to early November, closing during the winter months.

Sometime today, stop by the backcountry desk and obtain a permit for the Thunder River Trail on Days 16–19, if you want to take that trip. Rangers may advise against it, unless you have prior experience on the Kaibab or Bright Angel Trails. In that case, save this hike for future years, and day-hike or backpack instead on the North Kaibab Trail. Be aware that the Thunder River Trail may be closed because of extreme temperatures during the summer months. For all Grand Canyon trails, it is prudent to write long in advance for reservations. Contact the Backcountry Reservations Office, Box 129, Grand Canyon, AZ 86023.

Day 15: NORTH RIM DAY HIKE

- **Hiking and driving to matchless overlooks**
- **Picnicking on the rim**
- **Camping at the North Rim Campground or at Monument Point**
- **Gas, groceries, showers, and laundry available in North Rim**

Today's hike should help acclimate you to the higher elevations of the North Rim. Although its mileage is long, the trail is in good shape and can be walked quickly.

Day Hike: Widforss Trail

> **Distance: 10 miles round trip**
> **Time: 5 to 6 hours**
> **Map: topo for Grand Canyon National Park**
> **Difficulty: easy**

This popular day hike, mainly through forested country, culminates at Widforss Point. To reach the trailhead from Grand Canyon Lodge (see map, p. 234), drive north about 2.75 miles on AZ-67 to the dirt road across the highway from the head of the North Kaibab Trail. Turn left here and continue 1 mile to the parking lot. The trail begins by ascending a steep slope. In the next 5 miles, it first remains near the rim of the **Transept**, and then heads west into a more wooded area, where it dips into a couple of shallow drainages. Pack a lunch to eat at the picnic area near **Widforss Point.** From that breathtaking perch, you'll enjoy views into Haunted Canyon and The Colonade in the foreground and the South Rim in the distance. Double back to your car.

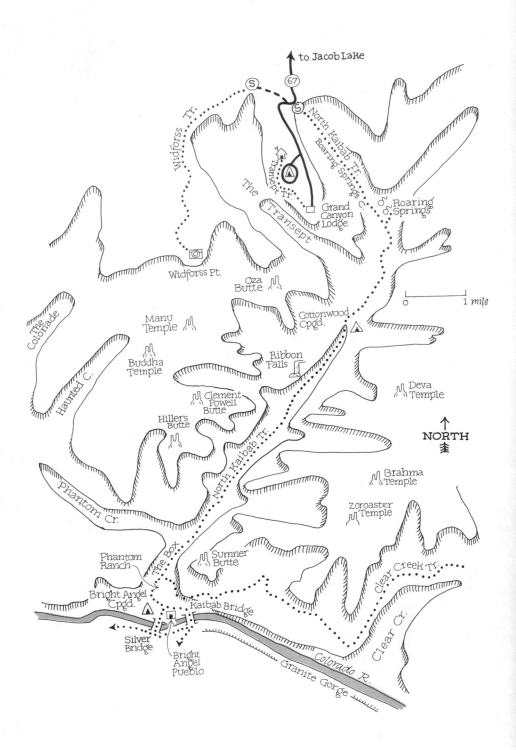

to Jacob Lake

Widforss Tr.

North Kaibab Tr.

Roaring Springs

The Transept

Transept Tr.

Grand Canyon Lodge

Roaring Springs

Widforss Pt.

Oza Butte

Cottonwood Cpgd.

1 mile

The Colonade

Manu Temple

Buddha Temple

Ribbon Falls

Deva Temple

Haunted C.

Clement Powell Butte

Hillers Butte

North Kaibab Tr.

NORTH

Phantom Cr.

Brahma Temple

Zoroaster Temple

The Box

Sumner Butte

Phantom Ranch

Bright Angel Cpgd.

Kaibab Bridge

Clear Creek Tr.

Clear Cr.

Silver Bridge

Bright Angel Pueblo

Colorado R.

Granite Gorge

At the conclusion of the hike, purchase 4 days' worth of supplies for the upcoming backpack excursion. Those who plan to hike the North Kaibab Trail (see below, Days 16–19, Backpack 1) can spend the night in the campground and the rest of the day visiting Point Imperial and Cape Royal. The road leading to these overlooks branches off AZ-67 just north of its junction with the Widforss spur. Turn east here and continue for 5.5 miles, arriving at a fork. **Point Imperial** (the highest Grand Canyon overlook) is 2.75 miles down the left fork, while a right turn takes you to **Cape Royal,** 14.5 miles distant. Although farther, Cape Royal—considered the supreme Grand Canyon vantage-point by some—merits attention. A very easy trail (0.75 mile round trip) leads to an arch called **Angels Window** and treats you to views of Wotans Throne, Vishnu Temple, and Freya Castle.

Those who have secured permits for the Thunder River backpacking trip (see below, Days 16 through 19, Backpack 2) should fill

The forested North Rim overlooks desert lands below.

their water bottles before driving to the trailhead. Water will be needed for tonight's campsite at Monument Point (1 gallon per person), for drinking and caching along the trail (2 gallons apiece), and for storage in the car (0.5 gallon apiece). Autumn and spring hikers will probably not need so large a carrying capacity; the rangers will advise you on this.

From Grand Canyon Lodge, allow about 2 hours to drive to Monument Point, where your trail begins. A road map for the Kaibab National Forest (North Unit), issued by the Department of Agriculture's Forest Service, proves helpful in locating the trailhead. Drive to the North Rim entrance gate and proceed north for about 4 miles. Just before reaching Kaibab Lodge, turn left on Forest Service (FS) 422, a gravel road. Continue for about 20 miles, and then turn left on FS-425, where there should be a sign for **Monument Point,** still about 10 miles distant. When you pass Big Saddle Camp, take FS-292A, a short dirt road that deteriorates markedly in its last mile or so. However, even a regular passenger car should be able to make it all the way to the rim, where other vehicles doubtless will be parked. The view from Monument Point at sunset and sunrise amply repays you for whatever this campsite may lack in privacy and amenities.

Days 16–19: INNER CANYON BACKPACK

- **Showering in the spray of a desert waterfall**
- **Watching rafts tackle the Colorado's thrilling rapids**
- **Camping at expansive overlooks or along a cool stream**
- **Gas and groceries available in Kanab; showers at Coral Pink Sand Dunes State Park**

The above list applies equally to the North Kaibab and Thunder River trips. Whichever you choose, the experience of a lifetime is in store for you.

At the conclusion of your hike, your first priorities probably will be to eat and shower. For this, you can backtrack to North Rim village or else drive north on AZ-67 to Jacob Lake and pick up US-89A north to Fredonia and Kanab, on either side of the state line. Just up the road is **Coral Pink Sand Dunes State Park,** the camping spot for Day 19.

To enter the state park, drive north from Kanab for 15 miles and turn left at a signed junction. The park, in which movies have been filmed, boasts sand of an unusual hue. For obvious reasons, it receives heavy weekend use from all-terrain-vehicle buffs. An interpretive trail extends into the dunes on a boardwalk. Views here are lovely.

Backpack 1: North Kaibab Trail

Distance: 28.5 miles round trip
Time: 4 days
Map: topo for Grand Canyon National Park
Difficulty: strenuous

Drive 2.25 miles north of Grand Canyon Lodge to the parking area for the **North Kaibab Trail** (see map, p. 234), one of the two maintained trails descending into the inner canyon. Shared by hikers and mule trains, the trail passes through five life zones on its 5800-foot drop to the Colorado River. It is steep for the first 4.75 miles, which follow Roaring Springs Canyon to its junction with Bright Angel Creek below the Redwall cliffs. Water scarcity does not pose a problem, since there is water at both campgrounds and along Bright Angel Creek between miles 5.25 and 8, but do remember to bring purifying equipment.

At its start, the trail swings significantly to the west as it cuts through the Kaibab Limestone stratum. Near where it enters the Toroweap Formation, it traverses east, and then drops down to **Coconino Overlook** at mile 0.75. This is a popular day-hiking destination, affording views into both Bright Angel Canyon and its subsidiary, Roaring Springs Canyon. The trail now switchbacks boldly through the Coconino Sandstone, down to the Hermit Shale. Straightening out, it bears west before continuing its southward progress toward Supai Tunnel, at mile 1.75. Look for seep springs in the next half mile.

The trail meanders through pinyon and juniper vegetation to hit the top of the Redwall at mile 2.75. A bridge crosses the creekbed, and the trail remains suspended above the drainage as it descends, at mile 3.5, past a spectacular monolith called the Needle.

At mile 4.75, where the Muav Limestone and Bright Angel Shale layers meet, a short spur trail (0.25 mile one way) heads east toward the dramatic waterfall, **Roaring Springs.** The springs, which emerge from caves deep in the earth, serve as the main water supply for both the North and South Rims.

Rejoining the main trail, you pass a pumphouse and helicopter landing pad near the mouth of Manzanita Canyon. In this vicinity the trail finishes cutting through Tapeats Sandstone narrows. Within an hour or so of walking you reach **Cottonwood Camp** at mile 6.75, where you should plan to stay on your first and third nights in the canyon. The campground has water, shade, toilets, and a ranger station. This area, like Indian Garden on the Bright Angel Trail across the river, was once farmed by the Anasazi, and evidence of their habitation can still be found here. Take care not to disturb ancient artifacts.

Past Cottonwood Camp, the trail proceeds in a southwesterly direction toward the river. About 1.25 miles beyond the campground, a cairned spur trail (0.25 mile one way) crosses a bridge over the creek and leads to **Ribbon Falls** (0.5 mile round trip). The waterfall's environs are exceptional, featuring hanging gardens and travertine formations.

Returning to the main trail, you can expect the canyon to narrow considerably on its way to Bright Angel Campground (mile 14) near the river. In a zone of contraction known as the Box, cliffs composed of Vishnu Schist—the canyon's oldest rocks, dating back 2 million years—frame the streambed. The trail crosses the creek a few times on bridges through the spectacular narrows. Phantom Creek comes in at mile 12.5, and 0.5 mile later is the intersection with the Clear Creek Trail. The rustic **Phantom Ranch,** which accommodates a limited number of overnight guests, is just above **Bright Angel Campground** (mile 14); reservations are essential (phone 303-297-2757).

After you establish camp, walk down to the footbridge over the Colorado's **Inner Gorge.** Look for Bright Angel Pueblo, an Anasazi

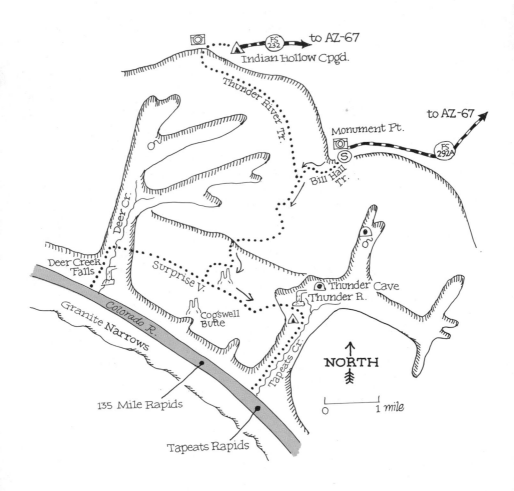

site named by John Wesley Powell, just off the trail about 100 yards north of the bridge. On your third day out, you'll begin the tedious climb back toward the rim. Get an early start in order to beat the heat.

Backpack 2: Bill Hall and Thunder River Trails

> **Distance: 25 or more miles round trip**
> **Time: 4 days**
> **Map: topo for Grand Canyon National Park**
> **Difficulty: very strenuous**

Thunder River—a cold and beautiful waterfall emerging from 3000-foot-deep Thunder Cave, in a limestone formation below the Redwall—feeds into Tapeats Creek, which can be followed to the Colorado River. The unmaintained route to this wonder is very scenic but dry and dusty, with little shade and no water for the first 9 miles. Make a carefully hidden water cache along the way in preparation for the tiring 5800-foot ascent from the river.

The **Bill Hall Trail,** a shortcut into the Thunder River country, starts at Monument Point (see map, p. 238, and Day 15 for driving directions). The route plummets through the Kaibab Limestone, and then contours around at the top of the Coconino Formation, a prominent band of white sandstone. Heading in a westerly direction, you come to a break in the Coconino, where the trail drops down a talus slope dotted with pinyons and junipers. After you intersect the **Thunder River Trail** on the Esplanade, originating at Indian Hollow Campground a few miles to the west, things level out. Walk on bare rock for a while, passing a boulder garden to your left, before reaching the notch where the trail, taking advantage of a rockslide, begins its 1000-foot Redwall descent. At the bottom is **Surprise Valley.** Here the trail veers to the right of a large butte and arrives at an important fork. The left fork, which is the one you want, leads to Tapeats Creek; the right goes into the Deer Creek drainage.

At the lip of Surprise Valley, the trail again switchbacks steeply down to **Thunder River**—said to be the world's shortest—where you can pause to enjoy an ice-cold drink (or shower!) from deep within the earth. Cottonwoods near the spring offer shade. From Surprise Valley to the designated campsites along **Tapeats Creek** is an additional descent of 1000 feet, paralleling Thunder River. Under normal conditions, you should have little trouble continuing all the way to the Colorado along Tapeats Creek, though you may have to ford the cold, fast stream once or twice (a dangerous practice at high water levels). The western bank tends to be steeper and more hazardous, though for the last plunge to the river, you will want to locate the established route on that side of the creek.

At the river there's a sandy beach where you can watch rafts run Tapeats Rapids. If the river level permits, turn right at this point

and pick your way through the Granite Narrows for about 2 miles to the exquisitely sculpted canyon of **Deer Creek,** a favorite (in fact, overused) stopover for river runners. For about the first 0.5 mile negotiate a boulder field along the river before ascending a rudimentary trail to some rocky terraces. Once you reach Deer Creek Canyon, you must walk upstream on some hair-raising paths until the route intersects the creek about 0.75 mile above the Colorado. Bring along ample water if you attempt this, and exercise caution. The safer and surer way to visit Deer Creek is from the trail in Surprise Valley. A large waterfall at Deer Creek's mouth cascades 100 feet to the river. Beyond the falls lies the creek's narrows section; the canyon becomes less scenic as it opens up.

Split the climb back to the rim into two segments, especially if your visit occurs during the summer months. In the evening after an early dinner, you can hike to the top of the Redwall, finishing the arduous ascent to Monument Point after breaking camp in the cool of the morning.

Day 20: ON THE ROAD AGAIN?

- **Heading home**
- **Or hiking the Zion Narrows**
- **Gas, groceries, showers, and laundry available in St. George**

For most of you, it's time to head home. You can complete the circuit by driving back to St. George on either of two routes. The first is to take US-89 north to UT-9 and then east through Zion National Park to I-15. The second is to double back through Fredonia and pick up AZ-389 west, which turns into UT-59 across the border. This route goes through the Kaibab Paiute Reservation, allowing a stop at **Pipe Spring National Monument,** a Mormon pioneer site complete with historic buildings and a pleasant, 0.5-mile trail that climbs 150 feet to the top of an escarpment.

A side trip to the **Tuweep** (or **Toroweap**) section of Grand Canyon National Park is also possible from AZ-389. The easy-to-miss turnoff onto Route 109, the Tuweep Road, is 6.5 miles east of Pipe Spring on AZ-389, between mileposts 24 and 25. Following signs carefully, drive south on unpaved roads for 55 miles through lonely, wide-open country to the park boundary. Tuweep offers primitive camping at its best, a few trails of varying quality and difficulty, and a matchless overlook. The Grand Canyon here is a deep, narrow gash in the earth, and the Colorado River is vertiginously visible, 3500 feet directly below. The Lava Falls Trail, the ascent to Vulcans Throne, and the Tuckup Trail are all difficult and somewhat dangerous. The best hikes here are two

Toroweap Overlook, Grand Canyon's longest rim-to-river drop

short, easy ones: the 1.5-mile, round-trip **Saddle Horse Trail**, from the park road to a viewpoint of Saddle Horse Canyon, and the 3-mile **Esplanade Loop Trail** through the campground to the Tuckup 4-WD Road, returning on the main park road.

For hardy hikers with time to spare, a piece of unfinished business remains: the Virgin River Narrows trip. If this prospect intrigues you, check with rangers to see whether the canyon is open to foot traffic. This decision is generally made on a day-to-day basis. Hikers must be at least 12 years old and 56 inches tall.

Optional Backpack: Virgin River Narrows

> **Distance: 16 miles one way**
> **Time: 1 very long day (12 hours or more) or**
> **preferably 2 days**
> **Map: topo for Zion National Park**
> **Difficulty: variable; very strenuous at high water**
> **levels**

In the minds of many backpackers, the **Virgin River Narrows** trip (see map, p. 212) offers the ultimate in canyon-stream hiking. The river snakes through unbelievably beautiful country. The settler who "discovered" it in 1872 called it "the most wonderful defile it has been my fortune to behold." Awe-inspiring red, black, and gold sandstone cliffs rise 2000 feet above the chasm, which is lined with cottonwoods and box elders for much of the way. This largely trackless wilderness features grottoes, fern gardens, pools, and some incomparable side-canyons. It is one of the most memorable of backcountry trips in all respects, but it should not be underestimated. Especially in high water periods, the hiking can be extremely fatiguing and difficult, since the river gets faster and deeper as it descends. Most of the way the river tends to be fairly shallow, perhaps 6 inches or less, but in a few spots it is sometimes necessary to swim across pools that, at high water, may be up to 50 feet long. Because of the cool water temperatures and minimal sun penetration, hikers can develop hypothermia even in midsummer. In fact, the canyon is closed most of the year partly for this very reason, but also because of flash-flooding, which has caused fatalities here. The best times to attempt the trip are late June, late September, and early October. Old boots are the recommended footwear, and a walking stick is a must.

The Park Service requires that all hikers—even day hikers— register at the visitor center the day before starting out. Current information about the weather forecast, upstream water releases, and the swiftness, depth, and temperature of the river may be obtained at the visitor center. Some people complete the entire hike in one very long day. And this plan does have advantages. It means that you can

Backpackers must wade through Virgin Narrows' shadowed gorge.

travel light, carrying only a daypack containing a full canteen (the river water, because of upstream grazing, is not potable without treatment), your lunch, a waterproof camera, and a change of clothes, in case you get wet. Moreover, it reduces the danger you will be caught unawares by a flash flood. On the other hand, completing the hike in one day will make you feel rushed and quite likely exhausted.

To get the greatest possible enjoyment from the trip, seek permission to spend a night in the canyon at one of the 12 designated campsites, assigned to you by the rangers. Line each compartment of your backpack with heavy duty plastic garbage bags and put your sleeping bag, also wrapped in plastic, inside the main compartment. A pack lined in this manner will float, should it become necessary for you to swim; you can push it along in front of you.

Most hikers stay in one of the park campgrounds the night before the trip and arise before dawn in preparation for the 1- or 1.5-hour drive to the trailhead. Because this is a one-way hike, you will need to set up a car shuttle or hire an authorized driver through T. W. Recreational Services, which operates out of Zion Lodge, to take you out to Chamberlain's Ranch, where the hike begins; phone (435) 772-3213.

On UT-9, drive through the park 2.5 miles past the East Entrance, where an unpaved road branches off to the left. Take this road for about 18 miles, enjoying fine views, until you cross a wooden bridge over the North Fork of the Virgin River. Turn left here and proceed 0.5

mile to the gate of the ranch, where you must sign in at the register box. Drive 0.5 mile past the gate (the road has some bad spots) to reach the parking lot.

On foot, follow the dirt road across the river and continue on it for a few miles. The canyon here is wide and shallow, and the walking is easy. You pass a small cabin on your left at mile 1.5 as the river winds through hillier country. Where the road crosses the river again and starts to peter out, drop several feet down into the canyon and walk in the streambed. From here you'll be descending all the way, but the 1300-foot elevation loss to the Temple of Sinawava area is barely perceptible.

For the first half of your hike, from Chamberlain Ranch to Deep Creek at about mile 8, the river should be relatively shallow. The canyon walls grow progressively higher and closer together. About a mile before Deep Creek you reach a very narrow, bankless section, where you probably cannot avoid wading, and also a falls, which you can skirt on the left side. **Deep Creek,** which comes in at an angle from the right (northwest), serves as a good landmark. It usually carries a lot of water, making the river considerably colder, deeper, and swifter. From here on you are likely to be in water much if not most of the time. Within the next 2 miles, two other tributaries—**Kolob** and **Goose Creeks**— also join the river on your right. These creeks are easy to miss because their mouths are smaller than that of Deep Creek. The designated campsites are concentrated in the area between Deep Creek and just below Goose.

It's impossible to fail to recognize **Big Spring** on the right at mile 11, a luxuriant and beautiful spot where you can refill your canteens. Below this point, the true narrows begin, and camping is forbidden because of the flash-flood hazard. Here the going becomes very rough, since you must cross and recross the deepening river countless times over slippery rocks. These cobbles often aren't visible below the water's surface, so twisted or sprained ankles are a distinct possibility. Your walking stick will prove indispensable along this obstacle course.

Between Big Spring and **Orderville Canyon** (a large but often waterless tributary entering from the left at mile 13), there may be chest-high pools that require you to swim. Around the mouth of Orderville you start to meet day hikers coming up from the Riverside Walk. At mile 15, pick up this paved, 1-mile trail to the Temple of Sinawava parking lot.

FURTHER READING

Edward Abbey, *Desert Solitaire* (Ballantine, 1968). A polemical memoir of the author's seasons as a ranger in Arches National Monument. Indispensable.

Edward Abbey and Philip Hyde, *Slickrock* (Peregrine Smith, 1987). A writer's and photographer's gorgeous love poem to the high desert.

Ron Adkison, *Hiking Grand Staircase-Escalante and the Glen Canyon Region* (Falcon, 1998). Trail and route descriptions for southcentral Utah.

Stewart Aitchison, *A Guide to Exploring Oak Creek and the Sedona Area* (RNM, 1989). With color photos.

Steve Allen, *Canyoneering: The San Rafael Swell* (University of Utah, 1992). Detailed route descriptions for this little-known region.

Douglas and Barbara Anderson, *Chaco: Center of a Culture* (Southwest Parks and Monuments Association, 1981). A fascinating account of Chaco's natural and human history.

Douglas and Barbara Anderson and Charles Supplee, *Canyon de Chelly: The Story Behind the Scenery* (KC Publications, 1988). Part of a handsome, inexpensive series on national parks and monuments in the region.

Fletcher Anderson and Ann Hopkinson, *Rivers of the Southwest: A Boater's Guide* (Pruett, 1987). A blow-by-blow account of raft, canoe, or kayak travel on the region's major rivers.

John Annerino, *Hiking the Grand Canyon* (Sierra Club, 1986). A goldmine of trip possibilities.

John Annerino, *Outdoors in Arizona: A Guide to Hiking and Backpacking* (Arizona Highways, 1987). Most of this book, with its lavish color photographs, concerns desert and mountain wilderness areas outside the Colorado Plateau.

Donald Baars, *The Colorado Plateau: A Geologic History* (University of New Mexico, 1983). The title says it all; one of the authoritative works in its field.

Fran Barnes, *Canyon Country Arches and Bridges* (Canyon Country, 1987). Definitive treatment of the formation, measurement, and discovery of natural spans.

Fran Barnes, *Canyon Country Hiking and Natural History* (Wasatch, 1977). A complete and highly informative guide to routes and trails in southeastern Utah.

Fran Barnes and Michaelene Pendelton, *Canyon Country Prehistoric Indians* (Wasatch, 1979). Southwestern archaeology for beginners.

Joseph Bauman, Jr., *Stone House Lands* (University of Utah, 1987). Geology and history of the San Rafael Swell.

Jack Bickers, *Canyon Country Off-Road Vehicle Trails: Maze Area* (Canyon Country Publications, 1988). A thorough introduction to this remote and fascinating area, written by a born explorer.

Jack Bickers, *The Labyrinth Rims* (4-WD Trailguides, 1989) . Detailed discussions of 60 accesses to Green River overlooks. Numerous hiking ideas included.

Eric Bjornstad, *Desert Rock* (Chockstone, 1988). Route and rock information for climbers.

Thomas Brereton and James Dunaway, *Exploring the Backcountry of Zion National Park* (Zion Natural History Association, 1988). Off-trail routes for experienced hikers.

Dee Brown, *Bury My Heart at Wounded Knee* (Washington Square Press, 1984). A sad and shocking account of how several Native American tribes, including the Utes and Navajos, were massacred, expropriated, or dispirited.

Harvey Butchart, *Grand Canyon Treks, I, II, and III* (La Siesta, 1970, 1975, and 1984). The classic works on Grand Canyon hiking and route-finding by a retired professor whose exploits and accomplishments are almost legendary. His estimated times for completing hikes, however, seem overly optimistic.

Canyonlands Natural History Association, *Dark Canyon Trail Guide* (Canyonlands Natural History Association, 1994). Complete and authoritative.

Robert Casey, *Journey to the High Southwest* (Globe Pequot, 1988). This half-guidebook, half-memoir is exhaustively researched; besides its historical and geographical material, it includes motel and restaurant recommendations.

Frank DeCourten, *Shadows of Time: The Geology of Bryce Canyon National Park* (Bryce Canyon Natural History Association, 1994). A beautiful volume, with color photos and diagrams.

Natt Dodge, *Flowers of the Southwest Deserts* (Southwest Parks and Monuments Association, 1985). A guide to identification; nicely illustrated.

Natt Dodge, *Poisonous Dwellers of the Desert* (Sundance, 1976). No-nonsense examination of the habits of creepy crawlers, and the preferred methods for treating bites and stings.

Francis Elmore, *Shrubs and Trees of the Southwest Uplands* (Southwest Parks and Monuments Association, 1976). Plant identification made easy, with beautiful pen-and-ink illustrations.

Colin Fletcher, *The Man Who Walked Through Time* (Vintage, 1971). An account of the author's solo hike from the western to the eastern boundary of Grand Canyon National Park.

Dave Ganci, *Desert Hiking* (Wilderness, 1987). A comprehensive introduction to the mechanics of preparing for desert excursions.

Dave Ganci, *Hiking the Southwest* (Sierra Club, 1983). Brief descriptions of hundreds of routes in Arizona, New Mexico, and west Texas.

Paul Geerling, *Down the Grand Staircase* (Westwater, 1981). A primer of Southwestern geology.

Bruce Grubbs and Stewart Aitchison, *The Hiker's Guide to Arizona* (Falcon, 1987). Describes 60 desert and mountain hikes in the Grand Canyon State.

Dave Hall, ed., *The Hiker's Guide to Utah* (Falcon, 1982). Thorough descriptions of trips in all parts of this incomparable state.

Dorothy Hoard, *A Guide to Bandelier National Monument* (Los Alamos

Historical Society, 1983). Complete historical and trail information, with gorgeous maps and illustrations.

Michael Kelsey, *Canyon Hiking Guide to the Colorado Plateau* (Kelsey, 1991). Photos, maps, thumbnail trip sketches, and geologic information on 120 canyons—he's hiked them all! For experienced backpackers.

Michael Kelsey, *Hiking and Exploring the Paria River* (Kelsey, 1987). Includes Bryce Canyon, which is part of the Paria drainage.

Michael Kelsey, *Hiking, Biking, and Exploring Canyonlands National Park and Vicinity* (Kelsey, 1992). "And vicinity" is liberally defined.

Michael Kelsey and Dee Ann Finken, *Hiking Utah's San Rafael Swell* (Kelsey, 1990). Incorporates historical material.

Joseph Wood Krutch, *The Desert Year* (W. Sloane, 1952). A naturalist's insights and observations concerning the desert ecosystem.

Joseph Wood Krutch, *The Voice of the Desert* (W. Sloane, 1971). Focuses on the Sonoran desert of southern Arizona.

Rudi Lambrechtse, *Hiking the Escalante* (Wasatch, 1985). Useful Baedecker on a beautiful Colorado River tributary.

Patricia Nelson Limerick, *Desert Passages: Encounters with American Deserts* (University of New Mexico, 1985). Reviews the experiences of several articulate desert lovers, including Abbey and Krutch.

Bob Lineback, ed., *Hiking in Zion National Park* (Zion Natural History Association, 1988). A guide to all the park's trails.

James MacMahon, *Deserts: Audubon Society Nature Guide* (Knopf, 1985). Field guide to plant and animal identification, with color photos.

David Mazel, *Arizona Trails: 100 Hikes in Canyons and Sierra* (Wilderness, 1985). Focuses mostly on desert mountains, but also includes careful and detailed descriptions of popular Grand Canyon routes.

Stephen Metzger, *New Mexico Handbook* (Moon, 1989). Complete and informative.

Gary Nichols, *River Runners' Guide to Utah and Adjacent Areas* (University of Utah, 1986). Covers all major waterways in its area.

David Noble, *Ancient Ruins of the Southwest* (Northland, 1981). Anasazi, Fremont, Sinagua, and other prehistoric ruins are photographed and discussed in this handsome, well-written volume. Highly recommended.

Norman Oppelt, *Guide to the Prehistoric Ruins of the Southwest* (Pruett, 1989). Informative coverage of over 200 archaeological sites.

Laurence Parent, *Hiker's Guide to New Mexico* (Falcon, 1991). Descriptions of 70 hikes, with maps and photos.

John Wesley Powell, *The Exploration of the Colorado River and Its Canyons* (Dover, 1961). The classic journal written by the captain of the first expedition (1869) down the Green and Colorado Rivers.

Marc Reisner, *Cadillac Desert* (Viking Penguin, 1986). A caustic study of the fiscally irresponsible and environmentally disastrous attempts by government, in conjunction with ranching and agribusiness interests, to "make over the West in the image of Illinois" by subduing its mighty rivers. Mesmerizing.

FURTHER READING

David Roberts, *In Search of the Old Ones* (Simon and Schuster, 1996). Explores various theories about Anasazi life and migration.

Ward Roylance, *The Enchanted Wilderness: A Red Rock Odyssey* (Four Corners West, 1986). Memoir of an environmental activist's life in Utah.

Ward Roylance, *Seeing Capitol Reef* (Wasatch, 1979). A thorough treatment, complete with road logs.

Rob Schultheis, *The Hidden West* (Random House, 1982). A beautifully crafted memoir of the author's desert travels in the U.S. and Mexico.

Sierra Club, *The Sierra Club Guides to the National Parks: Desert Southwest* (Stewart, Tabori Chang, 1984). Lavishly illustrated handbook on the history, geology, trails, and scenic delights of eleven national parks.

Sharon Spangler, *On Foot in the Grand Canyon* (Pruett, 1986). Memoir of the author's backpacking trips through the park.

Wallace Stegner, *Beyond the Hundredth Meridian* (Houghton Mifflin, 1954). Outstanding history of Major Powell's expeditions and his subsequent career as a Washington reformer and bureaucratic empire-builder.

William Stokes, *Scenes of the Plateau Lands and How They Came to Be* (1969). Layman's handbook of southwestern topography.

Tully Stroud, *The Bryce Canyon Auto and Hiking Guide* (Bryce Canyon Natural History Association, 1983). A slim volume with capsule trail descriptions, color photos, and sections on history and geology.

Tom Till, *Utah: Magnificent Wilderness* (Westcliffe, 1989). These desert and mountain images by one of the nation's premier landscape photographers are as magnificent as the state itself.

Bill Weir, *Arizona Traveler's Handbook* (Moon, 1987). Thorough coverage of all corners and aspects of the state.

Bill Weir, *Utah Handbook* (Moon, 1988). Another all-inclusive guide.

Stephen Whitney, *A Field Guide to the Grand Canyon*, 2d ed. (The Mountaineers, 1996). Covers flora, fauna, and geology, as well as hiking possibilities.

Terry Tempest Williams and John Telford, *Coyote's Canyon* (Gibbs Smith, 1989). A beautifully crafted appreciation of the Colorado Plateau.

John V. Young, *State Parks of Utah* (University of Utah, 1989). Useful historical and geological material about 48 parks.

Ann Zwinger, *Run, River, Run: A Naturalist's Journey Down One of the Great Rivers of the American West* (University of Arizona, 1975). Observations of an articulate, perceptive woman who traveled the Green River from Wyoming's Wind River Range to Canyonlands National Park.

Ann Zwinger, *Wind in the Rock* (Harper & Row, 1978). A naturalist's exploration of Grand Gulch and other ruin-studded tributaries of the San Juan River.

INDEX

ABOUT THE AUTHOR

Sandra K. Hinchman grew up in Endicott, New York. Her first experience backpacking in the Southwest ended in blisters, sunburn, heat exhaustion, and muscle cramps. The haunting beauty of the area, however, persuaded her to try again, and for over two decades Hinchman has considered the Colorado Plateau her true home. She wrote this guide so that others might love this land, too, and work to protect it. She is currently Professor of Government at St. Lawrence University in Canton, New York, where she specializes in political theory, but she returns to the Four Corners states as often as possible.

Founded in 1906, The Mountaineers is a Seattle-based non-profit outdoor activity and conservation club with 15,000 members, whose mission is "to explore, study, preserve, and enjoy the natural beauty of the outdoors . . . ." The club sponsors many classes and year-round outdoor activities in the Pacific Northwest, and supports environmental causes by sponsoring legislation and presenting educational programs. The Mountaineers Books supports the club's mission by publishing travel and natural history guides, instructional texts, and works on conservation and history. For information, call or write The Mountaineers, Club Headquarters, 300 Third Avenue West, Seattle, Washington, 98119; (206) 284-6310.

Send or call for our catalog of more than 300 outdoor titles:

 The Mountaineers Books
1001 SW Klickitat Way, Suite 201
Seattle, WA 98134
1-800-553-4453 / e-mail: mbooks@mountaineers.org

Other titles you may enjoy from Mountaineers Books:

MOUNTAIN BIKE ADVENTURES IN THE FOUR CORNERS
REGION, McCoy
A complete guide to off-road cycling in the four corners region of New
Mexico, Arizona, Utah, and Colorado.

AN OUTDOOR FAMILY GUIDE TO THE SOUTHWEST'S FOUR
CORNERS, Wharton
A comprehensive guide to family-friendly outings in the region.
Includes special tips on family safety and ways to help protect the
environment of the parks. With complete trail descriptions, plus flora,
fauna, history, safety, and more.

GRAND CANYON PLACE NAMES, McNamee
An entertaining, anecdotal history of 325 place names in Grand Canyon
National Park and adjacent areas. Tells the story behind naming of
Grapevine Canyon, Guinevere Castle, Kangaroo Headland, and many
others.

A FIELD GUIDE TO THE GRAND CANYON, 2nd Edition, Whitney
A comprehensive history to the natural history of the Grand Canyon.
Illustrated with 71 plates containing complete species information on
more than 480 plants and animals. Also presents the geologic history of
the Canyon.

LET'S DISCOVER BRYCE & ZION NATIONAL PARKS, Diamond
LET'S DISCOVER CAPITOL REEF, ARCHES, AND CAYONLANDS
NATIONAL PARKS, Diamond
LET'S DISCOVER PETRIFIED FOREST NATIONAL PARK, Diamond
LET'S DISCOVER THE GRAND CANYON, Diamond
The Let's Discover series are children's activity books for ages 6-11.
Games, puzzles, projects, pictures to color, and more to entertain
children and teach them about the area, its wildlife, its history, and
environmental responsibility.

ANIMAL TRACKS OF THE SOUTHWEST, Stall
Tracks and information on over 40 animals common to the region.
Poster available also.

MAC'S FIELD GUIDE TO SOUTHWEST CACTI, SHRUBS, AND
TREES, MacGowan & Sauskojus
MAC'S FIELD GUIDE TO SOUTHWEST PARK/GARDEN BIRDS,
MacGowan & Sauskojus
Two-sided plastic laminated cards developed by a teacher of marine
science. Color drawings, providing common and scientific names with
information on size and habitat.